# Immigration and the American Dream

# Immigration and the American Dream

## Battling the Political Hype and Hysteria

Margaret Sands Orchowski

ROWMAN & LITTLEFIELD PUBLISHERS, INC.
Lanham • Boulder • New York • Toronto • Plymouth, UK

ROWMAN & LITTLEFIELD PUBLISHERS, INC.

Published in the United States of America
by Rowman & Littlefield Publishers, Inc.
A wholly owned subsidiary of The Rowman & Littlefield Publishing Group, Inc.
4501 Forbes Boulevard, Suite 200, Lanham, Maryland 20706
www.rowmanlittlefield.com

Estover Road
Plymouth PL6 7PY
United Kingdom

Distributed by National Book Network

British Library Cataloguing in Publication Information Available

**Library of Congress Cataloging-in-Publication Data**

Orchowski, Margaret Sands, 1941–
  Immigration and the American dream : battling the political hype and hysteria /
Margaret Sands Orchowski.
    p. cm.
  Includes bibliographical references and index.
  ISBN-13: 978-0-7425-5874-8 (cloth : alk. paper)
  ISBN-10: 0-7425-5874-6 (cloth : alk. paper)
  1. United States—Emigration and immigration—Government policy. I. Title.
  JV6483.O73 200
  325.73—dc22                                                    2008000885

Printed in the United States of America

⊗™ The paper used in this publication meets the minimum requirements of
American National Standard for Information Sciences—Permanence of Paper
for Printed Library Materials, ANSI/NISO Z39.48-1992.

# Contents

# Part I

## BACKGROUND

# 1

## Introduction

In April 2006, the president of the Women's National Democratic Club (WNDC) in Washington, D.C., expressed the perplexity of many American civic leaders over the immigration issue in her introduction of a featured luncheon speaker. "Everyone knows I am an extremely opinionated person. I have an opinion about everything," she said. "But I don't know what to think about the immigration issue. We have asked Dr. Peggy Sands Orchowski here—journalist and the author of *Immigration and the American Dream*—to help us clear up the confusion in order to help us decide for ourselves what stand to take."

The president of the WNDC is not alone in her confusion. Feelings of frustration, even agony, are what many Americans admit they feel when they are asked privately about their stance on immigration, particularly on what to do about the tens of millions of illegal immigrants living in and continuing to pour into the United States. This is especially true of many mainstream Democrats who identify themselves with inclusiveness, social justice, diversity, and the American Dream. As a party, they hate the immigration issue.

"The Democrats are split across the board on immigration," Rahm Emanuel (D-Ill.), head of the Democratic Congressional Leadership Committee, said to me in the fall of 2006 at a presentation of his new book *The Plan: Big Ideas for America* (which did not include any plan on immigration).[1] Immigration reform was not included in the Democrats' priorities for the first "100 hours" when the 110th Congress opened in January. Immigration reform was not part of the "Top Ten Next Priorities" of Speaker of the House Nancy Pelosi (D-Calif.) for the rest of 2007, introduced just after the 100-hour agenda was completed in January. Nor was immigration part of the "Top Ten Issues" that Senator Hillary Clinton (D-N.Y.) introduced at a New America's Foundation conference in early February 2007.

"The Democrats were fine when they were in the minority party in 2005–2006 to stand back and watch the Republican Party rip itself apart over immigration. But now they have to face those same splits themselves," Norm Ornstein, political analyst at the American Enterprise Institute and coauthor with Thomas Mann of *Broken Branch: How Congress Is Failing America and How to Get It Back on Track* told me in February 2007.[2]

Even the great expectation that comprehensive immigration reform—including the legalization of millions of illegal aliens in the United States—would be the one big domestic issue that the Democratic majority and Republicans led by President George W. Bush could come together on blew up shortly after the Democrats took control of Congress in 2007. First it puffed out in early January at the much-hyped 2007 State of the Union Address. President Bush spent exactly 1 minute and 57 seconds talking about immigration in his 45-minute speech. And he never once mentioned the words "legalization" or "a pathway to citizenship" for foreign nationals living illegally in the United States—the issue that many Democratic activists deemed the nonnegotiable line in the sand for "comprehensive" immigration reform. "We need to resolve the status of illegal immigrants already in the country without amnesty, without animosity" was all Bush would say, however. This was hardly opening the door to bipartisan agreement on an issue on which clearly no party has a single message.

Then the much-ballyhooed "Grand Compromise" Senate bill, developed after months of secret meetings between no less a senior Democrat than Ted Kennedy (Mass.) and President Bush, was pulled from the Senate floor in June 2007—twice. Comprehensive immigration reform was declared dead for the rest of the 110th Congress, and the Democrats were left scratching their heads. What happened? Surely so many good middle-class Americans who believed in the American Dream could not suddenly have become such bigots, xenophobes, racists, and full of hate toward immigrants and immigration as some Latino immigrant advocate groups proclaimed they were.

I understand the dilemma. I am a lifelong Democrat who believes in inclusion and equality for all law-abiding Americans. I welcome people of all nationalities who have made the huge decision to leave their homelands permanently and to become Americans—to support and contribute to the American Dream. I advocate and am grateful for the rich blend of national traditions that makes up the diverse American culture. The United States is indisputably enriched by our heritage as a nation of immigrants. But we also are a land of the rule of law. The illegality of millions of people who stepped ahead of those trying to immigrate legally stokes my indignation and sense of justice and fairness as it does for most good-hearted, proud, and internationally minded Americans.

What is clear is that the issue of immigration is a core American issue. It touches our people's most basic beliefs about our freedom to move to new opportunities, about our national identity and sovereignty. It touches our personal experiences and family histories and our philosophies about inclusion, economics, and especially the role of government. It is to most people and even experienced politicians "surprisingly emotional."

We all have our immigrant stories. I have been involved with international cultures since I was a young child, growing up in beautiful seaside Santa Barbara, California, its southern California culture sweetened by its old and new Hispanic roots. It's a town proud of its Spanish heritage—the Iberian architecture and streets all with Spanish names (I grew up on Puesta del Sol), many named after Santa Barbara's most prominent Spanish families, such as the Cabrillos, Carrillos, Castillos, whom we all knew in school. My father was a professor since 1946 at the third branch of the University of California. His specialty was the history, philosophy, and international differences in education systems throughout the world. As young girls, my identical twin sister and I spent months living abroad with our parents when dad had sabbatical leaves to do research—in Europe, in South America, Central America, and the Caribbean. We also often hosted foreign students and scholars in our home. I grew up with the goal of being an American Citizen of the World. Three major life experiences affected my awareness and attitudes about immigration.

# 1. LIVING ABROAD: EXPERIENCING
# THE CONSEQUENCES OF MIGRATION

When my twin and I were 19 years old, we spent a year in Peru with our parents. Dad was a Fulbright scholar and lecturer there. Three years later, after graduating from the University of California, Berkeley, in journalism and Latin American affairs, I returned to South America as a journalist for several years and met my husband, a German national, in Argentina. After our marriage in Santa Barbara, we lived for a year in France, returned to Santa Barbara for eight years while he was a foreign student getting his Ph.D., then moved to Geneva, Switzerland, with our children for five years where we worked for the United Nations. We traveled often to Germany to be with family and my husband's lifelong friends. We spoke German and English at home with the children, they learned French in their Swiss (public) schools, and my husband and I saved Spanish as our own language. I learned to be as comfortable in the German and Swiss cultures as I had in the Peruvian and Argentinian cultures before. I came to realize that there are many differences in the way other cultures do things, and I saw my own American traditions in perspective. I realized that there are many good and not so good ways of doing things—traditions and habits—in all national cultures, including my own.

Some things about the U.S. culture I particularly came to appreciate, love, and be proud of. The American Dream is a real inspiration to Americans and to the whole world: everyone believes it to stand for justice, fairness, inclusiveness, opportunity, and security—all under the rule of law. Two unique U.S. institutions that I loved to tell people about when I lived abroad are the following:

1. The community college system, which allows any adult of any age and educational background to obtain training and advanced education in a community context; community colleges epitomize for me American opportunity and equality.
2. The U.S. tradition of volunteerism and philanthropy—to the point where it is expected that all Americans (especially women and children) spend some of their time each week in a volunteer activity.

I also learned that there are consequences when one emigrates.

One of those consequences is having to learn another language and to learn another way of doing something that you just assumed was "normal" (like how to hold a knife and fork and to do laundry in an automatic washing machine—yes there are big differences). To immigrate is to learn to eat and cook and shop and visit and go to school in a different way than in your home country. But the biggest adjustment of all is to learn another language.

In order to function well in another country, immigrants, like I was, have to integrate into their adopted country's daily life. The best way to do that is to learn its language. It is especially important for the children of immigrants to learn well the language of the country in which they are living and going to school. The kids also need to learn their heritage language so that they can talk to their grandparents, relatives, friends, and old neighbors of their parents.

American can do this, too. Learning another language is a skill that greatly enriches your life. Almost everyone in the United States has a heritage of another language and culture in their family, and learning to speak this heritage language helps us all to understand our multicultural backgrounds. One of the biggest advantages to marrying into another language and culture is that your children will have a motivation for learning another language.

Learning that I could learn to speak another language fluently (as an adult) was a life-changing experience for me. I had been a very poor language student in high school. But that first year in Peru, I learned to speak, read, and write Spanish fluently. In fact, I learned several things about language learning that have affected from then on my attitude about being multilingual:

- It is possible as an adult to learn, master, and enjoy the rich life experience of immersing oneself in another language and using it easily and fluently in all aspects of your life.
- Learning another language is learning another culture. Speaking another language isn't just replacing one word for another but learning a whole new way of thinking. The key is the grammar, and I became a real grammar wonk.
- Knowing just English and Spanish was indeed only a minimum accomplishment for a global citizen. Learning a third, fourth, and more languages is easier once a second language has been mastered.

- No matter how well you learn other languages, most multilinguals master only one. But it doesn't matter if you speak another language with an accent (think Henry Kissinger). You still can be fluent and greatly enrich your life by learning as many other languages as you need to. All will enrich your life and those of your family members, even if you can't read, write, and translate into and out of them equally.

All in all, to live in another culture and to learn its language and ways of life is a deeply changing experience. Some things you will like, and some you won't. After a while, however, you can hardly say what is "better" or "worse" about your way of life in another country—it is just different. And it changes you. You will never be "purely" of one country or another. Wherever you end up, you will miss something of your other life. While that can be unsettling at times—and even my children at times express anger that they didn't "completely fit in" to America even years after we had returned—it still is one of the most enriching experience of a lifetime. Best of all, being an immigrant gives you a new perspective about your homeland. There is so much I came to know and appreciate about America by living abroad for so many years. I heartily recommend to everyone to grab the chance if you can sometime in your life to go live in another country for an extended period of time and immerse yourself in its language and culture. You will never be the same again.

## 2. 1984 OLYMPIC VILLAGE DIRECTOR: EXPERIENCING "IMMIGRATION" MANAGEMENT UNDER THE SPOTLIGHT

The second profound experience I had that affected my understanding of immigration was when I worked for almost two years as an Olympic Village director for the Los Angeles Olympic Organizing Committee (LAOOC) in 1983 and 1984. As director of the National Olympic Committee (NOC) Department of the Olympic Village at the University of California, Santa Barbara (UCSB—one of the three Olympic Villages of the 1984 Games), I was in charge of 125 bilingual staff (bilingual in 38 languages and English) to deal with the Olympic team managers from throughout the Olympic world.

My first job was to assure the NOC delegations from all over the world that we had a strong security system at the Olympic Villages. There were triple fences surrounding each of the villages (the middle one being a movement and sound barrier); a number of identity cards, badges, codes, and passwords for various levels of village access; hundreds of colorfully uniformed, highly visible, friendly security personnel armed only with walkie-talkies (this was the 1980s and no cell phones as yet) posted throughout the village and at village entry gates trained to observe and report any unwanted access; and dozens of unseen, powerfully armed sharpshooters and SWAT teams stationed on rooftops and peripheral outposts surrounding the entire village. The 1984 Games were of course only the third Olympic games after Munich, where in 1972 the Israeli team had been tragically slaughtered by terrorists. We at the LAOOC wanted to ensure that our villages were totally secured. Still, in the spring of 1984, just weeks before the Games were to begin, the Soviet Union announced they were pulling out all their bloc's Olympic teams from the Games. Their stated reason? Security was not good enough!

What became clear after weeks of soul-searching and secret meetings with the Romanian Olympic members (after which the Romanian team became the heroes of the Games because they defied the boycott—the only Soviet NOC to do so) we learned that the security that the Soviets was so worried about was not security of anyone getting into the village. No, the weak (truly almost nonexistent) security the Soviets objected to was that administered toward those exiting the village.

We used to make the analogy that our Olympic Village system was like an independent country. We had a government (the International Olympic Committee) with state governments (the NOCs) and departments of housing and health and education (training). We offered a unique "national" communication system (e-mail was introduced to the world at the 1984 Olympics) accessible to every "citizen"—everyone with an official Olympic pass. My own NOC department was like the State Department, with "ambassadorial" attachés to liaison with each team, translators, and a full array of "diplomatic hosts" who were bilingual in dozens of languages. And like every country in the world, we had borders. And like every country in the world, we had rules about who could enter "our country." These rules were fully accepted (demanded even) and strictly enforced because of security concerns. However, like every free country in the world, we had no rules or regulations about who could leave. Anyone could leave our village at any time.

What became clear to me after my experiences working for five years at the United Nations in Geneva and then at the LAOOC is the ultimate *paradox of immigration*; that is, it is an absolute human right to be able to migrate from any country—no nation-state has the right to forbid its residents or visitors to leave (unless they are imprisoned justly as felons). But it is the sovereign right of any sovereign nation-state (or group of nation-states, such as the European Union) to decide who can enter, stay, and work in their country—in other words, to immigrate. No individual has the human right to move to, stay, and work in any sovereign state simply because they want to.

## 3. JOB INSECURITY IN THE UNITED STATES: THERE ARE NO JOB PROTECTIONS EVEN IN YOUR HOME TOWN

The third experience that affected me was job security. The main raison d'être of immigration—to work and to have better job opportunities than in your homeland—became one "challenge" that seemed to haunt my immigrant husband and our family continually after he had finished his Ph.D. in engineering at UCSB and started his career as an engineer in the United States. During our 20-plus years of marriage, my highly educated and dedicated engineer husband was "laid off" five times from jobs that he loved and was totally committed to. Losing one's job is always devastating, especially in the 1970s and 1980s when most professional jobs were supposed to be "lifelong" and before "outsourcing" of engineering and science jobs to young lower-paid foreign engineers both out of and inside the United States became common. Now the insecurity of engineering jobs in the United States, combined with the long years of study and the depressed wages and decreasing benefits (which I know for a fact, extremely personally), ends up discouraging many young Americans from even pursing studies in these "no future" fields.

The immigration lesson that became clear to me from the always-traumatic layoffs and painful moves we had to make from Santa Barbara because of job loss was this. Even though we lived in my hometown with lifelong friends and contacts and where we and our children were active in and (I believe) valuable to many community organizations, none of this mattered when it came to jobs. Nobody (including a hometown native) has an inalienable right to a job anywhere one wants to live just because they *want* to live there or because they live there already or because they have an established home and even a lifetime history there. We had no right to demand any preferential consideration for a job in Santa Barbara over anyone else in the country. In the real world, the only legal preference one has to get a job you're qualified for in a country (including in the United States) is legal residency in the nation-state.

This is the cardinal rule behind immigration laws. Among the protective roles of government, the core one for labor in every country of the world is that the national government recognizes and enforces laws that allow only its citizens and legal immigrants to have the right to work in the country and no one else. This is a basic protection that most every country in the world gives to its native workers (at the Associated Press in Peru where I worked in the 1960s, only a small percentage of the staff could be foreign), and it is usually rigorously enforced. But amazingly, in the United States, while legislating immigration and labor laws prohibiting the hiring of foreign nationals without the legal right to work (including hundreds of thousands of temporary visitors, such as tourists and foreign students), the fact is that for the past decade, there has been almost no enforcement of any kind of these basic labor protection laws.

## IMMIGRATION LAWS VERSUS OPEN BORDERS

Everyone recognizes—though some not agreeably—that there is almost no country in the world today that has absolutely open borders. It simply isn't practical, although as an ideal it is certainly attractive. (Indeed, even I used to believe in that ideal.) But even America's well-known friendliness, inclusiveness, and pride in its heritage as a nation of immigrants does not mean that it has open borders. Even the American Dream does not mean open borders.

Since no country in the world has open borders, that means that every country in the world has immigration laws. That means that every country has had to decide whom it will let in and whom it won't and who can stay in the country for how long and who can't. Immigration laws fulfill the most basic function of a government: to protect its people.

Immigration laws also reflect the values of a nation. In choosing whom to let in, whom to let stay, and whom to keep out, countries may decide that they want to open their doors to some of the world's poor or to victims of disaster or to people who can fulfill jobs that are needed and lack a national labor market. In the United States, we pride ourselves on being a nation of the rule of law. But we also have a weak history in protecting labor. As a nation committed to open-market capitalism (even most Democrats support it), we do not traditionally favor many laws that regulate commerce and labor markets in any way.

But immigration issues force us to consider such regulations; they force us to choose who can come in and who can't. And we hate that kind of a choice. As a highly diverse democratic and compassionate nation of immigrants, making such choices is extremely difficult and one that lots of people want to avoid—especially politicians and especially open-market capitalists.

It is similar to parenthood. Sometimes being a parent means having to institute tough love when the child becomes out of control (usually because the parents and other authorities were too lax until it was too late) and harms not only him- or herself but you and all that you value. Tough love is difficult to do. But enabling an out-of-control kid—or out-of-control immigration flows—to continue is not acceptable, sustainable, or good for anyone (child or immigrant) in the long run.

This is the dilemma over immigration policy that Americans find themselves in at the moment. Democrats had hoped the immigration issue would go away quickly by rushing through the legislative process (i.e., no committee hearings) and forcing (with their new congressional majority and the help of President Bush) passage of a gigantic omnibus immigration bill that included everything for everyone in some 1,000 pages of legislative proposals and amendments in the summer of 2007. That of course did not work. It is now obvious that immigration will be a major issue of the 2008 presidential elections.

## THE PURPOSE OF THIS BOOK

Americans have to talk about immigration in a serious and not just an emotional way. "I'm instinctively, emotionally pro-immigration. But a review of serious, nonpartisan research reveals some uncomfortable facts about the economics of modern immigration, and immigration from

Mexico in particular. If people like me are going to respond effectively . . . , we have to acknowledge those facts," wrote the liberal economist Paul Krugman in March 2006 in his *New York Times* column.[3] That is what I hope to do with this book: bring honest and frank facts and details to the debate on immigration so that a fair solution can be found— a solution that is just and good for the country, for American citizens and legal resident-workers, and for future new legal immigrants.

This solution in the form of a fair and enforced immigration system will be developed and supported by the American people only if we know and can debate the facts of immigration openly and honestly— without the blinders of narrow lobbying group interests and political correctness. Openness will happen only if the labels, spin, myths, and mantras now deeply embedded in much of the rhetoric on immigration issues are recognized and eschewed for what they are—mind blocks to an honest debate. It is important to see immigration in its true historical context and from the point of view of the two major players:

1. The immigrants who want to immigrate
2. The sovereign nation-state willing to host (and manage) them (no open borders, remember?)

A just immigration law that is fair to both the native worker and the immigrant worker is the goal of all legislators. But the politics of interest groups skew the mix.

The purpose of this book is to cut through all the complicated history, language, issues, and legislative politics of immigration to enable a more open and honest debate for a fair immigration policy that reflects the American Dream. No one should be made to feel like he or she is a bigot or a racist for wanting to control immigration in the United States. Democrats particularly should be able to acknowledge that controlled immigration can be part of the American Dream.

I think most Americans agree on at least three immigration-related points:

- As a nation founded by immigrants, immigration is essential to our very core being. It is part of the American Dream.
- It is impossible to have open borders, and we obviously need to have immigration laws—especially because we pride ourselves on being a country that functions under the rule of law.

- Our system of immigration laws is not working for various reasons (from a lack of will to enforce them to that they are the wrong laws) and needs "to be fixed" in some way (from enforcing the laws we have to changing the laws to fit a consensus on immigration policy).

There is, however, much disagreement among American leaders and the public on how immigration policy should be shaped and enforced. Much of the rhetoric from the immigrant advocates' side tends to frame the issue as being one between the good guys who are "pro-immigrant/ immigration" and the bad guys who are "anti-immigrant/immigration." But I strongly believe that this simplistic way of framing the issue is distorting it for a political agenda. The real issue underlying immigration is who should be allowed to come into the country legally. The issue is not about being pro- versus anti-immigrant or anti-immigration. The issue is about legal versus illegal immigrants and revitalizing immigration law. "Of course *no* one can openly say they are for illegal immigration," Arizona Governor Janet Napolitano likes to point out.[4] The immigration issue then really boils down to who and how many immigrants should be allowed into the United States legally to participate in the American Dream.

The immigration issue has come to an emotional tipping point in the United States because tens of millions of foreign nationals have been allowed to live and work in the United States illegally—many for a decade or more. The impact of out-of-control illegal immigration in the United States is being felt in American communities across the nation and on the American psyche. The dilemma over legal and illegal immigration is splitting American politicians in states and communities. It touches our basic belief in who we are as a First World nation-state in a globalizing world.

I believe that there are 10 immigration issues that must be addressed:

1. Establishing criteria and methods for identifying all immigrants—legal and illegal
2. Finding a valid way to verify the true need for immigrant labor in specific professions and jobs that would supplement, not replace, U.S.-born and legal immigrant workers
3. Assessing the impact of illegal immigrants on the quality of American communities: costs and contributions
4. Instituting humane enforcement of immigration, labor, and citizenship laws

5. Finding a consensus among Americans on how to deal with millions of illegal aliens presently in the country (probably will not be one solution that fits all)
6. Enforcing valid national border security concerns
7. Confronting the growing dependency on foreign scientists and engineers in our universities and most innovative industries
8. Toning down the emotional rhetoric—especially that which implies racism
9. Incorporating lessons learned from multiple, often experimental federal, state, and community responses to negative impacts of illegal immigration
10. Becoming aware of and dealing with the negative impacts that illegal migration to the United States has on other countries, especially large source countries like Mexico

These issues are detailed in this book. I include factual background information, sources where you can get more details, and recent quotes from lawmakers, hearing witnesses, and involved parties. I also share my analysis and informed opinions on the matters in the appropriate chapters of the book.

In the end, the kind of immigration law you support may be quite different from the one I support. And while I am an active and lifelong Democrat, I will make the case in this book that immigration is not a partisan issue in the conventional sense—along a horizontal political spectrum from left-wing liberal Democrat to right-wing conservative Republican. I see the immigration issue as a vertical issue, not a horizontal one—a horseshoe, if you will, that actually splits both Democrats and Republicans along a vertical spectrum from libertarians to economic nationalists. The political immigration horseshoe explains why there are so many strange bedfellows in immigration politics, such as Ted Kennedy with President Bush and the Center for American Progress (a neoprogressive think tank) with the CATO Institute (a libertarian think tank). I demonstrate this in chapter 8.

I also identify the three different bases of immigration law throughout American history:

- In colonial days (immigration entry based on work skills)
- In the 1960s (immigration entry based on family unification)
- After 9/11 (immigration entry based on national security)

Throughout the book, I address the two essential components of a successful nation of immigrants: willing immigrants and a nation-state willing to welcome and to manage immigration.

In the last section, I take off my journalist's hat and put on the pundit's—to analyze where I see the future of immigration law in the United States and the "globalized flat world" is headed. For instance, Is the nation-state dead, as Alvin Toffler predicted it would be in his 1980 book *The Third Wave?*[5] Are we headed for a global labor market, as some libertarian writers suggested in a *New York Times Magazine* piece in June 2007?[6] Or are we headed for the destiny of other failed empires, as Cullen Murphy wrote in his 2007 book *Are We Rome?*[7]

Your conclusion is up to you. I will tell you mine in the final chapter, based on the facts as I judge them, my experiences, and my informed opinions. I will gladly share with you what I think the steps toward a fair immigration policy should be—what should be done first and what should be considered lastly. And I will provoke you I hope with questions, such as whether each state should have its own immigration labor and benefit laws depending on its particular labor and population needs and on how its constituents feel about using their state tax monies, as in the nation's early history and given the failure of the "Feds" to enforce immigration laws. Many states and communities are beginning to do it anyway.

While I intend for you to consider the facts on immigration that I present, I understand that, depending on your own background, experiences, and deep beliefs, you may end up with totally different conclusions than mine. But my goal is not to have you agree with me. Rather, I want to provoke you to think about immigration in a serious way. After all, I am a working journalist—not a public relations flack trying to get you to buy a concept or a product produced by a company. And I did develop my craft during the decade of the 1960s, when our mantra was to *question authority.* I want to urge you to take on the characteristics of a journalist when you hear, read, watch, and participate in discussions about immigration: be curious, be skeptical, and ask questions—even about your own beliefs.

# 2

## Opening Pandora's Box: A Surprising History of U.S. Immigration

Most writings about U.S. immigration usually include a history about the waves of eager immigrants who came to America. The United States is often called a "nation of immigrants." Many people believe that American prosperity was and continues to be built by immigrants and descendants of immigrants. But in order to understand immigration in America and how we have responded to it in the past and will in the future, there are two questions that need to be addressed:

1. Why did immigrants come?
2. Why and how were they received and regulated?

It takes two elements to have a successful nation of immigrants, of course: willing people from other lands who want to successfully move, live, and work permanently in another country, and that country's willingness to have them. But the nation-state's role in immigration is seldom considered.

The simple fact is that neither the early American colonies nor the sovereign nation of the United States ever had open borders. From our earliest colonial history, there were regulations about who could live and work in American farms, villages, and towns. To truly understand immigration in America, it is crucial to know on what basis immigrants throughout our history have come into our country. What rights did they have to work and reside in the colonies and then the United States?

What laws have there been throughout our history to regulate immigration? What legislative committees have been charged with developing immigration law? Which government departments have administered these laws, and who is in charge of enforcing them?

These are the two sides of immigration history that this chapter covers: the immigrants' side and the side of the sovereign state(s).

## THE IMMIGRANTS' SIDE

Most histories of U.S. immigration focus on the migrant "waves" at certain time periods. These migration surges have been assigned various historical reasons, including the following:

- The search for religious freedom of the Puritan Pilgrims in the 1600s
- Opportunities to build a new nation by white Europeans in the 1700s
- Flight from famine and starvation by southern and eastern Europeans and Irish in the early 1800s
- Lust to find gold in California by masses of fortune hunters (including many from China) in the middle and late 1800s
- Escape from depressions and social unrest in the nineteenth century
- Escape from the ravages of World War I and especially World War II by refugees (many of them Jewish) in the 1920s and 1940s
- The almost entitled search for the American Dream by millions of "economic immigrants" (millions of whom since the 1990s stay with impunity in the United States illegally from every country in the world), most of them from relatively wealthy countries like Ireland and Mexico who are seeking better-paying work in the United States than in their homelands

These are the rather romantic histories about waves of immigrants who came to our shores. They assume that all immigrants came *voluntarily*. But they ignore that a significant proportion of immigrants to America, especially in our early history, came *involuntarily*. They were enslaved persons, abducted from their homelands and forced to immigrate to the United

States for the rest of their lives. And they were—and are today—children, accompanying their parents to a new land without a choice.[1]

No matter how or why immigrants came, however, it is a brave act. Leaving one's homeland to live permanently in another country (which is what distinguishes an immigrant from a tourist and other so-called temporary visa holders) is a dramatic, life-changing act for any person. Its impact is no less when it is a decision made on the spur of the moment or after years of contemplation. Its impact is significant on a person's life, whether it was a voluntary or an involuntary act.

## IMMIGRANTS COME TO WORK

Despite all the romantic and dramatic stories about immigration waves, however—from escaping oppression to searching for freedom and democracy—there is really just one underlying reason why anyone migrates from one country to another: *work*. It is about money—about making a living and providing for the immigrant's family (or his or her owner in the case of slaves). Even the early Pilgrims who left their homelands ostensibly for religious freedom, as well as the early colonials who came as indentured servants, came because they had opportunities to make a better living in the New World than they had in the Old—especially the possibility to become land possessors.

In the first years of America's "discovery" and settlement by Europeans, work was done by the colonials themselves and mostly without the help of native Indians (apparently much to the chagrin of the rather entitled first settlers of old Jamestown in 1607). However, as colonial farms and villages started to grow, the need for labor increased. There was always a "labor shortage" in the New World.[2]

Looking at immigration history in the light of its most essential raison d'être—work—reveals how closely perceived labor needs and labor and immigration politics and policies are linked. After all, the mantras "immigrants come to work (or to accompany a working family member)" and "they do jobs Americans won't do" are constantly repeated today (see chapter 5). If true, that means also that immigrants would not come to the United States in the massive numbers they do (legally and illegally) if they were not able to get work (legally or illegally) and to stay with impunity.

The history of immigration into the United States then is about the migration of millions of people who were welcomed to enter the country as workers or family members dependent on workers. The immigrants' ability to work has always been their main value to their families, communities, states, and the nation that permit them to stay and work. It is no different for twentieth- and twenty-first-century immigrants than for those of earlier centuries. "Gettable" jobs and work are undeniably the main reasons that immigrants come by the millions to America—often to join family members who came earlier and set up job networks for their countrymen.

## STAYING FOREVER OR ONLY TEMPORARILY

In the early centuries of American history, because of distance and the difficulty of travel, most immigrants who came to the United States came legally—under contracts with permits and documents. Most knew it would be forever. Most came with the intention that they and their children would become American citizens. Most had only infrequent contacts with their families in the old country; the next generation of their children had almost none.

Today, the reverse is true. Many of the new global migrants, who find work in the United States through ever-expanding family and village networks, do not come with the intention of staying forever and "becoming Americans." Many first-generation immigrants today come originally to get work for much higher pay per hour than they can get in a day in their homelands. Many come in illegally. Most first-generation immigrants live frugally. They send money (billions of dollars in remittances) back to their families in their homelands. Most plan eventually to go back themselves. They have strong and frequent contact with their homelands.

Even if they become U.S. citizens, many immigrants today in the United States hold dual citizenship and vote in the national elections of their countries while in the United States. Living in the United States forever is not a concern for many immigrants. "Don't worry about that pathway to citizenship; hardly any Latino migrant is interested in becoming a citizen. They just want to be legal and be able to come back and forth to work and to build their homes in their homeland,"

Congressman Luis Gutierrez (D-Ill.) said at a press conference at the National Press Club on April 18, 2007.[3] "The idea of citizenship is looser now; what nationality you are does not mean the same anymore in the globalized world," said Yale University history professor Stephen Pitti before the House Subcommittee on Immigration, Citizenship, Refugees, Border Security, and International Law on April 19, 2007.[4]

Still, against their original intentions, even many temporary immigrants end up staying—some as citizens, some as permanent immigrants, many of them illegally. Time passes. They find partners, often from their heritage communities. It becomes easier to stay as their U.S. families grow and their parents, brothers, and sisters and families come into the United States on family unification permits. They are able to buy a home under easy banking and mortgage arrangements (immigration status is not asked), and their kids are entitled to go to public schools from kindergarten through grade 12, no questions asked. Many first-generation immigrants settle into communities dominated by the language and culture of their native lands where they feel more protected and comfortable. They end up staying for decades if not for life. "Many of us want to go home. Many of us say we hate living in the U.S. But we stay because our children are here. I stay here only because of my children," an immigrant from Cameroon told me frankly but off the record.

Some political analysts say amnesty in 1986 encouraged millions of subsequent illegal migrants to stay on illegally with the expectation of a future amnesty. Others say that stricter border enforcement (and just the talk of it) since 9/11 has forced millions of illegal migrants to stay on (illegally), afraid to go home because it would be harder for them to return back to the United States (illegally).[5]

## THE NATION-STATE'S SIDE: WHY AND HOW WERE IMMIGRANTS RECEIVED AND MANAGED

Immigrants can't come to a country in large waves unless the host country is willing to let them in, to let them make a living in the country (this does not include refugee deluges from neighboring countries in times of disaster). Just as it is a migrant's human right to be able to leave a country without restraints (unless he or she is an imprisoned felon), it is a nation-state's inalienable right to decide who can come into their land to live and to work. This is the reason for immigration laws, rules, and regulations. Such rules have existed since man first made communities.

Up until the 1970s, almost all immigrants (voluntary and involuntary, from the early Pilgrims on) came to the New World "legally." Almost all were recruited.

From early on, the colonies and the motherlands of England, France, and Spain that governed them had strict regulations about who could come in and who could not. Even the Pilgrims and the early colonists were given land grants from colonial authorities in the old country to work and claim parcels of land in the New World, although Nathaniel Philbrick, author of the 2006 book *Mayflower*, said at the Library of Congress Book Fair that the settlers of the Mayflower Compact missed their original destination up the Hudson River and were dumped off at Plymouth Rock at the last minute before the return crossing would be impossible, hence "becoming the first illegal settlers in the United States"—at least until their new location was documented and made official.[6] So it was that most all the colonials were well documented in the motherland, establishing themselves in small towns, small farms, and small businesses—all legal. Even the slave trade was legal, and the slaves who were brought to America were documented for the most part as "legal cargo."

When the colonies formed a nation, regulation of immigration (including slave immigrants) was largely a matter for the states. But in 1875, the U.S. Supreme Court ruled that the federal government had the exclusive right to regulate immigration. Congress began enacting immigration laws in the1880s, including the Chinese Exclusion Act of 1882 and Alien Contract Labor Laws of 1885 and 1887, which barred certain workers from immigrating to the country. The Immigration Act of 1882 charged a tax on every immigrant and prevented the entry of "convicts, idiots, lunatics, and persons likely to become a public charge." The list of persons who were excluded expanded quickly, and immigration law became increasingly complex.[7] By 1892, European immigrants to the United States now had to be screened through Ellis Island, where they were either granted entry or not (the new museum at Ellis Island has poignant exhibits of the immigrants who were not allowed in). At this time as well, the first federal immigration and, soon after, labor laws were legislated.

Our beliefs about labor and work—who does it, how much to pay for it, how stable and protected it should be—touch our basic philosophies about freedom and the way we organize our society economically and socially. These beliefs are different, often depending on one's background. And they do change over time. Changing trends in beliefs about labor often are reflected in changing political dynamics over immigration and labor policies.

In general, the Americans never had much of a history of protecting their labor. The guilds, unions, and apprenticeships of the Old World barely existed in the New World America. Only a civil war abolished slavery—32 years after England abolished it. Belief in free enterprise, free markets, and as free labor flows as possible is the historical theme of labor in America. The idea of freedom (see chapter 4) and free market capitalism affects how Americans in various sectors of society and regions of the country view immigration.

There is much in our immigration history that sounds familiar today. Some analysts see the 1920s' wage gap, labor policies, and push for stricter immigration laws as being similar to today's.

The history of U.S. immigration then isn't just about immigrant inflows. It is also about our nation's attitude toward hiring and protecting workers. It is about immigration and labor law—how and why it is made, who administers it, and how (and whether) it is enforced.

## COLONIAL IMMIGRATION HISTORY

### 1560–1600s: Native American Labor

American colonials looked to a variety of sources for their labor. At first they assumed that "primitive" native Americans would help to clear their land and to farm. But that did not last long. As historian and professor Otis Graham writes in his book *Unguarded Gates*, "Early colonists sought aid from native populations to survive in the new world; they fully intended that these primitives could serve as their labor force once their farms and towns were established—including the chance to proselytize them into the Christian faith." Instead, by 1600, 90 percent of the native population had died because of disease, warfare, and social disorganization brought on by European immigration—"a virtual if unintended genocide."[8]

"The romantic version of immigration certainly does not include what immigrants to America did to the native populations of the country. Eventually the surviving native population was driven first to violence and then into exile," writes Graham.

It wasn't long in our early history before American colonials turned to the ability of migrants to fill their need for cheap labor.

### Indentured Servants: The Temporary "Guest" Workers of Early America

According to Otis Graham, America's first dalliance with immigrant workers began with indentured servants.[9] Industrious immigrants from the Old World (mainly England, Holland, and Germany) were indispensable in expanding colonial enterprise and labor in the farms and towns of colonial America. But even colonial assemblies enacted restrictions against paupers and criminal immigrants, the lame, the impotent, or the infirm. As early as 1639, "The quality of immigrants from the Old World was a constant issue of concern," writes Graham.[10] Criminals convicted of a capital crime in England could be transported in lieu of a death sentence (for the theft of an item with a cost of as little as one shilling). Servitude also could result from indebtedness, where a person, a spouse, or parents who owed money could be indentured to recover a debt. A church parish could indenture orphans in order to keep them off the poor rolls. The poor sometimes indentured themselves just to survive.

In America, indentured servants were the first hired laborers. For a while they fit the bill perfectly—white, voluntary labor with a good work ethic. They worked basically unpaid for the length of their agreed-to bond, when they would then be free to establish their own businesses and hire indentured servants of their own.

According to Deanna Barker of the National Center for Cultural Interpretation, "One half to two thirds of all immigrants to Colonial America arrived as indentured servants."[11] At times, as many as 75 percent of the population of some colonies were under terms of indenture. Even on the frontier, according to the 1790 U.S. Census, 6 percent of the Kentucky population was indentured. This was a labor system, not a system of apprenticeship. Indenture grew out of English agricultural servitude and proved more profitable as a short-term labor source than enslaving Indians or using free labor.

In most cases, the work of the indentured servant would be household or agricultural unskilled labor. But there was also a great demand for skilled craftsmen. If an indentured servant had a skill that was in demand, like weaving, smithing, or carpentry, the chance of negotiating a shorter contract was quite good. In theory, the person is only selling his or her labor. In practice, however, indentured servants were much like slaves, and the courts enforced the laws that made it so. For instance, colonial laws in Virginia prescribed "bodily punishment for not heeding the commands of the master." Runaways were frequent. The courts realized this was a problem and consequently demanded that everyone have identification and travel papers. Indentured servants, however, differed from slaves in a significant way. Their bond was for a determinate period. For the employers, temporary indentured servants had the advantage over lifelong servants and slaves in that they did not require care from cradle to grave.

"It must be remembered that in England, bonded servitude was the future for the vast majority of Englishmen," said Karen Ordahl Kupperman, author of *The Jamestown Project*.[12] For the majority of England's low- and unskilled illiterate population, their dream was to someday be a "tenant" on a large estate. Only an elite few ever had a future of education. Indentured servitude for seven, five, or (eventually it became) four years in the New World was a dream opportunity because servants who worked their full indenture received freedom dues, which were based on Hebrew law from the Old Testament.[13] Many colonies also granted 50 acres of land to the newly freed servant. This was a dream opportunity for many in England, and they came eagerly (they were somewhat like the temporary work visa holders of today who are allowed to work for a certain period of time and then have a chance to "adjust" the temporary visa to a permanent one). While there were abuses, many workers from the Old World took the opportunity to be an indentured servant in the New World.

As the need for hard manual labor grew on the increasingly lucrative tobacco plantations of the South, indentured servants were found not to be sufficient. Black slaves became the preferred labor. "Eventually, the final attempt to ease labor shortages was enslavement of Africans. Wherever you find slavery, you first find indentures," according to Barker.[14]

There are many well-researched studies, books, reports, and other resources for anyone wanting details about the history of the people brought to the United States as slaves—the numbers, the conditions, where they came from, their families, their lives. In a few years, a national museum of slavery and black Americans will be open to all on the Washington Mall. Many universities have prominent scholars in black history, a field that is recognized as a significant part of American history. The legacy of slave immigrant labor in America is an important and unique part of American immigration history. But it is also a history of *involuntary* immigration, which should be distinguished, I believe, from that of *voluntary* immigration.

## Jamestown, Virginia, and the Introduction of Free Enterprise

In 2007, the 400th anniversary of the founding of Jamestown brought the history of the New World's first English colony into focus, especially with the visit of Queen Elizabeth of England. Jamestown's second-rate image in American colonial history is not disputed, according to a *Washington Post* article on April 8, 2007. "Blame Thanksgiving. Blame the Civil War. Blame Harvard University and the educational hegemony of New England. Or blame the colonists and their conduct. The [Plymouth] Pilgrims are seen as pious seekers coming for religious freedom, but the Jamestown colonies were high society fops and lower-class ruffians hoping to strike it rich." Even John Smith, the colony's bona fide hero, famously complained that some of his fellow colonists preferred to "starve rather than work."

But while Plymouth is considered to be the cradle of America's soul, ironically the Jamestown colony experiences actually became the model of "America's foundation principles," said former governor and senator George Allen (R-Va.) in a *Washington Post* interview.[15] Jamestown seesawed from one catastrophe to another until its fortunes were turned around by the discovery of tobacco—a transatlantic cash crop. The financial success of the tobacco industry was the basis of the Jamestown area's importance in establishing the legacy of free enterprise, which also was much encouraged by Jamestown's lure to companies by offering them original Virginia Company stock certificates. The destruction of Virginia's Indians and the importation of African slaves is part of the story that clouds this legacy however, concludes the article.

## The Early Republic—Slavery and Chinese Immigration in America: 1760s–1870s

"As the new nation's economy was driven by southern plantation productivity, slavery replaced entirely the indentured servant labor," write Otis Graham. It became "a philosophical problem that was set aside, in the 1780s in order to form the union. But slavery continued into the 1800s to split the country"—even as England passed its abolition of the slave trade laws in 1807.

The Founding Fathers "do not reflect a 'divided' mind but rather a principled ambivalence towards immigration," writes Otis Graham.[16] Most thought that natural population growth would provide enough economic incentive for growth for the developing United States:

- George Washington wrote to Irish immigrants that "America is open to receive not only the opulent and respectable stranger but the oppressed and persecuted of all nations." But he often was of a different mind, writes Graham. "I have no intention to invite immigrants, even if there are no restrictive acts against it. I am opposed to [it] altogether," Washington wrote in a private letter.
- John Adams stated, "My opinion w. respect to immigration is that except of useful mechanics and some particular description of men and professions, there is no use of encouragement."
- Thomas Jefferson, in his *Notes on the State of Virginia*, recorded that a "natural population increases would provide VA with a maximum population for the state (4.5 million) and possibility too large a number in 82 years; there seems no need to accelerate that growth by the importation of foreigners."
- Alexander Hamilton agreed with Jefferson, according to Graham.

Naturally they felt that "immigration was not the same as the slave trade," writes Graham.

### Early 1800s

No national records of immigrants were kept until 1820s, but they numbered less than 10,000 a year in the first three decades of the Republic and consisted almost entirely of Englanders and involuntary slaves. The latter were increasingly preferred in the southern plantation fields than indentured white servants for almost two centuries, according to a PBS February 2007 account on slavery.[17]

### 1820–1840s: The First Great Immigration Wave

A surge of mainly Catholic immigrants from Germany started in the 1830s and from Ireland in the 1840s and reached some 120,000. This was augmented in the 1850s by previously rare immigrant populations from eastern and southern Europe—Catholics, Orthodox Christians, and Jews—all propelled to migrate by chronic unemployment in the Old World due to exploding population growth, wars, famine, and religious persecution of ethnic subsets, especially of Armenians and Jews out of eastern Europe.

### 1848–1850s: The Gold Rush and the Railroads in California

The new state of California in 1850 saw an explosion of migrants, especially from Asia—especially China—seeking their fortunes in the gold fields. California was a thriving and chaotic new state, with little or no labor or immigration laws or laws of any kind that were enforceable. "The California mine owners and railroad builders in the region were desperate for cheap and docile labor," according to Graham.[18] They began importing large numbers of Chinese "coolie" labor. California citizens described them as "sober, industrious, and inoffensive." As their numbers increased, Chinese workers became the prime day laborer hired by California-based "robber barons" to build the cross-country railroad (Chinese labor was similarly recruited into Peru and Bolivia decades later to build the first inter-Andean railroad line). Chinese "coolies" became the equivalent of bonded indentured servants of the colonial days, in the mines, railroad construction crews, and lawless gold-rush towns of the new chaotic state of California.

### 1850s–1860s: The Civil War

By the mid-1800s, over 50 percent of the population of the seven "Lower South" states were black slaves, according to William Freehling.[19] But the South was not a monolith about slavery in the 1800s. In his account of the decades leading up to the Civil War, Freehling writes that there were actually "three Souths": the Lower South, the Middle South (Virginia, North Carolina, Tennessee, and Arkansas, where there were large regions of nonslaveholding whites), and the Border South (Delaware, Maryland, Kentucky, and Missouri, where slavery was in decline).[20] By 1850, movements in the Lower South were actively pushing to acquire new slave territories in newly emerging states, to reopen the slave trade, to reenslave free blacks in their area, and to support secession. In the Middle and Border South states, there were active abolition movements. "Secessionists only succeeded because of a series of coincidences and incidents, including the joining of Savannah GA with Charleston SC by a railroad," according to Freehling.

Immigration rates diminished significantly because of the Civil War and the consequent economic depression, writes Graham.[21]

## 1868

The Fourteenth Amendment, voted in along with the Thirteenth Amendment, states, "All persons born or naturalized in the United States, and subject to the jurisdiction thereof, are citizens of the United States and of the State wherein they reside."

It has been interpreted that this means birthright citizenship for *anyone* born in the United States, but it is not clear if the civil rights advocates of the 1860s really meant to include children of people illegally in the country. It has been argued that the words "and subject to the jurisdiction thereof" could be interpreted as pertaining to the jurisdiction of the parents of the child—their citizenship and legal residency. Otherwise, why were those words included if the law meant that anyone would be given citizenship at birth?

## 1870s

The romantic version of Pilgrims and nation-building immigrants on the East Coast often misses the fact that "the real immigration issue was happening on the West Coast," according to Otis Graham.[22] In California in the 1870s, feelings toward Chinese coolie labor turned hostile when the gold rush waned, the Union Pacific Railroad was completed, and Asian immigration continued—reaching 10 percent of the state's population, one-quarter of its labor force in 1879. Chinese labor was seen as a low-wage labor pool beginning to compete with American labor. "They awakened fears of a new kind of slavery in a nation already convulsed by the struggle over African slavery."[23] Organized opposition to Chinese labor came from coalitions of workers (many of them Irish immigrants), small farmers, and shop owners energized by the depression of the mid-1870s. Employers came in for harsh criticism for using the Chinese as pawns.

In 1875, a Supreme Court ruling—*Henderson v. the Mayor of the City of New York*—became the landmark case that recognized the superior

authority of the federal government over the state government in respect
to immigration.[24] Specifically the case upheld the right of immigrants
in transit to other states and to Canada to pass through the city of New
York without paying the state's immigration bond. In 1876, the House
Committee on Immigration chose Ellis Island in New York harbor to be
the site of the U.S. immigrant screening station.

## Immigration Waves and Immigration Laws: 1880s–1920s

*1882*

The first national law restricting immigration, the Chinese Exclusion
Act, was passed in 1882. It suspended the admission of Chinese laborers (although not Chinese professionals, such as teachers, students,
merchants, government officials, and other professionals). "It was a
fumbling start on the necessary task of gaining national control over
the country's demographic destiny and labor markets over West Coast
Americans' 'understandable' concerns over an unlimited flow of cheap
oriental labor," writes Graham.[25]

The Chinese Exclusion Act of 1882 was the first effort to restrict U.S.
immigration through federal policy.

*1890s*

The high unemployment and social tensions of the 1890s building
from the increasing wage and economic gap between rich and poor in
the United States "gathered a powerful coalition for immigration restrictions," according to Graham.[26] The coalition consisted of organized labor, intellectuals, social reformers, most Republicans, and the southern
wing of the Democratic Party. Large business interests remained mostly
neutral against a background of a huge labor surplus through the long
depression of that decade. Also favoring the status quo was tradition—a
history of openness to immigrants and a record of successful assimilation of diverse European peoples.

## 1900–1920s: The Greatest Immigration Wave

The next decades would see an unprecedented immigration rush
to the United States. It corresponded to the period that is variously

known as the "Jazz Age," the "Age of Opulence," the "Jubilee Years," and "the period of excessive wealth" and a historic period (until the twenty-first century) of unprecedented earning gaps between the rich and the middle- and low-income workers. This also was a period with unprecedented growth in the number of uneducated, basically un-skilled, low-wage immigrant workers. They poured into the country from the famine-stricken and revolution-torn regions of southern and eastern Europe. They were employed with few if any regulations in the burgeoning industries of America—coal, steel, automobiles, textiles, and agriculture in the West—as well as in the townhouses and country mansions of the exceedingly rich elites of America. The average annual inflow of immigrants prior to 1921 was 176,983 from northern and western Europe and 685,531 from other countries, principally southern and eastern Europe.

Political pressure grew to do something about the surge of new im-migrants. According to Graham, "as the new century arrived, the 57th Congress received 5,082 petitions in favor of restricting of immigration; they came from every state in the Union."[27]

What did Congress do? They decided to study the issue—to do many studies in truth:

- In 1895, an immigration investigating commission reported to the secretary of the treasury, who administered the Immigration Bureau.
- In 1901, a 957-page report on the whole immigration question was produced that led in 1903 to the Immigration Bureau's transfer to the Department of Commerce and Labor (and eventually to the Department of Labor when it attained separate status in 1913).
- In 1906–1907, immigration from Asia, most especially from Japan, which was surging in the West Coast states, was restricted in Presi-dent Teddy Roosevelt's second term through a "gentleman's agree-ment," according to Graham;[28] the Japanese settlers were seen "as a competent high-fertility non-culture that presented impossible economic competition to the Caucasian race."
- In 1907, a preliminary Immigration Act was passed excluding per-sons "likely to become a public charge," and Roosevelt appointed a commission to study immigration and come up with a plan for "a definite solution to this immigration business."

- Three years later, the Dillingham Commission produced a 42-volume report on the economic and social impacts of immigration and affirmed that "further general legislation concerning the admission of aliens should be based primarily upon economic or business considerations—especially restricting unskilled labor for which there was already an oversupply in the U.S."[29] It also recommended a much disputed literacy test requirement for potential immigrants.

### Immigration Law of 1917

According to Otis Graham, in the 1912 election, all of the three main candidates had pandered to the immigrant vote.[30] The main issue was over the literacy test, and Taft and Wilson had virtually promised ethnic politicians that they would reject it and any other plan to limit immigration. Yet it passed the House of Representatives five times and the Senate four times and survived three presidential vetoes—all overridden—on its tortured route to passage in 1917. In the end, the 1917 law to limit immigration, including the literacy test, came in a wartime context when the country was concerned about national security and during a period of extremely high immigration waves (it is often pointed out that the percentage of immigrants compared to the native population was greater then than it is now, although the actual numbers were much smaller).

In 1921, Congress passed the Emergency Quota Act. In it, the incoming immigrant population was limited to 198,082 from northern and western Europe and 158,367 from principally southern and eastern Europe (including other countries). This represents a 3 percent reduction of immigrants and a drastic reduction in immigration from southern and eastern Europe.

### Immigration Act of 1924

In 1924, Congress passed America's first comprehensive immigration law: the Immigration Act of 1924, also known as the "National Origins Act," and the "Johnson-Reed Act." It limited the number of immigrants who could be admitted from any Eastern Hemisphere country to 2 percent of the number of people from that country who were living in the United States according to the 1890 Census. The selection of immigrants was determined by "nationality"—meaning the country of birth.

But within the national quotas, certain skills useful to the United States were given preference. Family reunification was limited to spouses and minor children. The goal was to permit only a small amount of annual immigration that would basically replicate the nation's ethnocultural and nationality base.

The 2 percent level dropped immigration levels to 140,999 from northern and western Europe and 21,847 from other countries, principally southern and eastern Europe. No numerical limits were placed on Western Hemisphere immigration. The act passed with strong congressional support in the wake of intense lobbying. There were only six dissenting votes in the Senate and a handful of opponents in the House. Most proponents of the law were concerned with upholding the ethnic status quo of the United States (i.e., white European) and avoiding American workers' growing competition with foreign workers.

The Dillingham Commission had predicted that immigration would be cut to approximately a 360,000 "quota." But it was only temporary. Eight hundred thousand immigrants were admitted in 1921, followed by 310,000 in 1922, 523,00 in 1923, and 707,000 in 1924—mostly from Mexico and Canada (nonquota countries) although quota-country immigrants from non-English-speaking southern and eastern Europe still predominated. And the law was not restrictionist for some African American leaders.

### 1930s: The Depression, FDR and the New Deal, and World War II

"The 1930s arrived with vast and chronic unemployment and the American people wanted nothing from immigration," writes Otis Graham.[31] Compounding that was the growing national security threat of concentrated numbers of immigrants from countries against whom the United States and its allies were going to go to war. It began with the election of FDR and the New Deal and ended with the entrance of the United States into World War II in 1941 after the attack on Pearl Harbor. Immigration declined to less than 50,000 during the war.

### 1940s: World War II Refugee Immigrants

In 1942, the war would bring purported temporary labor shortages in southwestern agriculture and unprecedented refugee issues, but the laws permitting only a few thousand Europeans in as permanent immigrants would not change. To confront the reported agricultural worker shortage in the Southwest, Public Law 45 was enacted inaugurating the bracero program—a seasonal worker contract program. This program allowed temporary admission to Mexican agricultural workers. This was not intended to be an immigration program.

### Post–World War II

The refugee problem—especially after the world learned about the ghastly Holocaust—became a global problem. In the United States, President Harry Truman urged that Jewish refugees be given priority within immigration quotas.

In 1948, Congress passed the first refugee policy measure in U.S. history, the Displaced Persons Act, allowing 250,000 visas over two years and a federally supported relocation program coordinated with volunteer religious and civic groups. (Eventually some 450,000 European refugees, about 40 percent of the total, were relocated into the United States.) Other refugees from China were allowed in as well.

In 1949 and the next 10 years up to Cuban Revolution, 250,000 refugees from Cuba were allowed in by President Dwight Eisenhower under a "parole authority." After that, quotas were officially ignored when it came to responding to future refugee crises in Southeast Asia, the Middle East, and Africa.

## The Second Immigration Wave and the Civil Rights Movement: 1950s and 1960s

### 1952

The Immigration and Nationality Act (INA), also known as the McCarran-Walter Act, restricted immigration into the United States. Prior to the INA, a variety of statutes governed immigration law but were not organized within one body of text. Some provided for a broader policy of family reunification.

Nationally, the attitude toward immigration and minorities was changing, and immigration was gaining interest in the highest circles. It was in the 1950s that Catholic Senator John F. Kennedy (D-Mass.) "cautiously stepped out on the immigration stage," according to Otis

Graham.[32] He sensed that a liberalization stance would gather vital ethnic voting blocs for his long-planned run for the presidency. Kennedy's work on a refugee bill caught the attention of officials at the Anti-Defamation League (ADL) of B'nai B'rith, a major Jewish activist group.

The ADL agenda for years had included opening America's immigration gates wider to increase "ethnic heterogeneity" (now called *diversity*, but in those days it mainly meant increasing the number of Jewish refugees from Europe and North Africa). In addition, the ADL wanted to reduce the chances of a populist mass that might embrace anti-Semitism. With Kennedy, the ADL produced a pamphlet, "A Nation of Immigrants," in 1958 that praised the contribution of immigrants and called for the end of the national origins system.

As president, John F. Kennedy was no crusader on immigration, but he was comfortable with immigration reform as part of his agenda. He was nominated to be the Democratic presidential candidate on a Democratic Party platform that pledged elimination of the national origins quotas system.

But in 1960, Kennedy was elected by a very narrow margin. So he moved slowly on sensitive issues. The immigration reform he proposed had only a minimal increase in total numbers—from 157,000 to 165,000 a year. Its selection system was based on individual skills and a first-come, first-served policy for family reunification.

After Kennedy's assassination, President Lyndon Johnson inherited the policy, but the American Jewish Committee lobbyists in Washington were pessimistic about it. "There is no great public demand for immigration reform," they reported.[33] Immigration was a minor issue compared to the exploding social issues of civil and feminine rights and a war in Southeast Asia. Especially in the smaller cities and towns, there was widespread condemnation of political elites' attempts to "liberalize immigration policy," observed historian Betty Koed.[34] A Harris poll released in May 1965 showed that the public opposed easing of immigration laws by a two-to-one margin.

But while Congress was engaged in the passage of the 1964 Civil Rights Act, immigration laws discriminating against specific nationalities were seen as related and unacceptable. During a Senate debate, Senator Robert Byrd (D-W.Va.) protested that every other country attractive to immigrants practiced selectivity without apology. "Why should Americans be the only ones who feel guilty about a selective immigration policy?," he asked.[35] But the core interest groups had changed since the 1920s.

In the economically robust 1960s, even the AFL-CIO labor union leadership no longer expressed concerns about job and wage competition from immigrants as they had in an earlier era—"although there is evidence that the rank and file of the unions still largely favored limiting immigration," Graham notes.[36] Even patriotic societies began to sense the inevitability of immigration reform, especially as African Americans were intent on extending civil rights globally and did not want to appear unwelcoming to immigrants. *Wall Street Journal* editorials supported the view that family reunifications in the new system would ensure that the new immigration patterns would not stray radically from the old ones.[37]

The Hart-Celler Immigration Act of 1965 ended quotas based on national origins. It was supported enthusiastically by all those who had also supported civil rights legislation and saw immigration issues as related. No congressman wanted to risk being seen as "racist" by opposing the legislation or even questioning the demographic consequences. The *New York Times* called the law "an intellectual victory."[38] No countries had preference. Administratively, the new immigration law set an annual immigration "ceiling" of 170,000 from the Eastern Hemisphere. But immediate family members and refugees were admitted outside the cap. And thanks to Senator Sam Erwin, a ceiling of 120,000 per year was set for the Western Hemisphere—with no cap for immediate family. In practice, "there was no upper limit," writes Graham. The worldwide cap of 290,000 was a fake.[39]

As a result, the major source countries of immigration radically shifted from Europe to Latin America and Asia. The numbers of immigrants tripled by 1978. Preferences for immigrant applicants switched from the historic labor market and skills criteria to one of family reunification and kinship—a feature that came to be known as chain migration and that is still a priority today. "Instead of immigration decisions being made on labor flow needs as is customary in almost every other country of the world, in the U.S. immigration is a private decision to bring relatives into the country," wrote Senator Eugene McCarthy (D-Minn.) ruefully a decade later.[40]

The 1965 bill also coincided with the greatest global population growth in world history. In every region of the world, the population was growing, and people were desperate for paid work. Concurrently, capitalism was strengthening in every nation. Union power was waning in the United States. To be competitive, America's globalizing businesses sought the cheapest labor possible—regardless of residency status—in order to make the cheapest products for the world's markets.

Consequently, this period saw for the first time in American history the migration of millions of foreign nationals to the United States who ended up staying on to work illegally and with impunity.

By the mid-1970s, illegal immigrants had become what journalist Roberto Suro (a founding director of the Pew Hispanic Center) called "a hot second tier issue."[41] They came mostly from Mexico entering Texas and California, displacing some Americans at the bottom of the wage scale. California labor leader Cesar Chavez and his United Farm Workers tried in vain to stem the tide of illegal workers employed by farmers who "held down food prices by holding down farm workers' wages. They undercut the economic and social gains of Americans of Hispanic descent."

### 1982: Free Public Education for Minor Illegal Aliens

Certainly, illegal immigration could be said to have been encouraged by a number of very liberal rulings by the Supreme Court giving educational, medical, and other public benefits to illegal aliens and their children. One such case is *Plyer v. Doe*.[42] In 1982, the Supreme Court held, in a five-to-four vote, that children living illegally in the United States have the same right to a free public education as American citizens. The case originated in Texas five years earlier. Lawyers for a group of children illegally in the state filed a class-action lawsuit seeking a free public education. Lawyers for Texas school districts argued that an influx of illegal students would ruin the public schools. A district court ruled in the plaintiffs' favor. The ruling was upheld on appeal, first to the Fifth Circuit and then to the Supreme Court in 1982. Under the ruling, "schools have to be careful of any unintentional attempts to document students' legal status which could lead to the possible 'chilling' of their Plyer rights."[43]

### 1986: The Immigration Reform and Control Act

Signed by President Ronald Reagan on November 6, 1986, the Immigration Reform and Control Act (IRCA) resulted from debates about how best to control "'undocumented' migration," said Yale University history professor Stephen Pitti at a congressional hearing in April 2007.[44] In presenting his historical context for IRCA, he focused entirely on "undocumented" (i.e., illegal) immigration of Latinos, presenting it as a migrant flow unstoppable by enforcement and fairly dealt with only by amnesty. "Migration to the United States proved critical to the economic strategies of many Latin Americans and many Latin American policymakers after WWII," said Pitti. "Wages earned in the U.S. and sent back to the homelands of immigrants were becoming one of the leading sources of foreign revenue [read, dollars] in many parts of South and Central America: Yet after 1973, U.S. residents faced many new labor market challenges," he offered. Unemployment rates soared, wages stagnated, and government programs were cut back considerably. By 1979, the worsening distribution of family income was clear. The number of U.S. residents who fell below the poverty line soared from 23 million in 1973 to 35 million in 1983, with African American suffering disproportionately.

IRCA reflected many of the immigration reform proposals of President Jimmy Carter in 1977. It emphasized new border enforcement, sanctions against employers hiring illegal workers, a restructured foreign worker (H-2) permit program to import temporary agricultural laborers, and amnesty for foreign nationals who had long lived and worked in the United States. The Senate passed a version of this bill in August 1982 and May 1983, but Hispanic congressional representatives, such as Edward Roybal (D-N.Y.), and members of the Congressional Black Caucus blocked its passage in the House. The bill was successfully reintroduced by Senators Simpson and Rodino in 1985 "in anticipation of midterm elections," wrote Pitti, and signed by Reagan in 1986.

## The 1990s: Irrational Economic Exuberance and the Libertarian Age of Immigration

By the early 1990s, corporate downsizing, the end of the Cold War, and new computer technologies hurt many white-collar employees in the Southwest. From 1990 to 1993, California lost more than 830,000 jobs, most of them related to the defense sector. Economic uncertainty prompted new citizen efforts to control "unauthorized" border crossing and to limit benefits given to "undocumented" residents already in the United States. This was a particularly visible political issue when California voters passed Proposition 187 in 1994; the new law would have restricted all public benefits to illegal aliens but was challenged immediately in court and given a restraining order. In November 1998 the appeal process was dropped by the newly elected Governor Gray Davis, killing the law. "Even the most vocal plaintiffs against Prop 187 said they were afraid that if it went to the U.S. Supreme Court, it would be held to be constitutional, reversing *Plyer v. Doe*," according to the California Coalition for Immigration Reform.[45]

In 1996, President Bill Clinton signed the Illegal Immigration Reform and Immigrant Responsibility Act (IIRIRA). Its underlying concern was national security. "It was driven by the 1992 terrorist attack on the World Trade Center and the change of the Congressional majority control to the Republican party after the midterm elections of 1994," said Paul Virtue, former Immigration and Naturalization Service (INS) general counsel before a subcommittee on April 20. "It took a one-size-fits-all approach to immigrants and treated otherwise law-abiding legal permanent residents the same as dangerous criminals."[46]

The alleged inequities and injustices of the IIRIRA are constantly brought up as reasons for immigration reform today, even as immigration has now become a national security concern, opined Mark Krikorian, director of the Center for Immigration Studies.[47] After 9/11, the INS was reorganized into two bureaus—one to service legal immigrants, the U.S. Citizenship and Immigration Services (USCIS), and the other to focus on enforcement, Immigration and Customs Enforcement (ICE)—both administered under the new Department of Homeland Security. Laws regulating immigration are as likely now to come out of the new Congressional Intelligence Committee and Homeland Security Committee as from the Judiciary Committee. "It is clear now that the United States must focus on individuals who pose a serious threat to Americans; we cannot afford to have our immigration enforcement resources diverted to the prosecution and deportation of *legal* immigrants who committed minor crimes many years ago, as IIRIRA does. That law did not have the punishment fit the crime," Virtue said.

But "there was one very large mistake made by Congress in the 1996 law," said Krikorian. That was rejecting the late Barbara Jordan's recommendations to cut overall legal immigration by one-third. The Jordan Commission recommended elimination of the unskilled worker category and the immigration lottery, which are incompatible with the goals and characteristics of a modern society. It also recommended tightening the family reunification portion of the immigration law by eliminating categories beyond the nuclear family—spouses and minor children. In 1995, Barbara Jordan told the House Subcommittee on Immigration that "credibility in immigration policy can be summed up in one sentence. Those who should get in, get in; those who should be kept out, are kept out; and those who should not be here will be required to leave."[48]

"Any evaluation of the 1996 Act needs to look closely at its impact on U.S. citizens," said Hiroshi Motomua, of the North Carolina School of Law at Chapel Hill at a House Judiciary Subcommittee hearing on April 20, 2007.[49]

### 2001: 9/11, Immigration, and National Security

After the terrorist attack on the World Trade Center on September 11, 2001, the nation suddenly focused on the "broken" immigration system as a threat to national security since all the terrorists were immigrants, several of them illegally in the country. (The USCIS has a detailed report documenting the exact status of each terrorist.[50]) As a result, the INS was reorganized into two completely new immigration service and enforcement agencies in the new Department of Homeland Security. A flurry of new immigration laws were also passed, tightening up consular interviews, foreign student data system, driver's license standards, and law enforcement retention centers and duties, to name a few.

President Bush came into office in 2001 and again in 2005 with immigration reform as a top priority. In 2006 and 2007, immigration became one of the priority issues for Congress.

## HISTORY OF IMMIGRATION MANAGEMENT

Immigration history in the United States also comprises the history of how immigration laws were legislated, administered, and enforced. There have been many changes in immigration management jurisdictions throughout U.S. history.

Legislative and administrative jurisdictions are at the core of how any law is made and eventually enforced. Being aware of which committees deal with immigration and which government departments administer and enforce it are signals about Americans' changing attitudes and concerns toward immigration.

In brief, then, here is a chronological history of how immigration was managed throughout our history:

- Through the seventeenth century, immigration was regulated by land grants and labor contracts from the colonial motherlands—especially in the form of indentured servant bonds in the 1600s. The colonial authorities and trading companies invested in colonial development for commercial profit. They restricted immigrants to the New World to those who could provide best the necessary labor (skilled and unskilled) and comfort for those laborers (i.e., women who would marry and bear children) to build the colonies into viable economic entities.

- In the 1700s, immigration patterns and jurisdictions were different according to regions. In the South the slave trade ruled immigration policies, and slaves were brought in as legal cargo to build the southern tobacco industry, while some skilled labor (including Jewish settlers) was allowed to settle in the burgeoning towns to provide tradesmen skills. In the mid-Atlantic colonies such as Virginia and Pennsylvania, many Scottish and German Protestant immigrants flowed in to the low-skilled labor market and rich farmland. These colonies became the "best states for the working poor—especially former indentured servants who had earned the right to fifty acres of land," according to historian Karen Ordahl Kupperman.[51] In New England, "the healthiest place in the world," according to Kupperman, the population was vigorous and grew rapidly. Natural regeneration and strict adherence to Puritan church and community laws discouraged much migration into the region.

- Throughout the first three-quarters of the 1800s, immigration was considered mainly a state matter involving labor. Various states passed laws to restrict immigration that were hotly contested by labor groups and chambers of commerce—especially in California.

- In 1875, the Supreme Court declared that immigration was a federal matter. In Congress, bills, resolutions, and petitions relating to immigration matters were referred to the Committee on Commerce or sometimes to the Committee on Foreign Relations if they involved diplomatic officials. The Immigration Acts of 1875 and

1882 were the only significant legislation passed: they excluded Chinese laborers, paupers, and criminals.

- In 1889, Congress created the House and Senate Committees of Immigration.
- In 1890, the House Committee's chosen site of Ellis Island in New York Harbor as the primary location for federal immigration screening officially opened.
- The Immigration Act of 1891 established an Office of the Superintendent of Immigration within the Department of the Treasury. It trained and hired "immigrant inspectors" who were responsible for processing and admitting or rejecting all immigrants seeking admission to the United States. They were responsible for implementing national immigration policy, including an immigrant "tax" of 50 cents per migrant. Inspectors were stationed at major U.S. ports of entry.
- The 1900s saw significant changes in immigration law jurisdictions. In 1903 the Department of Commerce and Labor was established, and immigration operations were placed there. With the passage of the Immigration Act of 1924, immigration laws were based on a concept of quotas of "desirable national origins" (meaning mainly European and educated Asians), and the focus was more on protecting American labor than on revenue. The laws were administered by the INS.
- In the mid-1920s, the State Department was charged with interviewing potential immigrants through their consular offices abroad and issuing entry visas allowing holders to come to a port of entry where their permits would be validated and registered.
- In 1940, the Commerce and Labor departments were separated, and President Roosevelt moved the INS to the Department of Labor's jurisdiction.
- In the late 1940s, after the reorganization of the government following World War II, the new administrative and legislative jurisdictions for immigration switched to the Justice Department.
- By the 1960s, the civil rights movement was being born, and the nation's immigration laws focusing on "desirable nationality quotas" now were viewed as "racist," according to Otis Graham.[52] The new immigration laws of 1965 and 1986 focused on extended family reunification and amnesty of all illegal aliens, respectively—not

on work skills or nationality quotas. The two often-competing roles of the INS became more of a problem: servicing legal permanent immigrants and enforcing immigration law against abuses. No one really knew what to do about the growing number of illegal immigrants coming and staying in the country, many of them distant relatives of legal immigrants with green cards.

- In the 2000s, after the attack on the United States by foreign terrorists, immigration became a national security concern. The INS was broken up, and its two conflicting roles were placed into two bureaus—one for immigration services (USCIS) and the other for immigration and customs enforcement (ICE). Both bureaus were placed under the administration of the brand-new Department of Homeland Security, remaining under the Judiciary Committee's legislative jurisdiction but also under the Intelligence, National Security, and the newly created HSL committees as well. As the economy boomed and the number of illegal immigrants became known through the 2000 Census (the first one to count them), enforcement of immigration and labor laws and especially sanctions against employers hiring illegal aliens became almost nonexistent.

## IMMIGRATION AS FOREIGN POLICY

It is interesting to note that jurisdictionally, immigration matters were only indirectly considered to be about foreign policy and under scrutiny of congressional foreign relations committees. The only major temporary permits that come under the State Department are certain university and research scholar exchange programs—particularly the J visas—for which the department has the responsibility mainly to vet the American host institutions. They also administer some of the temporary work exchange programs.

Of course, it is the duty of the U.S. Consular Services to interview applicants and to accept or deny visa applications for temporary programs and permanent immigration permits and to issue all visas for foreign nationals to enter a U.S. port of entry legally. Politically, it is true that consular officers often are "encouraged" by U.S. ambassadors and especially university lobbyists to favor certain visa applicants in order to wield America's considerable "soft power" in diplomatic relations—as well as to expand the increasingly lucrative and unlimited-in-number foreign student university programs. Delays in visa approvals caused some hearings on student permits in the Senate and House Education and Foreign Relations Committees to hear complaints by university officials and foreign student lobbyists. But foreign student visa policy does not come under those committees' jurisdiction. Even the enforcement of the Student and Exchange Visitor Information System is located in ICE, the enforcement arm of the Department of Homeland Security for temporary visas and customs matters.

Still there is a popular view, particularly among Americans who are "international" (particularly former foreign service officers and Peace Corps volunteers), that immigration is a major source of "soft" foreign policy power. Immigration and even the granting of temporary permits such as H-1Bs (temporary high-tech workers, including nurses and health care specialists) and those for foreign students is seen as the way to keep the goodwill of potentially difficult foreign governments. Harvard sociologist Joseph Nye's 2005 book *Soft Power* has had wide play on the television talk shows, especially of the more "liberal" media.[53]

## IN SUM: IMMIGRATION IS ABOUT WORK

For American employers, immigration has almost always been about getting the most readily available and best labor possible for the cheapest cost—about being able to employ people who are willing to work for the lowest wages and the most minimal benefits possible. Throughout our history, immigration has been about building our nation's prosperity—usually on the backs of "cheap labor." Workers in America almost always have been considered philosophically and in accounting practices to be a cost, not as an asset or an investment. In our entrepreneurial profit-oriented culture, of course, costs are to be kept as low as possible. That has often meant turning to the newest immigrant (today often illegal immigrant) labor.

Because of this labor and economic freedom in America, workers in America have not had the historical protection of guilds or even strong unions as they had in Europe. "Freedom" for American employers has meant largely freedom from regulations, tariffs, and labor controls. This libertarian view of labor (which is addressed in chapters 7 and 8) also affects a libertarian view toward immigration among both Republicans and Democrats.

History shows that during periods of war, immigration becomes a national security concern. Certainly this was true during the Civil War, both world wars, and especially since 9/11. But I don't believe that most Americans today consider illegal immigration across the southern border to be only a national security (i.e., terrorism) concern. Most Americans are worried about jobs and the quality of work in our country, especially since our labor union system is so weak (the majority of union members today are highly protected tenured government workers where citizenship documentation is carefully checked). For many Americans, illegal immigration is seen as a threat to Americans' wage and job security.

It seems to be just common sense to recognize that the basic underlying issue of immigration is *work, labor,* and *making a living.* "Being able to get paid work" is a definitive statement that also is intimately connected to the American Dream. But the fact that a large job market exists in the United States is not the deciding factor for most migrants to move here. Many highly developed countries have large job markets—often paying better and with far better work benefits than jobs in the United States. But in countries of the European Union, for example, few immigrants—and certainly not illegal immigrants—are able to get those jobs. The European countries are highly regularized with identity cards required of everyone, active labor unions, and well-enforced labor laws that inflict heavy sanctions on employers that dare to hire workers without the legal right to work in the country.

The United States is unique in the world in that we have uncounted millions of people working and living illegally in the country. Why? Because employers can hire workers illegally with impunity. Simply put, illegal immigrants work illegally in the United States simply because they *can.*

It can be said that Americans are addicted to cheap labor and even feel entitled to it—from the very early beginnings of our history. This addiction, this entitlement to cheap labor that enables employers to hire immigrants, whether legal or not, is a major force underlying our vigorous immigration history.

Following are some brief chronological highlights of the history of American labor protection.

## VERY BRIEF HISTORY OF AMERICAN LABOR PROTECTION

The first local unions in the United States formed in the late eighteenth century, but the movement came into its own after the Civil War, when the National Labor Union (NLU) became the first federation of U.S. unions. It only existed a few years. The NLU was followed by the slightly longer-lived Knights of Labor, which has been described as "a broadly-based federation of labor interest groups." The Knights movement collapsed in the wake of the Haymarket riots. It was followed by the American Federation of Labor, founded in 1886 by Samuel Gompers. It was a national federation of skilled workers' unions. Unskilled labor (especially black workers) was not admitted into unions until the 1940s during World War II, when women industrial workers were also accorded union protection.

Before World War I, President Taft helped set national labor policy that reduced strikes and generated union support for the national cause. In 1921, he became chief justice and helped make the federal courts much more powerful in shaping national policy. He was a leader of the progressive conservative wing of the Republican Party in the early twentieth century, a pioneer international arbitration and scion of the leading political family in Ohio. Although he had been nominated by his good friend Theodore Roosevelt, "Teddy" eventually broke with Taft for being "too reactionary."

The 1920s (that famous "Jazz Age" era of huge wage disparities between elites and working Americans) ushered in the period of America's first powerful labor union. John L. (Llewellyn) Lewis (1880–1969) was the autocratic president of the United Mine Workers of America (UMW) from 1920 to 1960. In 1920, the House Committee on Immigration received many petitions, some in response to the violent labor dispute in Centralia, Washington, involving the International Workers of the World, favoring the restriction of Communists and other subversives.

During the New Deal 1930s and 1940s, labor unions in the United States became "official." In 1935, with the passage of the Wagner Act, a federal agency—the National Labor Relations Board (NLRB)—was established with the power to investigate and decide on charges of unfair labor practices. It also could conduct elections in which workers would have the opportunity to decide whether they wanted to be represented by a union.

That year, the UMW became the driving force behind the founding of the Congress of International (then Industrial) Organizations (CIO). Using UMW organizers, the new CIO established the United Steel Workers of America and organized millions of other industrial workers in the 1930s. They were so powerful that under boss John L. Lewis, during the midst of the war, the union voted its boss the legal right to shut down their mines' war production to get their demands.[54] The CIO provided most of the revenue to support CIO organizing drives for the United Automobile Workers (UAW), UMW, the Textile Workers Union, and other newly formed or struggling unions. According to general labor history, Lewis hired back many of the people he had exiled from the UMW in the 1920s to lead the CIO and placed his protégé, Philip Murray, at the head of the Steel Workers Organizing Committee. Lewis played the leading role in the negotiations that led to the successful conclusion of the Flint sit-down strike conducted by the UAW in 1936–1937 and in the Chrysler sit-down strike that followed.

It was well known that Lewis's UMW was one of FDR's main financial supporters in 1936, contributing over $500,000 to the successful presidential campaign.

The NLRB still remains in effect today, but the labor union movement has passed its prime. Some blame McCarthyism and the Cold War's fight against communism, which tainted the ideals of the "worker state" in America. Some blame America's success with a relatively free market economy now emulated throughout the world. Many blame globalization and foreign competition. "The role of organized labor has changed for two simple reasons," writes labor journalist Philip M. Dine in his 2007 book *State of the Union*. "First, some employers have become more enlightened and treat workers better witout a union. Second, a combination of employer-friendly labor laws discourage workers from voting for unions."[55] Corporations and employers have grown more emboldened ever since President Ronald Reagan's government took on the Professional Air Traffic Controllers Organization in 1981.

Whatever the cause, it is true that today in the United States, the labor union force is mainly powerful in the service sector, albeit that sector is "inherently difficult to organize because of the transient nature of that type of employment, the dispersal of work sites and the typical low pay and high sense of vulnerability often tied to a large immigrant presence," Dine writes.[56] The American Federation of State, County, and Municipal

Employees and the Service Employees International Union are two of the country's most powerful service sector unions. Their attitudes are somewhat confused toward immigration and the unfettered waves of illegal labor flooding the service sector jobs. "Labor's self interest involves representing American workers and their jobs and wages, while also protecting (illegal) immigrant workers from exploitation," Dine concludes. [57] "The labor movement occupies a rather lonely perch."

## CONCLUSION: LABOR NEEDS AND IMMIGRATION LAW

Compared to other "developed" or "First World" countries, the United States is a very labor-intensive country. For instance, you rarely see human beings taking parking tickets in a parking lot or a freeway stall in Europe or killing animals in a gut-filled loathsome poultry or swine slaughterhouse—those jobs are done by machine in most other developed countries. And labor in America has always been relatively less protected than in the "Old World."

Labor guilds were always fairly weak in the United States even in colonial days, and in the past decades, U.S. labor unions have been weakening in all but the service industries. In addition, employer sanctions against hiring people who do not have the legal right to work in the United States have almost been ignored since instituted in 1986, whereas in Europe national identity cards and strict employer regulations and monitoring of hirees have been strong for over a century. There is a direct correlation between the rising and falling waves of immigration (legal and especially illegal) and the establishment of labor and immigration laws throughout our history, in my opinion.

I have observed that throughout our immigration history, immigrant surges are determined by employment crises abroad and at home, our changing immigration and labor laws, and how much these laws are enforced. Where once there was a correlation between immigration waves in America and world crises, in recent decades (especially the last), the correlation now seems to be between immigration surges and the enforcement or not of our immigration and labor laws. When immigration and labor laws are enforced, immigration waves decrease. When laws are not enforced, immigration surges (especially of illegal immigrants) increase.

The past decade has seen the demise of labor protection organizations and labor policies. The United States will not even sign major international labor conventions, and attempts to put labor standards into international trade agreements have often killed the pacts. It seems clear that enforcement (or not) of labor laws clearly affects the flow of especially illegal worker immigrants and their families as much as the lack of enforcement of immigration laws.

# 3

## The Facts: Who, Why, Where, What, How, and When?

"You're entitled to your own opinion but not your own facts." How often have you heard this on the talk shows and among sniping experts on a panel? The problem is that even facts can be twisted and spun, pieces omitted, and numbers interpreted in various ways.

It seems to be especially difficult to find agreement on "facts" in the vociferous and emotional debate over immigration—even when the "facts" involve numbers. For instance, here are some typical simple questions asking for facts about immigration on which experts on all side of the issue do not agree and even spin for their own benefit:

Question: How many foreign nationals currently live and work *illegally* in the United States?

Answer: Between 11.5 million to 20 million, depending on who is talking.

Question: How many family members does each legal immigrant bring in?

Answer: Between two and over 100 per legal immigrant, depending on who is talking.

Question: Do illegal immigrants impact the economy negatively or positively?

Answer: There are economists who show charts, graphs, and numbers arguing both sides; however, there seems to be some agreement that the wages of unskilled American workers have been depressed in some areas.

Despite all the nuances of the immigration issue, however, there are some basic facts about immigration that can be clearly defined. This chapter addresses some of them. Then we can at least start on firm ground before driving through the twists and turns and different levels of immigration spin, the myths, and the mantras, before we get to the details about immigration issues, politics, and legislation, followed by the prognosis of the future of U.S. immigration policy.

## THE QUESTIONS

Who is an immigrant, and who is not? There are three categories of migrants and visa holders:

1. Legal permanent resident (LPR) (i.e., a green card holder)
2. Temporary visitor/nonimmigrant (i.e., tourists, students, H-1B workers, agricultural workers, and so on)
3. Illegal alien (the legal term for a foreign national living and often working in the country illegally, no matter how he or she entered)

It is generally agreed that in 2005, the numbers of "foreign-born individuals" (the Migration Policy Institute's word for "migrants") totaled about 36 million of whom roughly 35 percent were naturalized, 33 percent were legal noncitizens—not specified if temporary or permanent—and 32 percent were living and working illegally in the country.

In general, an immigrant is a citizen of one country who moves to another country with the intention of staying (and, for most, working). Obviously a foreign national who is just traveling through one country to go somewhere else or who comes to a country for just a short time (weeks or months) to visit, study, do business, or stay with family members temporarily without the intention of staying and working long term is not an immigrant.

In addition, normally once an immigrant has been naturalized and is a U.S. citizen, he or she is not referred to as an immigrant anymore. He or she came in as an immigrant, and most Americans have an immigrant heritage, but once citizens, they are no longer officially immigrants (some may disagree and consider first-generation naturalized citizens still to be immigrants; this is why some journalists may report that "legal immigrants" can vote, confusing "legal" for "naturalized").

"Migrant" and "migration" are used for any person who moves within a country as well as outside of one. "Labor migration" is often heard in international circles—but it could also mean within a country or a region. But "immigration" is used always (as far as I know) in the international context; it means to migrate from one country into another with the intention of staying and working (the less used term "emigration" refers to a citizen who is moving away from or out of the homeland to be an immigrant in another country).

## WHAT IS A VISA?

Before going into the details of the various categories of migrants and the permits they hold, one misused word has to be clarified. It is the term "visa." Almost everyone, including lawmakers and immigration officials as well as most people in the media and in the public, refers to the kinds of legal documents migrants are given as a "visa." But that is not really what a visa is. While the term probably will creep into this text as well instead of "permit," "document," or "status," just for the record it needs to be stated what a visa really is.

Officially, a visa is a signed document by a U.S. consular officer that only allows a citizen of another country to present him- or herself to an immigration official at a U.S. border entry point. That's it. A visa neither guarantees entry nor states the status of the migrant when (and if) he or she is allowed to enter.

Until recently, citizens of certain countries (namely, western Europe and Canada) did not need a visa to come to a U.S. port of entry if they were intending to stay no more than 90 days; they were from the "visa-waiver countries." They could just come to the port of entry and present their national passport showing that they were indeed a citizen of a visa-waiver country; they do not have to show a visa from a U.S. consular officer. Still, however, they must be issued a permit document—an I-94W—showing their status and their authorized duration of stay.

Since 9/11 and changes in the intelligence and homeland security regulations, the conditions even for visa-waiver-country citizens are tightening. Efforts in the summer of 2007 to increase the number of visa-waiver countries to include mainly the new eastern European countries of the European Union failed despite the fact that many amendments were proposed for the Immigration Reform, Homeland Security Spending, and Defense Authorization bills, among others. A bill to implement the rest of the 9/11 Commission Report recommendation includes some loosening of standards in the visa-waiver program and has some legs. The visa waiver remains a highly controversial subject at the time of this writing.

A visa is normally obtained at a U.S. embassy or consular office outside the United States. While it has always been law that anyone applying for a visa should have an interview by a consulate officer, in fact during the 1990s this regulation was often waived to reduce workload and to streamline processing. In fact, for citizens of certain countries considered important to the United States but not one of the European visa-waiver countries (such as Saudi Arabia), visas for certain kinds of permits were, in practice, waived. By 2001, only about one-fifth of all nonimmigrant visa applicants were interviewed, by some accounts. For instance, college students who were accepted into a U.S. institution of higher education on a foreign student temporary permit from some countries (including Saudi Arabia) often were allowed a "fast-track" visa process where they were to be considered eligible by definition—no interview needed. In 2004, portions of the intelligence bill not only ended fast-track visa arrangements but also required that almost every visa applicant be interviewed (except young children and the elderly).

This reinstituted mandatory interview requirement (together with required screening of certain types of applications, such as young men from countries of interest in the war on terror and students in certain academic fields) undoubtedly has caused an increase in the number of delays and visa denials. The significant issue for interviewers, according to consular officers, is to determine if applicants for temporary permits have the intention to immigrate. If they cannot demonstrate that they qualify for the type of visa they are seeking, that their application is credible, and that—with a family or bank account in the homeland, for instance—they are likely to return when their authorized stay is ended, the officer is obliged to deny the visa. This rule applies as well to all those who are reapplying for a temporary visa after the one they had been on had expired. These required interviews obviously cause some significant inconveniences and delays, especially for applicants who have to travel to capital cities to an embassy in order to have their interview with a consular officer (rather than a foreign designee). Secretary of State Condoleezza Rice in 2006 extended U.S. consular offices into secondary cities of many prime visa applicant source countries, such as India, at the rather vocal urging especially of university presidents who had become dependent on foreign students for their revenue and their body counts. Some university officials complained that the new regulations had increased the number of denials of foreign students and scholars, but some had long-expired visas that had just been ignored previously. These overstayers had returned home for a family matter, found they had to reapply for an entry visa, and then were deemed to have immigrated illegally and were denied entry. By 2007, however, foreign student applications had reached record highs, and delays had decreased.

Often a visa document will be designated "multiple-entry visa good for 10 years." This means only that the recipient can come to a U.S. port of entry multiple times during a consecutive 10-year time period. It does not mean that the holder can stay in the United States for 10 years, coming in and out. It does not mean that the holder can get a job and work in the United States for 10 years. It is not officially a status document or a work permit, although it is often used to demonstrate legal status such as it is.

Once the applicant is accepted for a visa, the immigration inspector at the port of entry will give him or her an I-94 form on which it is marked clearly what classification of stay the holder has: tourist, business, temporary workers, student, religious worker, and so on. Each of these specific classifications has its own limitations for length of stay and permit to work. Many (such as tourist permits) do not allow the holder to work at all. On the I-94 form, a warning is printed: "A nonimmigrant who accepts unauthorized employment is subject to deportation." On the I-94W form, the visa-waiver country holder is warned in addition, "You may not attend school or represent the foreign information media during your visit under this program, nor apply for a change of nonimmigrant status or adjustment to temporary or permanent resident." Both documents state that they must be retained in the possession of the holder until they exit.

A visa does not even guarantee entry into the United States. A visa is issued by a Department of State consular office abroad, but a separate

U.S. agency, the U.S. Customs and Border Protection Agency (CBP) out
of the Department of Homeland Security, has the ultimate authority
to deny admission at the port of entry. The period for which the visa
holder is authorized to remain in the United States is determined by the
CBP at the port of entry, not the Department of State consular office.

Green card holders do not need a visa to enter into the United States,
but they still need to show their national passport as well as their green
card in order to reenter the country—just as anyone from a visa-waiver
country must do.

### Legal Permanent Resident

In the United States, "immigrant" is the term usually applied to a
foreign national—also referred to in legal parlance as an "alien"—who
has a legal and official U.S. permit to live and work permanently in the
United States. This permit is known popularly as a "green card."

In recent years, the U.S. Citizenship and Immigration Services (USCIS)
has granted over 1 million new permanent immigrant legal permits a
year—more than any other country.

A legal permanent resident (LPR) immigrant can stay their lifetime
in the United States with almost no restrictions on working (except
perhaps in positions requiring top-secret clearances), traveling, owning
property, doing business, or receiving public benefits and other privileges of permanent residency. The main thing he or she is not allowed
to do is to vote; the right to vote remains the exclusive privilege of a U.S.
citizen. The green card can be revoked if the LPR commits certain crimes
or is found to have "abandoned" their green card by living abroad for
more than six months without notifying the USCIS.

The green card is the only status from which a foreign national can
apply for citizenship. It is not a requirement. No permanent resident
is ever required to become a U.S. citizen, and permanent residents
can (and most do) live their entire lives in the United States without
ever becoming a citizen. According to the Pew Hispanic Center (PHC),
in 2005 about 12.8 million foreign-born residents (52 percent) were
naturalized citizens out of a total of 288 million at that time. By 2007,
the U.S. population had grown to over 300 million—mainly through
immigration and births to foreign-born mothers. That summer, immigration activist groups (especially Latino) announced they would

be pursuing active campaigns to get the some 8 million eligible legal immigrants to apply for citizenship and to subsequently register to vote. The number of green card holders who obtain citizenship (i.e., are "naturalized") each year is increasing from an average of about 150,000 a year in the 1970s to over 600,000 in the 1990s. Immigrant activists in 2007 hoped to see that number climb to 1 million from all over the world (although only a small proportion are Latinos or Mexicans, as they "have a comparatively lower tendency to become U.S. citizens than other nationalities" according to the PHC). Certainly proximity of their homelands has much to do with this. "Latinos aren't that interested in becoming citizens," said Congressman Luis Gutierrez (D-Ill.) to a group of Latin American journalists at the National Press Club on April 18, 2007. "Most of them just want to be able to go back and forth from their homelands to work in the U.S. with ease."[1]

In general, in order to apply for citizenship, a foreign national must have been in the United States on a permanent residency status green card for at least five years (spouses three years) with a clean criminal record. The application processing time can take up to a year and includes a test on U.S. history and constitutional principles and an English exam (usually oral). Both tests were upgraded in 2006 and 2007. The application fee was also raised in 2007 from $330 for adult applicants and $255 for minors plus a $70 fingerprinting fee to $595 for adults and $460 for minors plus a $80 fee for biometric identifiers. There is no fee for military applicants. "The high costs for naturalization may be one factor that discourages low-income immigrants from naturalizing at the same rates as higher-income immigrants," stated an "Immigration Facts" report of the Migration Policy Institute in February 2007.[2]

About 20 percent of green cards every year (some 200,000) are granted to a primary worker in a family. The rest are granted each year on the basis of family kinship to the primary worker as well as a few to refugees and lottery winners. The primary green card holder normally obtains green cards first for a spouse and minor children, and there is no number restrictions on those relations. But since the Immigration Reform and Control Act (IRCA) of 1965, the primary permanent immigrant also can apply for green cards for his or her adult children and their spouses and children, adult brothers and sisters and their family members, grandparents, and other dependent relatives including cousins—in other words, extended family members (this is often referred to as "chain migration"). These "preference visas" are limited in number (minimums) by prioritized criteria including relationship, age, and status of the family sponsor.[3]

Outside of these restrictions, the United States does not discriminate in granting green cards on the basis of age, disabilities, gender, and/or cultural differences. A little-known fact about new permanent immigrants is that senior citizens and disabled family members who are granted green cards are immediately eligible for Social Security insurance benefits regardless of whether they or any family member ever paid into the system.

Since 1965, IRCA eliminated all national quotas for green cards. There is in general no preference for any particular nationality, and some skill and achievement requirements are still in place for certain employment categories. Since the terrorist attacks of 9/11, however, immigrant applications from foreign nationals from designated "terrorist harboring countries" have been scrutinized with additional attention, and applicants from those countries may have a higher likelihood of being denied. "National security" has now become a focus of some of the immigration reform debate but not yet much of a factor affecting the acceptance of green card applications.

The number of green cards given out to any one specific country is also restricted. To be inclusive and fair, the Immigration and Nationality Act caps the number of annual "family preference" green cards so that citizens from no one country can receive more than 7 percent of the total minimum number of 226,000 employment-based green cards given out each year.[4] According to Michael Hoefer, director of the Office of Immigration Statistics for the Department of Homeland Security, at a hearing on government immigration statistics before the House Subcommittee on Immigration on June 6, 2007, "No more than 25,620 green cards can be granted to family members of employment-based immigrants from ANY one country. Dependents are limited to 7,320 or about two percent of the total. Completed applications are counted in the order received on a first come first serve basis. Once a country's numerical limit has been reached, any further completed applicants received from citizens of that country will be put on a wait list in order of receipt."[5]

The waiting list of eligible completed applications is years long for countries where visa demand exceeds the per country limit (the "oversubscribed list"). Countries at present that are on the so-called visa pro-rated list are Mexico, mainland China, India, and the Philippines. For other countries like Iceland, for instance, there is rarely a waiting list based on that nationality. But once the total number of limited preference categories (some 400,000) have been accepted for any year, all other applications received are put on the waiting list by country and date of receipt. "It is impossible for us to accept all the eligible applications we receive from family members alone every year. There is an agreed upon total number of around one million—the most generous country in the world. Anyone who is denied or who has been on a waiting list or who has a family member on a waiting list for years complains that this is unfair, but do you have a better idea? We can't have open borders."[6] This explains the often-heard complaint of legal residents that they have been waiting for years to bring in their adult children or parents, aunts or uncles, grandparents, and so on, all of whom are totally eligible to come in but have to wait their turn for a green card. They are frustrated, of course. They are doing things legally and feel that they have the right to bring in their numerous relatives when they want.

From the immigrant's point of view, waiting years for a legally eligible family member to get a green card is heartbreakingly unfair.

But to the nation-state, the other key "player" in immigration, it is the only fair way to deal with millions of wannabe immigrants. A universal fact is that it is a nation-state's inherent right to determine exactly who and how many and how foreign nationals can enter and stay in the country. This is what immigration laws and border enforcement are all about. It is an indisputable practice that all nation-states or unions of nation-states in the world maintain and mutually honor. This is even truer in the age of global corporate capitalism and twenty-first century communication and transportation devices that makes it far easier for migrants to leave their homelands than ever before. But nation-states and unions of nation-states with definable borders still exist despite many prophesies of their demise. The reality is that well-defined nation-states not only exist but are multiplying as well, and they set immigration rules for themselves as an unarguable right of a sovereign country.

For aspiring immigrants from high migrant source countries, immigration into any specific country is a numbers game.

There is one other category of immigrant that needs to be defined here: refugees. When most people think of refugees, they think of large groups of mainly helpless women, children, and aged people from specific geographic areas who are facing massive death because of a natural disaster or war in their home region and who must be moved in order to be saved. Refugees are the most desperate of migrants, and they pose a moral and a logistical challenge to all citizens in all nations of the world. The United States has also been involved—supporting world organizations such as the United Nations High Commission on Refugees, sending in U.S. military missions to protect and move refugees, and helping a variety of nonprofit organizations work in refugee camps throughout the world.

But the world refugee problem is tremendous. "Of the nearly 12 million in the world today, more than 7 million are warehoused—confined to camps or segregated settlements or otherwise deprived of basic rights lasting ten years or more," according to a May 2007 statement by the U.S. Committee for Refugees and Immigration.[7]

The U.S. refugee program is managed out of the departments of State, Health and Human Services, and Homeland Security. The refugee program is an immigration program that lies outside the regular green card system and has its own highly restricted numerical limitations that often have been set by the president. The program identifies, interviews, and accepts refugees who meet stringent refugee qualifications including that they can prove (or at least convince a judge) that they face likely persecution if they return to their homelands. Once passed, refugees (and often their families) are transported to a specific town where they are met by town sponsors (usually from local churches or nonprofit organizations), given a place to live and help for children and aged members to get into public schools and onto applicable public benefits, enroll in English classes, and get a job or into job-training or higher-education programs. After a year, the refugees are allowed to apply for a green card.

In 2007, the number of refugees allowed to come to the United States under the refugee program was 70,000 a year. However, only about 50,000 actually were accepted. "This is partly because many refugees coming out of war countries are found to have committed disqualifying violations, mainly in terms of accepting material support from an organization that the U.S. considers to be a terrorist support group," according to Kelly Ryan of the Bureau of Population, Refugees, and Migration.[8] The "material support" limitation was part of the REAL ID Act that was passed by Congress in 2005. "It paralyzes America's traditionally generous refugee admission program," *Washington Post* editorial writers charged in April of that year.[9]

By 2007, the Iraqi refugee problem was becoming an issue. "Iraqi citizens are fleeing their homes at the rate of 50,000 a month and they need help" was the headline of a *Washington Post* editorial in January 2007.[10] Legislation was introduced that year to resettle into the United States 15,000 "special immigrant status" Iraqis and their families for each of the next four years. It is likely that priority for Iraqi resettlement will be given to those Iraqis who worked for Americans during the war.[11]

There is another way for a foreign national to get a green card, though it has been so fraudulently used that it is a program that might well be in its last years. The congressionally mandated Diversity Immigrant Visa Program makes available 50,000 permanent resident visas annually, drawn from random selection among all entries to persons who meet strict eligibility requirements from countries with low rates of immigration to the United States.

## Legal Temporary Nonimmigrant/Visitors Permits

A temporary permit holder is a foreign national who enters the country legally on one of dozens of different kinds of temporary permits, such as tourist or visitor (three days to six months), professional or skilled worker (usually on a three-year H-1B permit), foreign student (F, J, or M permits good for the duration of studies plus a year of practical training), or season agricultural worker (H-2 permits). Nearly 2 million foreign nationals enter the United States legally every year on such temporary permits. Many of the temporary permit categories (such as tourists and foreign students) are unlimited in number. Others (such as H-1B and agricultural workers) are limited in number. But all temporary permits have the same kinds of conditions.[12]

As seen earlier, the kinds and numbers of temporary permits have grown exponentially since 1965 in part because of the elimination of the work skills that for 200 years had been the basis of granting immigrant status.[13] Because over 80 percent of the available green cards today are granted on the basis of family ties, not work skills, the need for foreign labor in certain job categories has increasingly been met by these temporary work permits. In the past few years, these permits have become controversial and maligned. "This guestworker program is the closest thing I've ever seen to slavery," Congressman Charles Rangel (D-N.Y.), chairman of the House Ways and Means Committee, has been quoted as saying.[14] "They create a permanent second-class tier of laborers in America," Latino activists pushing for citizenship for illegal and temporary workers often proclaim.

### Tourist or Visitor Permit

Foreign nationals who wish to visit the United States for leisure or tourism are normally eligible to receive B-2 permits. They are required for citizens of countries that are not included in the visa-waiver program. However, citizens of countries included in the visa-waiver program may also be required to obtain a B-2 visa if they plan to stay in the United States for longer than 90 days or change status to other immigration categories after entering the country. B-2 visas are also issued to individuals who are coming to the United States to undergo medical treatment. The application process is similar to that of a visitor for tourism, but there are additional documents that must be submitted to establish that the applicant qualifies.

Persons admitted to the United States on a B-2 nonimmigrant visitor visa are usually issued a six-month stay at maximum. The immigration officer at the port of entry determines how long each visitor is allowed to stay in the country. Most visitors have their I-94 cards stamped with a six-month stay; however, the immigration officer has the right to issue a shorter stay on a case-by-case basis. On entry into the United States, the foreign visitor has the right to request an extension of stay. Individuals who enter on B-2 visitor visas are normally eligible to change to another status if they qualify. But those who enter under the visa-waiver program are not eligible to change status—which is the major advantage of nonimmigrant visas over the visa waivers.

Anyone admitted to the United States under a B-2 visitor visa is not allowed to work or receive any kind of payment while staying in the United States. Foreign nationals who wish to work in the United States must apply for a work visa, such as an H-1B or H-2B permit.

## The H-1B Permit

This was once the most popular work visa in the United States, but its numbers were decreased from several hundred thousand in the 1990s to 65,000 at present.[15] It was established for professionals with a college degree (although it is often marketed as a way to keep the best and brightest of the world who go to American universities to stay in the country to found dot-com industries employing thousands of U.S. workers or brilliant biotech researchers working on cancer). But it has been used increasingly for lower-level tech workers in research labs and computer production companies as well as for skilled medical techs, teachers, semiprofessional trainers, and even stablemen and party valets. Most of the annual allotment of available permits is taken within the first week of offering, often by high-tech companies hiring large number of foreign tech personnel from Asia who are given the permits either abroad or when they graduate from U.S. universities.

In 2006–2007, a campaign was conducted by various universities to include an H-1B expansion piece in immigration reform bills. They argued in congressional hearings and in the press that the United States surely will lose its competitiveness, prosperity, and future if the number of H-1Bs is not increased by hundreds of thousands immediately. In a unique single-witness hearing before the Senate Education Committee in the spring of 2007, Bill Gates made a case to attach a green card to every foreign student's graduating with an advanced degree from a U.S. university in a science or engineering field (increasingly, more foreign students are graduate students than undergrads and earn the majority of science and engineering graduate degrees at many U.S. colleges and universities).

Many other categories of temporary workers are increasingly seen in the United States (sometimes under the special H-2B or J visas). Vacation employees mainly from eastern Europe are often hired by the thousands as hotel and shop workers and especially lifeguards in summer resort cities like Ocean City, Virginia, and Sun Valley, Idaho, and at most national parks and often at large condominium swimming pools throughout the country. Schoolteachers and tutors, especially in math and science, increasingly come to the United States from the Philippines, according to a *Washington Post* article, making 10 times more money than they could in their homeland.[16] Summer help for festivals and parties come increasingly from South America. In most cases, employers claim that it is impossible to find American teenagers to do this work and that they are forced to hire foreign workers from May through September. Often the eager young foreign workers take on two or three jobs during a summer to make money to live on the rest of the year, according to the *Post.*

### Foreign Student Permits

The foreign student visa is by far our most generous and positive and cherished temporary permit.[17] Since the 1940s, when it was established to allow bright young people from war-torn countries to have a chance to pursue their studies, it was always regarded as a temporary nonimmigrant visa. The numbers were few; most were elite students going to elite universities. Now, according to the 2007 Open Doors report of the International Institute of Education, "international education is our fifth largest service export, bigger than medical services."

There are three kinds of foreign student permits:[18]

1. M: For trade schools and vocational certificate programs offered by private "professional" schools and (decreasingly) by community college vocational education and language certificate programs (M2s are for spouses and children). Before 9/11, thousands of educational institutions, from trade schools to university extension programs, offered graduate "certificates" in bartending, cosmetology, flight training, graphic design, computer technology, and language classes and were loosely vetted by M visas. There are no work permits with the M visa, except for a short practical training for M visas.
2. F: Mainly for college degree programs (associate degree to Ph.D.) and English-language programs offered by colleges. Since 2004, more F1 college students are graduate students than undergraduates. F visas can also be used for exchange students in elementary and secondary schools.
3. J: For research scholars and visiting professors at universities, think tanks, and research labs. Usually these carry a three-year, nonrenewable limit.

## Seasonal Agricultural or Farmworker Permit

According to the Department of Labor, the only legal mechanism through which to contract people from outside the United States to work on farms here is the H-2A work visa program. A key prerequisite for issuance of H-2A visas is certification by the Department of Labor that the specific jobs for which foreign workers are sought could not be filled from the U.S.-resident labor supply. Agricultural employers have to demonstrate a labor shortage to import foreign workers on a temporary basis under terms and conditions that will result in no adverse effect to U.S. workers.[19]

There are many bureaucratic hurdles to meet before the permits can be granted. Beyond the certification that the foreign farmworkers are not taking jobs away from native and naturalized citizens and LPRs, employers must also meet several required terms of employment of H-2A workers, including provision of transportation from and back to their home country, housing while here, and a state-specific "adverse effect" pay rate generally higher than minimum wage.

It is not surprising, then, that most foreign agriculture workers do not come in under the H-2A program. According to Marcos Camacho, general counsel for the United Farm Workers at a congressional hearing,

Today, we have reached a situation in agriculture that demands urgent action. There are about 2.5 million farmworkers in this country, not including their family members. More than 80% of them are foreign-born, mostly but not all from Mexico. Virtually all of the newest entrants to the farm labor force lack authorized immigration status. The helpful reports from the National Agricultural Workers Survey by the U.S. Department of Labor state that about 53% of farmworkers are undocumented. But most observers believe the figure is 60% or 70%, and much higher in specific locations.

Many employers now hire farm labor contractors in the hope that they can shield themselves from liability for hiring undocumented workers in violation of our immigration law and from liability for labor law violations. The labor contractors compete against one another by offering to do a job for less money, and the cut-throat competition means that the workers must take lower wages. When one labor contractor is prosecuted for violating labor laws, he is easily replaced. Our current immigration system is causing employers to attempt to evade responsibility for their employees, while undocumented workers are too fearful of being deported to demand changes. In many cases, due to inadequate enforcement of labor laws, employers take advantage of undocumented workers by subjecting them to illegal wages and working conditions.[20]

Many proposals have been included in various immigration reform bills and in stand-alone bills, especially by Senator Diane Feinstein (D-Calif.), to make it easier for employers to hire foreign farmworkers, particularly for the bend-over agricultural labor on American farms. All these bills have failed to date, largely because they are usually included as part of a gigantic omnibus or comprehensive immigration package containing controversial elements such as legalization and a "pathway to citizenship" for farmworkers presently in the country illegally. After the first bill failed to pass cloture in early June 2007, Senator Feinstein remarked on the floor and on the record to an empty Senate chamber that the bill was "probably too massive and it might be best to break up some of the pieces and try to have them pass on their own."[21] She meant the agriculture bill part. But she tried that in December 2006, and her separate bill also failed; the bill included a "pathway to citizenship" for illegal workers (some 60 percent of whom are hired and working illegally, "without documents" or with fraudulent documents). Legalization of illegal workers poisoned the bill. On October 31, 2007, I asked Agriculture Committee Chairman Senator Tom Harkins (D-Iowa) if he was expecting Senator Feinstein to add the AgJobs amendment to the farm bill to be voted on the next week. He said very firmly, "She told me she would propose it and I told her I would not support it. Even though I supported it in the immigration bill, I don't want to drag down the farm bill with a filibuster or anything like that. It is an immigration matter. It is part of comprehensive immigration reform and we won't get to that until 2009 or after."

## Other Temporary Permits

The K-1, also known as the fiancé(e) visa, may be used by U.S. citizens who wish to bring their prospective husbands or wives to the United States with the intention of getting married. Minor children of fiancé(e)s can also accompany them to the United States as they can be issued K-2 visas. The U.S. citizen must file a petition with the USCIS on behalf of the foreign fiancé(e). After the petition is approved, the fiancé(e) can obtain a K-1 fiancé(e) visa. The K-1 visa is issued at a U.S. embassy or consulate abroad. The marriage must take place within 90 days of the fiancé(e) entering the United States.

Individuals who are employed outside the United States as executives or managers or in a position that requires specialized knowledge may qualify for an L-1 intracompany transfer work visa. If the applicant is already in the United States, a change of status might be possible. A change of status enables the individual to obtain L-1 status without leaving the country and having to apply for the L-1 visa at a U.S. embassy or consulate abroad. The process of completing and submitting a request for a L-1 intracompany transfer visa can be both costly and confusing. It has also been misused by companies to bring in foreign national workers to do jobs Americans could very well do. Recently the visa has come under close scrutiny, especially where American ports are managed by foreign companies.

The O classification is for individuals with "extraordinary" abilities within science, arts, education, business, or athletics at the national or international level. Individuals with a record of extraordinary achievements within motion pictures and/or television can also apply for the O-1 visa as long as the work performed is in an area of extraordinary achievements. O-2 visas are for supporting individuals of the O-1 visa holder, and the relationship between the O-1 and O-2 visa holder must have been long lasting. The spouse and unmarried children of O-1 visa holders are entitled to O-3 visas to come to the Unites States with the main O-1 visa holder. The work performed must be temporary. The individual must possess skills that are extraordinary within the field of sciences, arts, education, business, or athletics or within the field of the motion picture or television industry. Examples of proof of extraordinary ability can be contracts, awards, nominations, prices, published material, or similar documentation reflecting the nature of the individual's achievement. This visa has been commonly misused, however, especially by foreign students getting Ph.D.s in the United States and using their academic relations here and abroad to proclaim extraordinary ability that often may not be any more than an American Ph.D.

Individuals who are members of legitimate religious organizations may be eligible for a so-called R-1 religious worker permit allowing them to live and work legally in the United States for a specific period of time. These visas are made available to members of the clergy and also to key employees of religious organizations. R-1 visas can be obtained if the applicant has been a member of a legitimate religious denomination for at least two years. R-2 visas can be obtained for accompanying relatives of the main applicant (R-1 visa holder). This permit has come under considerable scrutiny recently.

Asylees are another large source of temporary permits. Asylees are accepted as expedited temporary residents after their country has suffered natural disasters or civil disorders or if they can demonstrate a credible fear of persecution in their home countries. Their status is often legislated by Congress. Their period of asylum is limited to a certain number of months or years and indicated on their asylum documents. The period can be extended. Immigrants in distress can also be granted a "temporary protected status" visa for a specified amount of time, which also can be extended. In the 1980s, hundreds of thousands of El Salvadorians were granted asylum in the United States after their country erupted into civil war. By 2007, their "temporary" protective status periods and "temporary" work permits had been extended so many times and for so many years that now the immigrants are demanding that they be given permanent residency status and the rights of citizenship. El Salvadorian consulate offices have recently sprung up all over Washington, D.C., where El Salvadorians are the largest Latino immigrant nationality.

### "Illegal Alien"

This is the official term for a foreign national who either snuck into the country illegally or entered the country legally on a temporary permit and stayed on after the permit had expired, leaving them in the country illegally. If they reside and work with the intention of staying, they could then be called an illegal immigrant.

It is estimated that there are some 12 million to 20 million illegal immigrants presently in the United States (as of 2004 Census surveys).[22] Twelve million is the minimum number that is admitted by just about everyone involved with the issue. It is a matter of concern since in 1986 the IRCA legislation was supposed to have stopped illegal immigration by granting a one-time-only amnesty to all illegal aliens in the country at the time. It was estimated then that about 1 million foreign nationals would be eligible for the amnesty. In fact, over 3 million have requested (and still are to this date) amnesty. Many experts strongly believe that today the number of illegal immigrants may also be double to triple the number counted by the 2000 Census—some 11.5 million. I consider the number of 16 million illegal aliens an honest estimate.

Experts also agree that approximately 55 to 60 percent of illegal immigrants snuck into the country illegally—about 50 percent over the Mexican border with the United States. But not all of these are Mexican nationals. Every year, about 13 percent of the some 500,000 people who sneak over the Mexican border every year are OTMs ("other than Mexicans"). Most are from Central America, a growing percentage are from Latin America and Brazil, and the rest are from Asia and the Caribbean. A growing number of OTMs (less than 1 percent are estimated to be from the Middle East).

The other 40 to 45 percent of illegal immigrants in the country, then, are foreign nationals who entered the country on legal visas. They overstay tourist and foreign student visas and come from throughout the world. Some 100,000 illegal aliens in the United States are Irish citizens, and they are vocal for "comprehensive" immigration reform that includes legalization of all illegal aliens. Often groups of young Irish adults who are in the country illegally attend the various immigration hearings in Congress and lobby especially the Irish-heritage members of Congress to demand that they "legalize the Irish"—the name of their organization that appears prominently on the backs of their Irish green T-shirts. The Irish youths often pass out bright green brochures proclaiming, "We need *Your* help to keep the Irish in America." The brochure includes quotes and photos of smiling Senators John McCain (R-Ariz.), Hillary Clinton (D-N.Y.), Ted Kennedy (D-Mass.), Sam Brownback (R-Kans.), and Charles Schumer (D-N.Y.). "You are really here on behalf of what America means," Clinton is quoted to say (let's hope she is not referring to their illegal status).

It is estimated that of the 600,000 foreign nationals studying on foreign student visas presently in the United States, at least 50 percent (or some 300,000) will stay on even though their permits require them to return home after their studies. Among graduate students, some 70 percent stay on. Many of these former students will at first seek to "adjust" their temporary permits to a green card or to another temporary permit, usually the H-1B. Some will marry U.S. citizens, some will win the lottery, and some will stay on as university and research scholars.

But many of these former foreign students will stay on illegally—as did some of the 9/11 terrorists.

The illegal staying-on of foreign students is not the part of the foreign student visa for which university officials feel responsible. Although they are vetted by the State Department to issue the foreign student visa and thereby receive the lucrative benefits of hosting foreign students, officials of the National Association of Foreign Student Advisors are clear that it is not their duty to enforce the "return home" part of the visa or indeed to even know where their foreign student is or whether he or she ever left the country. "We are not policemen," they say. But some do believe they have other duties other than being mere foreign student advisers, however. For instance, the welcoming sign at the office of my University of California's foreign student office for years displayed the services "International Student and Immigration Advisors." But certainly most of the university officials who enthusiastically welcome Bill Gates's proposal to tag every college STEM diploma with a green card would never agree that the numbers of such immigration degrees should be limited in any way. They certainly would not want their foreign student number to be limited by a U.S. law defining the number of green cards that could be given out in a year—even if those green cards would be determined by a point system prioritizing U.S. college degree earners first. Rather, colleges have come to depend on the increased revenue from foreign student tuition fees (three times that of U.S. students) and need to be able to keep encouraging foreign students to come to the United States and pay those high fees by enticing them with the promise of jobs and even green cards after their studies.

## Criminal Status

Legally, every illegal alien in the United States is committing at least a serious civil offense just by being in the country without a permit—punishable with removal or sometimes up to a year in prison and a fine of up to several thousand dollars. But the criminal status of an illegal alien can easily escalate to a felony if a crime is committed, if false documents are used, or if the foreign national reenters the country after having been forcibly deported—all punishable by deportation and a permanent criminal record making them ineligible to enter the country in the future.[23] The continued presence and employment of an illegal alien puts them and their families at risk of being declared such felons.

Again, both misdemeanors and felonies are punishable by deportation—voluntary or involuntary.[24] (If you think this is harsh, look at what other countries do. In Mexico, for example, as in most countries of the world, illegal residency in the country is considered to be a *felony*. Period. Most countries enforce their laws and punish accordingly.)

The status of an illegal alien gets stickier when the following occur:

1. A temporary permit has expired but the holder has applied for a permanent green card, which legally they should apply for only when abroad. American immigration lawyers make a lot of money from the "in-transition" immigrant (they particularly like the highly educated ones), and it can take thousands of dollars, many years, and a lot of tension to fix the status. It is allowable to make the adjustment if the H-1B employer is sponsoring the green card application or if they have married an American (legitimately).
2. An illegal alien has a child born in the United States. Legally the parents may have a "fast track" to citizenship once the child is 21, but having an American citizen child does not automatically give the parents either a green card or even the automatic right to a temporary work permit. Legally the parent should return to the homeland, and there is absolutely no requirement for parents to take their American children back to their native lands with them. Usually the child has dual nationality, and, as a citizen, he or she will always have the right to come back to the United States.
3. Illegal aliens who marry American citizens can adjust their status to a green card without falling into the 3/10-year bar and need only wait three instead of five years to apply for citizenship if they want. But recently, multiple marriages of foreign nationals with American citizens who are apparent strangers have come under scrutiny in courthouses throughout the country and have been exposed for the immigration scams they are.

## Legal Rights of and Benefits for Illegal Aliens

Illegal aliens have no legal rights to work or to collect most public benefits or get publicly funded loans for college, and they do not of course have all the civil rights of citizens or even permanent immigrants. Still, however, illegal aliens have many rights in the United States that they are not afforded in any other country in the world, including the right of habeas corpus and the right to a court trial if arrested for a criminal offense. Illegal aliens also have the right to certain federal public benefits, including the following:

- They can get free medical care in any public emergency medical facility—whether or not their condition is truly an immediate medical emergency and even if their condition is a minor ailment or a chronic disease like diabetes or cancer or even an organ transplant.
- The minor children of illegal immigrants are allowed to attend public schools for kindergarten through grade 12 for free and to obtain the required vaccinations free of charge.
- In some states, illegal alien young adult children who graduate from a state's public high school are allowed to attend the public colleges of that state for the in-state tuition rate, not the much higher tuition that out-of-state American students, legal foreign students, and the children of temporary permit holders (such as H-1B holders) must pay. There are pending lawsuits—University of California at Berkeley for one—against granting benefits to adult illegal residents that U.S. citizens don't have. The suit was brought against the university by students from Hawaii and is at the time of writing on appeal.

Illegal aliens in the United States also are protected by federal law from being asked their legal status by just about any public official (educators, medical personnel, and so on). But in some cases, federal law does allow law enforcement to ask for status if there are "articulable facts suggesting the persons they are pursing are noncitizens"—a lower bar than "probable cause." It depends on the jurisdiction. Some states and counties are allowing, even requiring, their law enforcement personnel to ask status of those stopped even for minor infractions, while other jurisdictions forbid it. Just a few entities are required to ascertain the legal status of an individual, including employers (including individuals hiring people to work in their private homes and gardens), U.S. immigration service and enforcement bureaus, state departments of motor vehicles, public colleges or universities, and Social Security offices (although most of these entities offer documents to legal temporary permit holders). Usually the requested status is to be designated in writing (usually by checking a box marked "citizen" or not) on a written application. If the box is marked "citizen" or if a status document (like a Social Security card or a state driver's license) that the holder asserts is legal is presented (even if it is fraudulent), most institutions like colleges are not allowed to query further. Usually most small employers never will ask for the holder to prove whether a presented document is valid.

In a number of American cities, local legislators have been pushed by constituents (particularly the Catholic Church and immigrant advocacy organizations) to make their cities sanctuaries for illegal immigrants.[25] In these communities they openly give illegal workers identity cards and offer them benefits such as free job training and searching, health services, language education for adults, and legal advocacy and protection (mainly noncooperation) and sanctuary against the U.S. Homeland Security Immigration Enforcement raids or investigations. They forbid their local law enforcement officers to ascertain the legal status of anyone, *including criminal detainees*, or to participate or help federal law enforcement officials in enforcing federal laws regarding labor law and employer sanctions.

The United States also offers an almost unique right to illegal aliens: birth rights citizenship. It allows that any child born to an illegal alien may nevertheless be considered to be a U.S. citizen. This has become very controversial and is increasingly being considered a misinterpretation of the Fourteenth Amendment, which states, "All persons born or naturalized in the United States *and subject to the jurisdiction thereof,* are citizens of the United States" (emphasis added).

It is a singular fact that the United States is the only country in the world where millions of foreign nationals live, some for decades, and are hired illegally with almost total impunity. The "unauthorized population" (as the Migration Policy Institute calls illegal aliens) was estimated to be growing by over 500,000 individuals per year.

## Why Do Immigrants Come? Why Do Americans Welcome Them— and Why Not?

There is no disputing that the United States issues more permanent and temporary visas to legal immigrants than any country in the world and has millions of foreign nationals living and working illegally in the country. Immigrants to the United States come from every country in the world, although Mexico accounts for the most (30.7 percent) followed by the Philippines, China, and India. According to the U.S. Census Bureau's 2006 American Community Survey, there were 37,547,789 foreign born in the United States, which represents 12.5 percent of the total U.S. population.[26] While the issue of immigration is complex and multifaceted, there is actually a consensus among all experts on immigration regarding the whys. It is all about jobs.

"Immigrants come to work" is heard so often that it is practically a mantra. It is the undisputed number one reason cited for immigration by almost everyone. Of course there are many other ways to say it. "Immigrants are hardworking people who come to provide for their families, to make a better life for themselves, to work hard, and to pursue the American Dream." These are all commonly heard and almost universally accepted as the primary reason immigrants come to the United States.

But of course work is also not the whole story of why immigrants come to the United States. Some say that legal and illegal immigrants bring their extended families to the United States precisely to get all the free benefits allowed them. As mentioned previously, even migrants who are in the country illegally nevertheless receive many taxpayer-supported benefits.

Many desire to immigrate to the United States for other less tangible but nevertheless extremely important benefits besides work. Two in particular are the following:

1. Freedom: Many immigrants appreciate freedom of educational and economic opportunity and freedom from the constraints of gender, age, family history, and historical relationships.
2. Law and order: America is known as a land of the rule of law; many immigrants come from countries rife with corruption and injustice (even some European countries do not have the legal protections of habeas corpus). Even middle America's adherence to laws covering such mundane activities as pedestrian crossings, traffic lights, and littering is an attractive alternative to their experiences in the native homelands.

All these benefits of living in the United States can be said to constitute the American Dream. And that is really what immigrants seek when they come to America.

### Why Do Americans Welcome Immigrants?

Not surprisingly, Americans actually have somewhat the same reason to welcome immigrants to the country and their communities as do immigrants for coming: it is about work or, in this context, labor needs. And it is about making money (building prosperity, if you want to make it sound nicer). From the time the colonists planted their flags and built their first farms, villages, and forts, they welcomed immigrants for the labor they could supply and the prosperity they could help build. There is no doubt that the primary reason immigrants have been welcomed (and regulated) in first the colonial states and then the federal ones was for the work they could contribute—as employee and then eventually, as expected, as employer.

In *Seizing Destiny*, Richard Kluger relates how our founders—the Puritans of New England, the tobacco planters of the South, and President Thomas Jefferson—believed that what truly set America apart was its virtually unlimited supply of land and the ability to attract the labor to work it.[27] Early colonists, including indentured servants and later homesteaders and land grantees from Europe, all were promised landownership as their prize for hard work and long hours of servitude. If they followed the rules, they got freedom and land. The magic of America is that from early on, former servants, workers, farm laborers, craftsmen, and even some slaves could become citizens and leaders if they worked hard enough and played by the rules. All were encouraged to exploit labor and land and to build prosperity just as their former masters had done.

This is the American Dream—equality and opportunity and inclusiveness for those who follow the rules and regulations. This is the basis of why immigrants come and why Americans welcome them.

## WHAT IS THE AMERICAN DREAM?

Most all of us will nod our heads in agreement as soon as we hear the phrase "the American Dream" when used in terms of immigrant and U.S. workers' aspirations. We all seem to know what the American Dream is, even while there seems to be some confusion about exactly who exactly should be called an "American."

A recent comprehensive study on the American Dream defines it well. "The American Dream is rooted in the workplace and it is tied to the job," according to Celinda Lake.[28] "Work is seen as a value, not just a means to an end. The American Dream is a powerful expression of values, not just an outcome of work. In America, work is a core value. Americans believe that hard work should be respected and rewarded—with wages that support a family, affordable quality health care, opportunities for your children and retirement security."

The American Dream, of course, is about more than just work. Most immigration experts and most Americans agree on this: the American Dream is also about keeping basic American values, such as justice and the rule of law.

When John Tirman wrote *The 100 Ways Americans Are Screwing Up the World*, he wanted to assure his readers that he really does hold America in high esteem.[29] In his concluding chapter, "The Ten Things America Does Right in the World," he stated that many of the "good" things relate to immigration:

1. The open door
2. Honoring diversity
3. Aiding the weary
4. Human rights
5. The rule of law—"a nation of laws not of men"
6. Fairness
7. Citizenship
8. Secularism
9. Creativity
10. Educational excellence

Similar values are identified as being inherently American by Anne-Marie Slaughter in her book *The Idea That Is America*.[30] The values she writes about are the following:

1. Liberty
2. Democracy
3. Equality
4. Justice—an American obsession fashioned by laws, adjudicated by the courts
5. Tolerance
6. Humility
7. Faith

Obviously being open about immigration reflects almost all American values and our vision of the American Dream—work opportunities and the rule of law. Both Tirman (professor at the Massachusetts Institute of Technology) and Slaughter (dean at Princeton University) emphasize that the rule of law makes America not only safe to live in but also a country that believes in and practices justice for all.

### Anxiety about the Economy

As we have seen, the American Dream is dependent on the contin-ued availability of work opportunities and security, both of which are dependent on the economic progress of the United States. "Americans believe in progress, that everything gets better, that things will always improve," said Celinda Lake.[31] "The American Dream means your chil-dren will do better than you do by working hard." Throughout history, ever-optimistic future-oriented Americans have included immigrants in that American Dream. Throughout our history, prosperity was built on moving up, often with new immigrants to take the growing jobs you moved out of or, in some places today (Silicon Valley, for instance), to build high-tech businesses that your children would prosper in. "Americans believe that hard work should lead to economic security and upward mobility for your family."

But what happens when that American Dream seems less obtain-able? "Nearly three out of four American workers believe the American Dream is becoming harder to reach; and two out of three believe it is harder for their generation and will be harder for the next generation to achieve," researchers found.[32] "Every demographic group [is] deeply pessimistic about the state of the country's economy," they write.

Almost everyone agrees these days that all the macroeconomic indica-tors (such as gross domestic product, productivity, and the unemploy-ment rate) portray the United States as having a strong and slowly grow-ing economy. Still most American middle- and working--class families have experienced wage stagnation and fear of (if not actual) job loss over the past five years. According to the American Dream study, "Work-ers are anxious and angry about the state of the economy. They believe strongly that despite the news accounts of economic growth, working families are falling behind. Their anger and anxiety is rooted in concern over the basics: health care (over 65 percent of workers have either recently or currently been without health care coverage), retirement, personal debt, paying the bills (including for gasoline, the mortgage and college tuition). Over three out of ten workers have had to incur debt to pay for basic expenses and a majority of workers now believe they will retire at an older age than they expected (closer to 70 years old)."[33]

Crucial to workers is the unemployment rate and the rate of job and wage growth. "The negative view of American workers is driven by stagnant wages and higher costs of living," report the American Dream researchers.

In 2007, the U.S. unemployment rate remained fairly steady at around 4.5 percent with blacks at 8.5 percent and Hispanics 5.6 percent as of October, according to a Bureau of Labor Statistics news release on November 2, 2007.[34]

For the American Dream and the immigration issue, it is important to point out other facts about employment rates:

• The difference between employment rates by gender has been shrinking.
• Unemployment rates of blacks continue to be significantly higher than those of whites and Hispanics.

"The labor market fortunes of African Americans continue to lag behind," according to the Migration Policy Institute.[35] "The data reveal that African Americans are doing worse than others in this recovery, and are faring worse than they did in the 1990s recovery," they reported.

"The proportion of the Latino working-age population that is gainfully employed is higher than the proportion of any other racial or ethnic group," reported the Pew Research Center in *Trends 2005*. Pew does not distinguish between Latino workers who are working legally or illegally—but it can be estimated to be around 50 percent.

### Job Growth

The Center for Labor Market Studies at Northeastern University issued a study finding that "all of the growth in the employed population in the U.S. between January 2001 through April 2004 can be attributed to recently arrived immigrants."[36] Following the gains of new immigrants and the losses of native-born and longer-term immigrant workers, the study found that "new immigrants acquired as many jobs as the other two groups lost and then some!" Even in the traditional area of manufacturing, the employment of new immigrants is significant even at a time when total wage and salary employment in these industries declined by more than 2.7 million positions.[37]

Most of the new immigrants entering the labor force were male, 70 percent under 35 years of age and 25 percent under 25. Fifty-six percent were Latinos, most Mexican and Central American citizens; 20 percent were Asian and 5 percent black. "I hope this study will spark a long-needed analysis of employment and immigration policies," said Andrew Sum, director of the Center and lead author of the study, though he warned against using the statistics for immigrant bashing.

College-educated middle-class workers appear to be holding their own in the current employment environment even though significant numbers are underemployed. Bob Herbert, a *New York Times* columnist, concluded that the situation is bleaker for high school graduates (who don't go on to college) and dropouts, especially males—black and white.[38] Even in Silicon Valley, where "life is good and money is pouring in, almost everyone is anxious," wrote *New York Times* reporter Gary Rivlin.[39]

Hispanics in the United States, especially recent arrivals, are the only group that have seen a rise in employment.

### Income Gap

Leading indicators like wages, consumer spending, and productivity are always variable and interpreted by different groups as being permanent trends or not.[40] But the indicators that are generally agreed on by almost all sides show that economic inequality has been growing. Robert H. Frank, Cornell University economist, writes about it in his 2007 book *Falling Behind: How Rising Inequality Harms the Middle Class*:

1. Between 1920 and 1960, incomes of U.S. households up and down the income ladder grew briskly and at about the same rate—almost 3 percent per year.
2. Since 1979, the incomes of families in the bottom 80 percent of the income distribution have grown by less than 1 percent each

year, and only households in the top 20 percent have enjoyed income growth comparable to that in the earlier period.

3. For a small group at the very top of the economic ladder, however, incomes have been growing explosively. For the past 25 years, *BusinessWeek* has conducted an annual survey of the earnings of chief executive officers of the largest U.S. corporations. In 1980, those executives earned 42 times as much as the average American worker, a ratio larger than the corresponding ratios for such countries as Japan and Germany even today.

4. By 2000, however, American chief executive officers were earning 531 times the average worker's salary. The gains have been even larger for those above chief executive officers on the income ladder.[41]

### Economic Mobility

But perhaps the most distressing economic and social indicator pertaining to the American Dream is the growing evidence that mobility in the United States is lower than in other industrial countries. This was the finding in a 2007 study by the Organization for Economic Cooperation and Development. The study, as editorialized in the *New York Times*, found that "mobility between generations—people doing better or worse than their parents—is weaker in America than in Denmark, Austria, Norway, Finland, Canada, Sweden, Germany, Spain and France. In America there is more than a 40 percent chance that if a father is in the bottom fifth of the earnings' distribution, his son will end up there too. In Denmark, the equivalent odds are under 25 percent and they are less than 30 percent in London."[42]

These findings show that cross-sectional inequality is a crucial statistic in terms of the American Dream that "anyone and everyone can make it rich in America." And that inequality is growing.

## INCREASING DEMANDS TO STOP ILLEGAL IMMIGRATION

There is probably no issue in America today that illustrates so visibly the desire of American workers for collective action and their anger at the federal government for not protecting them than the issue of illegal immigration.

The strain on local services—especially schools, hospitals, and community intervention services—has affected the welcoming attitude of many Americans toward especially illegal immigrants. There is no question that many community schools and hospitals throughout the United States are being overwhelmed by the annual doubling and tripling of illegal immigrants and their family members into their communities. While local business owners may benefit or even depend on the cheap labor they have imported, there is no doubt that community services are impacted negatively. Many county and Catholic hospitals have had to close because of bankruptcy caused by the overwhelming number of patients who do not pay for their services.

Governors, such as California's Arnold Schwarzenegger (R) and Arizona's Janet Nepolitano (D), have sought congressional support, and some have even initiated lawsuits against the federal government demanding payments for the costs of caring for illegal immigrants that the federal government did not keep out by enforcing border laws. All to no avail.

Thousands of legislative proposals have been considered by local legislators in states such as Arizona and certain counties and towns throughout the country to tighten restrictions on illegal immigrants. They range from strict new sanctions on employers and on landlords who hire and give leases to illegal aliens to making English the official language of the local governments to passing laws to deny local-, state-, and county-paid benefits to illegal immigrants—leaving of course the minimal required federal benefits, such as free public elementary and secondary education and emergency room treatment for emergency medical procedures, in place. There is no doubt that legislators and public administrators, pushed by a large and vocal constituency, are getting tougher about illegal immigration. They want it to end. A few cities—such as New Haven, Connecticut—have gone the other way, acknowledging that the concept of illegal immigration is unacceptable but needing to deal with those illegal aliens already in their communities, especially to know who they are.

Some immigrant activists (particularly advocates for the legalization of all illegal aliens) explain that the "harsh and cruel" local government penalties against illegal immigrants and their employers are due to anti-immigrant hatred, xenophobia, racism, and nativist protectionism against all immigrants. The *New York Times* seems to agree. In a recent editorial, they write that the "toughness" and "unprecedented crack-downs" on illegal immigrants using false documents is "shortsighted, disruptive and self-defeating" and will "unleash a flood of misery upon millions of illegal immigrants."[43]

Working Americans' choice of how many immigrants they want to welcome to their communities and job sites depends on their perception of how the American Dream is going to play out for themselves and their families, their neighborhoods, communities, states, regions, and country first. It is the same everywhere in the world—except Americans are a lot more idealistic about immigration than other places.

# 4

## The Vocabulary of Immigration: Buzzwords, Framing, and Spin

Immigration as a political and economic subject touches many hot buttons, biases, and basic beliefs. Many of the topics of immigration make people uncomfortable—particularly considering our Western sensitivity toward discrimination, racism, human and civil rights; capitalism and the market economy; and patriotism and the protection of "American jobs." The discomfort is caused because there is tension between our ideals about immigration—our pride in being a "special" country of inclusion and openness—running up against our inherent strength and tradition in being a nation that enforces the rule of law.

It is a given that unless a country has open borders, it must have immigration laws. And immigration law means having to legally enforce a national decision on who will be allowed to come into the country to stay and to work and to be granted citizenship. Immigration law forces citizens to make a choice—to discriminate, in the old sense of the word. And we Americans hate to make that kind of choice.

Immigration issues today are particularly a dilemma for those Americans who continue to regard immigration from the perspective of the 1960s—as a basic human and social right. They often confuse the individual's right to travel and migrate, with a sovereign nation's right to decide who may immigrate (stay and work) in the nation and enjoy the civil rights of citizenship. And of course, immigration law of any specificity is almost inherently anathema to libertarians on the right (who view the marketplace as the only real tool to limit immigration) and the left (who do not want any limits on an individual's freedom to move anywhere they want).

## BUZZWORDS AND SPIN

To tread among these political and ideological minefields, a particular immigration vocabulary has developed consisting of labels and buzz-words and spin. The language of immigration has been messaged, managed, and manipulated by the increasingly visible and popular technique of political "framing."

Recently, four popular books have let us all into the secrets of the framing of language—particularly political language. The technique is also known as spin.

The first notable book is *Words That Work* by Frank Luntz, a successful Republican communications consultant who framed, for instance, the concept of "death taxes" rather than the more benign "estate tax." In his book, he outlines the rules for developing effective words; he devotes a section of the book to how to frame words about immigration in a Republican way.[1]

The next two are books by Professor George Lakoff: *Don't Think of an Elephant* and *Whose Freedom?*[2] In the former, Lakoff shows Democrats how conservatives successfully used framing to win the 2000 and 2004 elections. He held conferences throughout the country and on Capitol Hill with Democratic political leaders to get them to change relatively banal Democratic concepts such as "global warming" (who doesn't like warmth?) to the more urgent and fearsome and perhaps action-eliciting "climate crisis" or "climate change." Much of what Lakoff writes about how conservatives and progressives think of freedom and the way they frame it is enlightening and relevant to how the political vocabulary of the immigration debate is framed.

The fourth book, *Un-spun*, is a collaboration between Brooks Jackson and Kathleen Hall Jamieson.[3] Jackson is a former CNN investigative reporter, and Jamieson is the director of the Annenberg Public Policy Center. Their book dissects the warning signals and the tricks of spin: how to be aware of it and how to challenge it with facts.

## Words That Work

To Luntz, using "effective" words is the goal of all communicators. Effective words are the "right" words that resonate so well with the public that they remember them and the words become a "buzzword," a stand-in, an unconscious connection for an entire concept. He has several rules for effective words, along with some examples on how they could be applied to the immigration debate (some examples are his, some are mine):

1. Use short sentences. No more than two commas, but none is best, and always have "you" or "your" in it. Example: This is about your schools and hospitals!
2. Credibility is as important as philosophy—and credibility is often obtained through empathy. Example: Our immigration system is broken. Don't blame the illegal immigrant or the business owner.
3. Consistency focuses attention. With the immigration debate, Luntz suggests always using the term "illegal immigrants," not "illegals." Focus on those who are hurt. Example: Illegal immigration hurts all those legal immigrants who followed the rules.
4. Quantitative facts are best for understanding. Example: A small-town mayor reported that in 2000, local taxpayers paid for five English-as-a-second-language teachers in their schools; by 2007 they now pay for 40.
5. Appeal to fairness. Example: Protect the wages, work standards, and quality of life for all American citizens and legal workers.
6. Offer something new. Example: Offer small business loans to illegal aliens who voluntarily relocate to their homelands so they can build their own prosperity and their country's, using the skills they learned in the United States.
7. Sound and texture matter. Words starting with "re" are particularly powerful. Examples: revitalize, renew, restore, rekindle, reinvent, rejuvenate, reenergize, return, relocate, repatriation, and reentry.
8. Hope and opportunity resonate (see table 4.1).
9. Visualize the message. In immigration, negative visuals of illegal aliens show families running against traffic or climbing over walls; positive visuals of illegal alien families might show them learning English or teaching soccer to American kids.

*Chapter 4*

**Table 4.1. Renaming of Immigration Terms**

| From | To |
| --- | --- |
| Voluntary self-deportation | Repatriation with a clean slate |
| Expedited application process | Urgent skills work opportunity visa |
| Exit payments | Homeland business opportunity grants |
| Enforce immigration laws | Revitalize rule-of-law legacy |
| | Rejuvenate U.S. labor fairness |
| Amnesty | Start over or second chance |
| Immigration reform | Revitalizing our immigration tradition |

10. Ask a question. Example: Since when did American families have to hire an illegal alien to mow their lawns and clean their toilets rather than doing it themselves? Are engineering and high-tech jobs now jobs Americans won't do? Why don't poultry slaughtering businesses in South Carolina use machines as in Europe rather than manual labor as in the Third World? Are we becoming a Third World country?

11. Provide context and explain relevance. Example: America has millions of illegal workers—many times more than in any other First World country. We're also the *only* First World country that does not have national identity cards, does not enforce labor laws, and gives free schooling and hospital care to anyone who is in the United States no matter their legal status and that gives citizenship to the babies of illegal aliens born in the country. That is why we have millions of illegal workers.

## Framing

Lakoff, on the other hand, looks at how ideas are "framed" to get people to think and do what one wants. Frames are boundaries, created by language, often using metaphors to illustrate big ideas—like freedom, climate change, or even immigration. In his book *Whose Freedom?*, he shows how widely differing views about freedom can be explained through a simple understandable metaphor—parenting.

Lakoff explains that most thought does not follow the laws of logic. "Frames can trump facts when the fact doesn't fit the frame," he writes. "But frames and metaphors define common sense."[4] People can agree on the core beliefs of a big idea. For instance, most people believe that "freedom" means "being able to do what you want to." Most people for instance would also agree that political freedom is "about the state and its role to maximize freedom for all its citizens." But it is the specifics about the big ideas that are the problem. "There are wildly divergent ideas about how big or small the government's role should be and how it should do it." It is the same with "economic freedom," which is about being able to earn, spend, and invest money as one chooses. Everyone agrees with the general idea, but anyone can come up immediately with wildly divergent ideas of how free or regulated society should be about money.

Here is where framing the language of the message through a metaphor helps people understand a point of view. Lakoff writes that points of view about a big idea like freedom generally are based on (or between) two radically different, well-structured conceptual frameworks. The metaphor that everyone uses is family. According to Lakoff, conservatives and progressives in the United States have two widely different beliefs about family—each group believes that families are either strictly controlled or loosely controlled, respectively.

Basic questions about freedom are conceptualized in these two beliefs. Regarding freedom in general, the basic question is, How much freedom does an individual have within and outside the family?

Regarding political freedom, where the nation-state is seen as a large (in America a highly diverse) family and government as the parent, Lakoff answers the question by stating that conservatives believe that the parent should be strict, while progressives believe that the parent should be less strict, a permissive parent. (Lakoff spins the terms toward his own bias by calling the conservatives' belief in family control as "strict father" and the progressives' belief in family control as "nurturing parent"—as if a strict father can't be nurturing and as if nurturers are both fathers and mothers.)

"Economic freedom" is viewed in just the opposite way by conservatives and liberals: economic conservatives view economic freedom as having little control (outside of natural market forces), whereas progressives tend to see government as having a stronger role in ensuring equal economic opportunity and helping individuals when the market system does not work—in other words, more control. It would seem that in economic freedom, the progressives are the strict-parent believers and the conservatives the permissive-parent ones.

It is not hard to see how the great idea of immigration fits the belief system of freedom since it comprises both political and economic freedom. Everyone acknowledges the core general concept of immigration is that the United States is historically a nation of immigrants built politically and economically with, by, and for immigrants and their descendants. But what about the specifics? Should there be few and flexible immigration laws—a permissive-parent attitude—or immigration laws that are strictly enforced—the strict parent?

You can ask the same questions of the labor economics of immigration: should it be controlled loosely by the market where employers can hire the cheapest labor possible—even below American standards—that immigrants from the poorest countries of the world will accept gladly because it improves their lot while they drain their homelands of their brains and muscles in order to send home foreign remittances? Or should laws be enforced to protect American wages and standards for legal workers? Here, while progressives may be "permissive parents" in immigration politics, they tend to be "strict parents" regarding labor and economic controls. Conservatives tend to split just the opposite.

It is no wonder that so many people say they are confused about what to think about immigration. The truth is that in immigration issues, both Republicans and Democrats are split almost in half. I see the political dichotomy in immigration as not between progressive Democrats and conservative Republicans but rather between libertarians (the permissive parents, if you will) and protectionists/restrictionists—what David Brooks calls "economic nationalists" (the strict parent). And there are Republicans and Democrats at both ends. I see immigration not as a horizontal issue on a spectrum of left to right (progressive Democrats to conservative Republicans) but as a vertical issue with the politics lining up and down a horseshoe with libertarians on the open-ended bottom and economic nationalists on the closed top.

It is interesting to see how the two different basic beliefs about immigration cause believers to frame the language about immigration in two different ways:

1. The strict-parent believers frame the immigration debate as being essentially about legal and illegal immigration.
2. The permissive-parent believers frame the immigration debate as being about people who are either pro-immigrant versus anti-immigrant.

## Word Spinning and Deception

In *Un-spun*, Jackson and Jamieson describe "spin" as a "polite word for deception." The degree of spin is considered harmless (like little white lies) and all political parties have always done some of it. But now the distribution of spin is much more ubiquitous through 24-hour cable television, the Internet, and year-round election campaigning. And now both sides are actively working to (knowingly) deceive the public. "They may even be deceiving themselves," write the Annenberg scholars, "because both sides tend to ignore evidence that doesn't favor their point of view."

Jackson and Jamieson detail seven warning signs of spin. It is interesting to see how much of the immigration rhetoric falls into their warning signs. Here are their warnings and some immigration spin examples:

1. If It's Scary, Be Wary. "If amnesty is granted, by 2020 there will be 50 million illegals who will become citizens, and we will no longer have an America that we know."[5]
2. A Story That's Too Good. "A pathway to citizenship will fulfill the American Dream of millions of hardworking people who sacrificed so much to come here."
3. The Dangling Comparative. "The largest invasion of immigrants ever!" dangling the obvious question "as compared to when and where?"
4. The Superlative Swindle. "'Draconian' employer raid."
5. The "Pay You Tuesday" Con. "We must legalize now all the hardworking people whose only crime is that they came over the border illegally to pursue the American Dream."
6. The Blame Game. "Illegal immigrants have brought crime, impacted our hospitals and schools, and taken jobs from native Americans."
7. Glittering Generalization. "Comprehensive immigration reform."

## BUZZWORDS: WORDS THAT WORK IN THE IMMIGRATION DEBATE—AND THEIR FRAMING

There are many buzzwords in the immigration debate. But two stand out as the most successful and the most effective. They have resonated with the public so well that they have become stand-ins—connections for an entire concept. "Amnesty" and "anti-immigrant" effectively frame the issues they address.

### Amnesty

"Amnesty" is the most effective buzzword in the immigration legislation debate. It is a stand-in and an unconscious connection for an entire concept: not only to forgive millions (estimates range from 11 million to 20 million) of foreign nationals who have broken U.S. immigration and labor laws by living and working in the United States without a permit to do so, but also to give them permanent immigration status and the choice to become citizens.

What is amnesty in legal terms? *West's Encyclopedia of American Law* defines amnesty as a governmental act that grants a group of persons who have broken the law immunity from prosecution. And amnesty can (and almost always does) have stringent conditions ("seriously qualified" in legal terms). Amnesty is

> the action of a government by which all persons or certain groups of persons who have committed a criminal offense—usually of a political nature that threatens the sovereignty of the government (such as sedition or treason) are granted immunity from prosecution. Though an amnesty can be broad or narrow, covering one person or many, and can be seriously qualified (as long as the conditions are not unconstitutional) it cannot grant a license to commit future crimes nor forgive crimes not yet committed.[6]

Amnesty allows the government of a nation or state to "forget" criminal acts, usually before prosecution has occurred. Amnesty has traditionally been used as a political tool of compromise and reunion following a war. An act of amnesty is generally granted to a group of people who have committed crimes against the state, such as treason, rebellion, or desertion from the military.

Amnesty is not a pardon. Both derive their legal justification from Article 2, Section 2, of the Constitution, which gives the president the power to grant *reprieves* and *pardons* for offenses against the United States. The main differences between the two actions, however, are the following:

- Amnesty is usually given to a group of people who have committed a crime against the United States but have not been convicted of the crime in a court of law; it is given before prosecution.
- A pardon is given by the president to a specific individual *following* a conviction for a crime.

Giving illegal aliens the chance to become U.S. citizens is the most controversial issue. It has become the line in the sand over which strong proponents and opponents will not compromise. Most of the mainstream media editorial writers and pundits are almost obsessed with the issue; there have been many editorials in the *New York Times*, for instance, that insist that no immigration reform is possible without the forgiveness. It has become the standard by which one's immigration stance is judged to be "pro-immigrant" or "anti-immigrant." And it has been the poison pill that has killed legislation that otherwise seemed deemed to pass.

Amnesty was a major focus of the 1986 Immigration Reform and Control Act (IRCA), which legislated it for the some 2.5 million illegal aliens in the country at the time.[7] Nearly everyone admits that the 1986 amnesty was a humane act that was supposed to be a "one-time legislation," as Senator Ted Kennedy (D-Mass.) promised.[8] But they were wrong. IRCA is considered by many to be a failure. Illegal immigration grew by multiples since amnesty was instituted. While the reasons for the failure are many—including especially the fact that none of the enforcement regulations were supported—it failed mainly because none of the other enforcement sanctions that were supposed to go along with the law were enforced. It is common sense to understand that amnesty without enforcement encourages more illegal immigration.

The present-day proponents for legalization and citizenship for illegal aliens will make every effort to deflect it from being called "amnesty." Instead they employ other language (e.g., earned citizenship, legalization, bringing "them" out of the shadows, following the American Dream, pathway to citizenship, or extension of temporary working visas).

In fact, those who favor legalizing the status and giving citizenship to foreign nationals presently in the country illegally insist that what they are proposing is not amnesty because their legislation imposes harsh conditions and requirements for an illegal alien to meet before getting legalization and citizenship. Conditions include registering the migrant and documenting work history, job skills, length of stay, family status, and arrest record. Some of the proposed legislation imposes complicated requirements such as "touchbacks" (returning to their homelands for a certain period of time and applying from there), going to a port of entry to be issued a temporary visa, or maneuvering a "pathway to citizenship" that takes years before being granted a permanent green card. Various fines have been proposed that have to be paid by the illegal alien before getting legalized; fees range from $500 to over $10,000. Imposing these conditions and requirements and punishment in the form of fines and fees is not giving amnesty to an illegal alien, proponents claim.

Columnist Thomas Sowell, however, wrote the following about the 2006 immigration legislation: "Republican Senators have come up with yet another disguise for amnesty. Under this new plan, its advocates claim, illegal immigrants would 'have to leave the country' and re-apply to come back in legally and get on a path toward citizenship. It sounds good but on closer examination it turns out to be a fraud."[9]

Still the term "amnesty" enraged editorial boards in many of the nation's elite newspapers, such as the *Washington Post* and the *New York Times*. Articles headlines "Debate Could Turn on a 7-Letter Word" and "Careful Strategy Is Used to Derail Immigration Bill: Amnesty Becomes Achilles Heel" ran in the *Post* during the weeks leading up to the vote on the legislation.[10]

### Silent Amnesty

In a desperate attempt to circumvent the extremely effective word "amnesty" being used by opponents of the "pathway to citizenship," proponents of legalization (across party lines) came out with a new talking point: "If legislators do not pass the comprehensive immigration reform bill to legalize hard working immigrants (meaning foreign nationals living and working in the country illegally of course) then they will be in effect granting silent amnesty to them and costing the taxpayers millions of dollars."[11]

The cleverness of this spin is breathtaking. It totally converts the negative of amnesty and the money that illegal aliens are costing American taxpayers into a positive argument for—amnesty. It was short lived but nonetheless a brilliant tactical ploy.

## Anti-Immigrant

This is the commonly heard charge assigned to those who favor strong enforcement of immigration and labor laws and who oppose "amnesty." It is so effective because it is short (one of the Frank Luntz rules), and it connotes being not only against something that is esteemed (immigrants) but also against them in an inherent way—not against a behavior but against a person, an immigrant, a status that almost everyone in American once held. The label "anti-immigrant" is seen often in leading newspapers and magazines not as quotes but as adjectives in news articles written by (so-called) top reporters. Other often-heard but not as effective labels of proponents of strict immigration law enforcement include "nativist," "racist," "xenophobic," "restrictionist," "un-American," "anti-Latino," and the overused and almost senseless words "Nazi" and "fascist."

Of course the label is completely disingenuous. It misinforms brilliantly. The truth is that almost everyone who favors strong immigration and labor law enforcement and border security is *not* anti-immigrant. They are not even against immigration. Some of the strictest immigration law enforcement advocates are immigrants themselves. Many agree that certain immigration visas should be expanded and more immigrants allowed in. But almost all are concerned about the large and increasing numbers of *illegal* migrants. Most do not want to "award" illegal behavior by giving illegal aliens a pathway to citizenship. Most do not blame the immigrant for coming—they blame the federal government for failing to enforce its immigration and labor laws and Congress for allowing gaping loopholes in the law.

"Anti-immigrant" is also brilliant in that this simple term frames the immigration debate entirely toward a position that the other side does not believe in at all. The antithesis of "anti-immigrant," of course, is "pro-immigrant." Those who use the term "anti-immigrant" purposely mean to frame the immigration debate into an almost impossible-to-lose battle position: between combatants who are pro-immigrant and those who are anti-immigrant.[12]

The other side has not been able to establish an effective buzzword for those who favor legislation that expands legal immigration and forgives foreign nationals who have broken immigration and labor laws by living and working in the country illegally. Almost every night for the past four years, Lou Dobbs, the CNN anchor who is the most visible spokesperson for the side that is strongly against illegal immigration, has labeled them variously as "the pro–illegal alien lobby," "pro-amnesty senators," "illegal alien supporters," "pro-amnesty open-border senators," and "pro–illegal alien amnesty advocates."[13] All these phrases lack the simple spin resonance of "anti-immigrant."

## Other Successful Buzzwords

*Draconian*

It is interesting to note how certain legislation gets labeled with a certain adjective or label and thereafter is always described by that adjective by commentators, pundits, editorial writers, and, unfortunately, reporters. For instance, the House bill passed in November 2005 was almost continuously described as "draconian." This negative adjective slants and biases the public perception of the bill.

*Comprehensive*

It is equally biased to label a bill with an overly positive label as with a pejorative one. By 2007, "comprehensive" became the buzzword for legalization of foreign nationals living and working in the United States illegally. For many (illegal) immigrant activist groups, comprehensive immigration reform came to mean not only easy, simple, and inexpensive legalization of (all) illegal immigrants as quickly as possible but also a pathway to citizenship by granting them permanent (not temporary) immigration status.

## Spin by Substitute Words

"Spin misleads people," write Brook Jackson and Kathleen Jamieson.[14] In the immigration debate there are two legal terms that are especially difficult for all sides to address honestly. They are the terms "illegal alien" and "temporary" permit. Both terms have elicited many substitute stand-in terms that also match the frame of the issue of immigration reform based on the framework of legality versus illegality or pro-immigrant versus anti-immigrant (see table 4.2).

**Table 4.2. How Immigration Terms Are Spun**

Illegal Alien
Illegal undocumented worker
Illegal immigrant
Illegal worker
Unauthorized worker
Migrant in transition
In the shadows
Underground workers in an underground economy
Visa overstayer
Foreign nationals living in the country illegally
Hardworking immigrants who have roots in our country and want to stay[a]
Slaves[b]
Honorable workers
The most vulnerable workers
Immigrant
People who are geographically challenged or border dyslexic[c]

Temporary Permit Holder[d]
Legal immigrant[e]
Guest worker
Hardworking immigrant
Foreign student
Visitor
Tourist
Probationary worker
H-1B permit holder
Agricultural worker
Business visitor

[a]"The vast majority of illegal immigrants are decent people who work hard, support their families, practice their faith, and lead responsible lives. They are a part of American life. America remains what she has always been: the great hope on the horizon, an open door to the future, a blessed and promised land" (President Bush White House Statement on immigration from the Office of the Press Secretary, May 15, 2006).

[b]Rangel is quoted in the article "Close to Slavery—Guestworker Programs in the U.S." in the *Bulletin of the NGO Committee on Migration* on June 7, 2007, as saying, "This guestworker program is the closest thing I've ever seen to slavery." Available online.

[c]Tongue-in-cheek reference to illegal aliens used by reporters in Arizona according to Jerry Kammer, Copley News Service, as related to the author, June 2007.

[d]There are dozens of permits that the U.S. Customs and Immigration Services stamp into the passports of millions of foreign nationals whose visas are accepted at a port of entry and who are given entry to the United States. All these permits (often called "visas") are temporary, nonimmigrant, and time and work limited. They include permits for tourists, guest workers, foreign students, H-1Bs, and so on. But you rarely if ever will hear them referred to as "temporary" in any debate on immigration.

[e]A "legal immigrant" is an immigrant who came into the country to live and to work with legal paper, with documents, with a visa that authorizes them to stay for a certain amount of time, or with a permanent resident visa. This is compared to an "illegal immigrant" who snuck into the country and lives and works here illegally or who overstayed the legal time limits of their visas and now is living in the country illegally.

## An American

"American" is, in general, a confusing concept. At 19 when I first lived in South America, some Peruvian colleagues pulled one of their favorite tricks on me. *"Que eres?"* they asked, meaning what nationality was I. *"Soy Americana,"* I replied. *"No,"* they said laughing. *"Somos Americanos tambien. Tu eres Norte Americana."* ("No. We are Americans too. You are North American.") I'm not sure whether my Canadian friends would agree with that.

The fact is that we citizens of the United States have no good word for our citizen designation. Despite my friends' teasing, they were of course Peruvians. If I asked them what they really were, they would have proudly said *"Peruanos,"* not *"Sud Americanos."* Throughout U.S. history, citizens have referred to themselves and have been referred to in every official document as Americans. In every country of the world, U.S. citizens are known as Americans.

While most of the world agrees what an "American" is, in the United States there seems to be real confusion about who is an American. Politicians and policymakers vow to give benefits to "hardworking Americans" and the like. But just who do they mean? American citizens? American citizens and legal immigrants? Illegal aliens? Illegal felon aliens?[15]

## Bilingual/Bicultural

For decades in the Southwest, the terms "bilingual" and "bicultural" were understood to refer solely to a Spanish-speaking person mainly from Mexico or Central America who also knew English. This Spanish/ Latino-only connotation has slowly begun to change as the media begin to cover immigrants from cultures around the globe.

The broader meaning of "bilingual/bicultural" is extremely important as we talk about adjusting immigration permits back to needed work skills. That will include many more immigrants from Asia.

## Official English

Whether to make English the official language of the United States is covered in detail in chapter 6. However, the spinning of "official English" needs to be included here. Many would argue that in order to progress as a worker in the United States, it is best to know English. But

**Table 4.3.  The America They See**

Those Advocating "Official English" Policies

- English-only government documents
- Ballots in English only
- No personal translators provided full time in any public facilities, including courtrooms and hospitals
- A requirement that only English be spoken at the workplace
- Passage of a stringent (oral) English exam to qualify for naturalization/citizenship

Those Opposing "Official English" Policies

- Translations necessary for public safety and civic participation
- Interpreters in the courts for even the most exotic languages in order to have a fair trial—even if a court defendant knows English
- A requirement that every American study at least one other language—often starting with Spanish
- The right for every employee to speak any language they want to at work and no requirement to speak or even know English
- "An immigrant does not need to know English in order to be a good American citizen."[a]

[a]Congressman Ron Ellison (D-Ill.) before the House Judiciary Subcommittee on May 23, 2007. Confirmed to the author in a personal interview.

how to address the issue has tied many politicians into knots. In two pieces of legislation dealing with the issue late in 2006, English was referred variously as "the national language" and "the most common language in the United States."

Official English, which refers only to government documents, has confused many, including the proponents and opponents. Spin terms and talking points for and against "official English" are across the spectrum in terms of reasonableness (see table 4.3).

## Spin by Omission of Key Words

Another common method to spin a message is to leave out crucial information and promote only that information which supports a particular viewpoint. In the immigration language spin world, there are many examples of spin by omission, even in simple sentences, phrases, and mantras so often heard that they are not even questioned. Here are a few often-seen examples:

"Our economy is dependent on immigrant workers." The missing word here is "illegal" immigrant.

"Rights for immigrants." The missing word again is "illegal" immigrant. "Huge waiting lists for English classes for immigrants." The missing word is "free" English classes.

## Spin by Partisanship

Some issues are so split by partisanship that an entire issue is seen completely differently by one side and the other. One such issue connected to the immigration debate is *voter fraud*. To Republicans, it often means noncitizens (including legal and illegal immigrants) registering and voting illegally. To Democrats, it means voter machine glitches, no paper trails, voter identity validation requirements, long waiting lines, glitches in voter registration lists, voter registration fees, and/or butterfly ballots and hanging chads.

## Sloganeering—for Democrats

On June 27, 2007, the *Politico* newspaper published a story with the headline "Tough, Fair and Practical: Magic Words." Reporter Carrie Budoff described how these "magic words" were being developed as a slogan for Democrats to use when talking about immigration—it was "a pithy phrase that was the product of months of research, 1,200 telephone interviews, and deepening concern among Democrats that they would lose control of the emerging wedge issue," according to Budoff.[16] The tagline, "Tough, Fair and Practical on Immigration!," was devised by Third Way, a centrist strategy group. It was stated often by Democratic senators Ted Kennedy (Mass.), Ron Wyden (Ore.), and Harry Reid (Nev.) days before the final vote.

# 5

## Six Mantras and Myths about Immigration: Often Heard, Rarely Questioned

Many phrases and statements about immigration have been repeated so often that they have taken on the status of mantras (which in Hinduism—where the word originates—means a sacred repeated verbal formula that "protects the mind" from other thoughts). After some time, many mantras that are repeated and unquestioned often enough become living myths. The mantras and myths about immigration need to be questioned by thinking citizens in order to develop informed opinion. Questioning mantras is also an interesting pursuit. It brings unexpected "aha!" moments as some of the misinformation as well as some of the truths underlying popular myths are uncovered. To question is to exercise our most basic freedom.

Seven common mantras regarding immigration in the United States are presented in this chapter. You probably recognize them. They are common beliefs and often repeated. Do you think they are irrefutable? What do you think after reading the provocative questions that accompany them?

### 1. THE UNITED STATES IS A NATION OF IMMIGRANTS

This is probably the most common statement made whenever immigration comes up as a topic of conversation, a presentation, or a debate. It is a mantra that is stated as a "given," often followed by silence, a linguistic shrug. It is as if once the mantra is stated, there is nothing more to say.

One reason the mantra is taken as an all-encompassing given is that as a simple statement, it is true. It is a fact. Yes, the United States was founded, developed, and eventually became a nation of, for, and by generations of descendants of immigrants. No question.

But it doesn't stop there. Thinking Americans—like good healthily skeptical journalists—must also open their minds to this mantra and ask at least two key questions.

## Is the United States Uniquely a Nation of Immigrants?

The simple truth is that being a "nation of immigrants" is not that unique. Most countries of the world developed as nations through immigration. Many, if not most, modern nation-states share the early history of the United States as a national entity developed for and by immigrants and their descendants—like all the nation-states of South and Central America, the continent of Australia, many of the nation-states of Africa, and some of those in Asia. (In fact, if you really want to get picky, most indigenous populations of every country of the world were themselves migrants in prehistoric times.) The past decade has seen global migration increase exponentially, as technology has made it easier for labor to move and as most of the world's nations have become, in varying degrees, open, free market capitalistic economies. Now immigrants come to make more money in the host country at jobs there. Some call this "globalization" and the "flattening of the world." Whatever the phenomenon is called, it is clear that most countries of the world are "nations of immigrants." The United States cannot really be considered "a unique nation" because of our immigration history alone.

There is a good consequence of not being a unique "nation of immigrants." We can learn from and teach other countries about immigration management. It is both valid and important to compare our experience with immigrant settlement, development, and assimilation with how other nations deal with immigration issues. There is no room for hubris about this international subject by any one nation.

## If So, So What?

Even if it is an indisputable fact that "the United States is a nation of immigrants," then what follows? Why do people repeat the mantra? What do they mean by it?

- Do they mean that since we started as a territory without a central government or immigration laws (outside of colonial licenses to settle certain land areas) or even "official" national borders that we have to continue to be that way, to have open borders?
- Does being a historic nation of immigrants mean we cannot make or enforce immigration laws?
- Is being a nation of immigrants a bad thing? Do mantra reciters mean that only indigenous cultures have validity and that all immigrants should go back to their heritage countries?
- Or does the mantra mean that as a historic nation of immigrants, we should be welcoming to all immigrants? The question is then, How welcoming? To how many and who exactly? Just certain immigrants? First come, first served? The mantra doesn't address that.

It is irresponsible to let such a simplistic statement as "We are a nation of immigrants" "protect our minds" from questioning what the person saying the mantra means. People who recite the mantra need to be asked questions. Response to the mantra needs to be a version of "True, but so what?"

## 2. IMMIGRANTS DO JOBS AMERICANS WON'T DO

This mantra was recited most visibly by President George W. Bush to support his position that guest worker visas need to be expanded. The mantra implies that there are millions of jobs in the United States that employers cannot find any Americans to do.

There are many questions to be asked and considered about this mantra. But before that, it is interesting and meaningful to consider *how the mantra is framed*. What does the choice of words imply?

### Why Is the Word "Immigrants" Used in the Mantra?

The use of the all-encompassing "immigrants" makes the mantra inarguable. It also makes it senseless.

Obviously, hiring *legal* immigrants with *legal* work permits is not an issue. Legal immigrants do needed jobs. The main question about legal immigration is how many work visas should be issued to keep our economy moving and our native and legal workforce fairly employed. That is what immigration laws, backed by labor laws and policies, are all about.

The real issue underlying the mantra therefore is the *illegal* hiring of foreign nationals who are in the country *illegally* and/or do not have legal work permits. The mantra is almost always used to imply that immigration and labor laws need to be changed and reformed by expanding work visas and legalizing all those who at present are hired illegally. In order to make sense, however, the mantra should be stated, "Illegal immigrants do jobs Americans won't."

But using the word "illegal" poses a problem for most proponents of the mantra—including a majority of news reporters and editorial writers. Almost everyone says that they are against illegal immigration. Most say that they believe, like every American, that the United States is a country guided by "the rule of law." But it seems to be extremely difficult for proponents to acknowledge that the good, hardworking people who serve in American homes, gardens, restaurants, and hotels are working illegally. It is easier to just lump all working migrants together under the word "immigrant" and not to mention the illegal part. In almost any article in the major newspapers about the dependency of American business on "immigrant" workers, the illegal status of the "immigrant" workers is rarely, if ever, mentioned. Most members of the press and punditry refer to all foreign-born workers simply as "immigrants" (some even say, "There is no such thing as an illegal immigrant," even as they advocate for the *legalization* of all illegal immigrants).

There is another image as well behind the use of the word "immigrants" rather than "illegal immigrants." Use of the word "immigrants" frames the basic immigration debate as being one between those who are *pro*-immigrant and those who are *anti*-immigrant rather than *against the illegal status*: pro–legal immigrant, anti being in (especially working in) the country illegally.

## Do Illegal Immigrants Really Do Jobs Americans "Won't Do" or "Aren't Doing"?

In April 2006, President Bush suddenly changed the phrasing of the mantra. He started referring to "jobs immigrants do that Americans aren't doing" instead of "won't do." The change seemed to be an acknowledgment that the American public—if not yet members of the press—universally were questioning the mantra's pejorative connotation that American "won't do" certain jobs, that we disdain doing certain jobs as being beneath us.

## Is It True? Do Illegal Immigrants Really Do Jobs Americans Aren't Doing?

There are valid questions and arguments on both sides—yes *and* no. First for the affirmative.

### Are There Some Skilled Jobs That Need Foreign Workers to Fill?

At a July 2006 hearing before the Congressional House Education and Workforce Committee on the "impact of illegal immigration on American students and job opportunities," five experts agreed that there probably are some jobs at any particular time that need an infusion of foreign workers—who should be able to come in on "temporary" visas (no one mentioned their becoming permanent immigrants). "Meteorologists and metallurgical engineers, welders and air solution technologists are in very short supply, as are refrigeration technologists, product design and power electronic engineers and various levels of security experts and technicians," said manager of global immigration services for Ingersoll Rand Company Elizabeth Dickson, testifying on behalf of the Chamber of Commerce.[1] "More H-1B visas are needed for these fields that require a college education," she said. "Demographics show that with the boomer retirement, in ten years we will not have a skilled workforce."

### Should Entirely New Guest Worker Visas Be Created for Some "Less Skilled" Jobs?

"Agricultural workers need whole new guest worker visa programs," said Luawanna Hallstrom of the National Council of Agricultural Employers at a congressional hearing.[2] "Of the 137,000 able-bodied (American) candidates identified by California's EDD department in the San Joaquin Valley for available agricultural jobs, only 503 applied for work and only 3 actually showed up," she reported. "A workable agricultural guest worker program will not take jobs from U.S. workers. Americans do not raise their kids to be seasonal workers. They want their children to have college educations and full time, year-round jobs," she said on the record.

## Do Mexican Workers Take Unskilled Jobs That African Americans Won't Do?

Apparently, Mexican President Vicente Fox believes this mantra. In May 2005, Fox stated in a public speech why he thought opening the borders to all Mexicans who wanted to work in the United States was essential. In his version of Bush's mantra, he said, "There is no doubt that Mexicans . . . are doing work that not even [American] Blacks are willing do there in the U.S." African American leaders were outraged. A contingent of them immediately traveled to Mexico City to demand an apology from Fox. While they did not get a direct apology, the cat was out of the bag as far as the mantra was concerned. It had become international and racist.

## Do African American Leaders Support the Mantra?

Despite African American leaders' irritation with Fox, it seems that most of these leaders also support the mantra that American workers won't do the jobs illegal Mexicans do. In the July/August 2006 issue of *Crisis* magazine (a publication of the National Association for the Advancement of Colored People since 1910), five black leaders were interviewed about immigration.[3] All were sympathetic to the plight of immigrants and equate it with the African American fight for civil rights in the 1960s:

- "This is a position that dates back to legendary Latino field worker organizer Cesar Chavez," writes *Crisis* editor in chief Victoria Valentine in her introduction to the cover story (although Cesar Chavez was actually opposed to illegal immigration).
- Human Rights lawyer Constance Rice of Los Angeles (cousin of Secretary of State Condoleezza Rice) said, "If you are talking about my friends the Buppies," referring to black yuppies, "we benefit

from illegal immigration because these folks [illegal immigrant hires] are mowing our lawns and taking care of our children."

- University of Maryland Professor Ronald Walters, while recognizing that Latinos and blacks compete for low-skilled jobs in construction and restaurants where wages and benefits have decreased, believes that "an effective political coalition (with Latinos who support illegal immigrants) is necessary because we legitimize each other's issues."
- "We don't want our people doing these jobs anyway," said Wade Henderson, executive director of the Leadership Conference on Civil Rights, which is an umbrella body of 180 civil rights groups. Black workers "should aspire higher and go to college," he said. "They need to be challenged to get off their butts and get through school," an African American lawyer at the Commerce Department (who did not wish to be identified) agreed.
- Congresswoman Sheila Jackson Lee (D-Tex.) agreed with other Black Congressional Caucus leaders that illegal workers doing jobs Americans won't do needed to be supported, not maligned. Her solution: setting a "fair federal minimum wage" for all.

*Do the Major American Labor Unions Support the Illegal Hiring of Foreign Nationals?*

In August 2006, the AFL-CIO did a 180-degree turnaround regarding illegal immigrants (*"unauthorized* workers" in the words of the *Washington Post*) by voting to join forces with a coalition of some 30 day laborer organizers. Prior to that date, the union had strongly supported sanctioning employers of illegal workers, In the summer of 2005, when its major branch union of service employees—the Service Employees International Union (SEIU)—embraced illegal hires as potential union members, the AFL-CIO and SEIU split up. Illegal immigrant laborers are seen by some as a solution to declining union membership and to revitalizing the civil rights cause. Although the agreement does not require illegal aliens to join the unions, the AFL-CIO stated that the new partnership was done to give "exploited day laborers the resources of union legal aid and work stoppage benefits against employers. Worker exploitation hurts us all," said union president John Sweeney.[4]

Turning to the negative in the "Do illegal immigrants really do jobs Americans aren't doing?" question.

### Don't Most Illegal Workers Do Bend-Over Agricultural Jobs?

The most efficient way to answer this question is to simply look at the relevant data about the job distribution of illegal workers:

- 3 percent work in farming (19 percent of all famworkers are illegal aliens).
- 33 percent work in construction, home repairs, and home maintenance (27 percent of all drywall installers are illegal aliens; 26 percent of all ground maintenance workers in the United States are illegal aliens).
- 33 percent work in the hospitality/service industry (food prep and production—25 percent of all butcher/poultry workers and 20 percent of all cleaners/dishwashers are illegal aliens).
- Over 40 percent of all illegal workers came into the country legally and overstay their expired temporary visas (many of them foreign student permits). These formerly legal but now illegal migrants work largely in white-collar and skilled jobs (10 percent of illegal immigrants are in management and business professions, and 13 percent are in sales and administrative support).[5]

### Are There Really Jobs Americans Won't Do?

In April 2006, the Center for Immigration Studies published a report that examined exactly who did agricultural fieldwork, construction, and hospitality jobs in America. Their conclusion: "There are no jobs that Americans won't do or aren't doing. In every job category, there are a majority of American citizens and legal immigrants who do those jobs, including farm farmwork."

### Do African American Workers Agree with Their Leaders That Illegal Immigration Does Not Pose a Threat to Them?

African American workers have a different view of Latino competition than their black leaders (especially the ones quoted in *Crisis* magazine).

Groups such as Choose Black America—a coalition of black activists from U.S. cities such as Los Angeles, Chicago, Detroit, and New York— are very much concerned about low-wage Mexican workers who are taking jobs that used to be unskilled black workers' ladder to the middle class. But following a press conference at the National Press Club in Washington, D.C., on May 23, 2006, there was no mention of it in the mainstream media the next morning. ("The editors did not consider the participants to be important Black leaders," said a *Washington Post* reporter who was there.[6]) Increasingly, black worker advocates express frustration that no African American legislator will take up the issue. "No Congressional Black Caucus [member] met with the Choose Black America group in D.C. in 2006," they said.[7]

*Have African Americans Been Denied Construction and Restaurant Jobs Because They Don't Speak Spanish?*

Increasingly, African Americans who are skilled construction and restaurant workers complain openly about not getting good jobs or being laid off because "they don't speak Spanish." Their stories fall on politicians' deaf ears. A black member of the Human Rights Commission of the City of Los Angeles told a C-SPAN Washington Journal audience on April 15, 2006, that "blacks in Los Angeles should learn Spanish; becoming bilingual would be a good career move for them!"[8] One laid-off black construction worker, a native of Washington, D.C., said, "This isn't fair! I'm not a racist! I'm not anti-immigrant! But this is my country and we speak English here."[9]

*Have Illegal Workers Replaced Native-Born Blacks in New Orleans Reconstruction Jobs?*

After Hurricane Katrina, hundreds of displaced longtime residents (especially African Americans) returned to New Orleans to take the federally funded reconstruction jobs. But suddenly in the spring of 2006, stories in the media reported that the jobs Louisiana residents took were now being done mainly by Mexican nationals, most of them illegally in the country. "The city is in danger of being over-run by Mexican workers," Mayor C. Ray Nagin was quoted by the *New York Times* as saying publicly. "The local guys are trying, but there's nowhere for them to stay. The workers' camps provided often by a government employer like the Naval Air Station at Belle Chasse looks like Little Mexico," said one electrician. "Many illegal immigrants came to the base every night on busses for the employer-supplied meals even though they didn't work there." That troubled the worker. He complained to the employer, then to the Immigration Services, and was laid off, according to a story in the *New York Times*.[10]

## How Does the Latino Unemployment Rate Compare to African American Unemployment?

In September 2006, the Pew Hispanic Center and Brookings Institution published reports that showed that Latino workers were the only group in the nation whose unemployment rate was dropping—to 5.3 percent—while the unemployment rate of the nation's white workers remained steady at around 4.6 percent and those of American black working-age males at around 8.7 percent nationally, according to the U.S. Department of Labor. However, according to Bob Herbert, a *New York Times* columnist, 33 to 50 percent of black male high school graduates in their 20s were unemployed and between 59 and 72 percent of black males who left high school without a diploma were jobless.[11] Latino workers were the only ones experiencing an increase in hiring. The report does not distinguish between those Latino workers who are legally in the country and those who are not.

## Is Illegal Immigration a Civil Rights Issue?

An October 2006, *New York Times* front-page story about tensions between black and Latino workers in Willacoochee, Georgia (making up 19 and 21 percent of the population, respectively), reported that "African Americans expressed anger and unease as immigrant groups hailed efforts to legalize illegal immigrants as a new civil rights movement."[12] The issue escalated when an illegal Latino migrant mother (Elvira Arellao) who had been deported three times and was now a felon took refuge in a Chicago church with her young son and declared herself to be the "Rosa Parks" of immigrants. A National Public Radio feature on September 7, 2006, "Some Bristle as Sanctuary Plea Draws Civil Rights Comparison," focused the show on whether illegal immigration was a civil rights issue.[13] Increasingly, black activists are seeing illegal immigration as a labor issue and perhaps a human rights issue but not a civil rights issue since civil rights pertains primarily to the rights and duties of citizenship (and legal immigration).

## Does American "Third World Kind of Dependency" on Cheap Foreign Labor Prevent Us from Investing in "First World" Technology?

The need for more legal work visas for foreign nationals to "do jobs Americans won't" has been challenged by university agricultural researchers. These academics are concerned about the will and ability of the United States to break away from a "Third World kind of dependency on (cheap) foreign workers" and instead to invest time and resources in research to develop labor replacement technology. "Support for such research and development is always a struggle, yet it is a way out of the labor dilemma," said Professor Phil Martin of the University of California, Davis, at a 2006 congressional hearing.[14] "Reliance on foreign labor takes away from the incentive for states and agricultural companies to invest in research to find ways to pick and pack crops mechanically—to get away from the dependency on low-wage unskilled manual labor," he said. "State agriculture payroll taxes should be devoted to research and development of new technological, mechanized and other labor force development."

## Can Genetic Engineering of Some Agricultural Products Ease the Problem of Dependency on Illegal Cheap Farm Labor?

Mark Krikorian of the Center for Immigration Studies makes the case for the need for biological genetic engineering breakthroughs to ease the problem of illegal hires in the farm fields of America.[15] He cites an example of this kind of innovation from the California tomato industry in the 1960s. At that time, the mega tomato ranches, consisting of hundreds of acres of fields growing tomatoes for sauces, stews, cans, and so on, faced the sudden termination of the bracero labor program that had supplied the ranchers for years with low-cost seasonal workers from Mexico. The California tomato ranchers were desperate for a way to plant, water, and pick their massive crops. They appealed to researchers at the two great agricultural universities of California—University of California, Davis, and Cal Poly state college—who within two years developed a hard-skinned tomato that could be sowed, picked, and packaged by machine. After an initial investment, farmers could produce more and higher-quality tomatoes with fewer personnel who were skilled and earned better money. This is an example of labor replacement technology doing away with the need for cheap labor from the Third World.

*What Are U.S. Companies Required to Do to Prove That No American Can Do a Job for Which They Hire a Foreign Worker?*

The answer is "minimally if at all," according to labor experts. "Existing visa programs for technical workers today—like the H-1Bs, L-1s [intracompany workers], and TNs [technical workers]—are generally less protective of U.S. workers," Rebecca Smith of the National Employment Law Project admitted at a July 2006 congressional hearing.[16] "They [the employers of technical workers] have fewer regulations on the amount and duration of work, wage levels, and transportation and recruitment fees for their foreign workers." And there are no regulations—none—requiring employers to make an extensive search for U.S. workers. However, employers of technical workers often do express concern about job verification requirements. They are worried that such regulations "can foster discrimination against anyone who looks foreign," Smith concluded.

*How Well Does the U.S. Enforce Its Labor Laws Sanctioning Employers Who Hire Workers Illegally?*

Unfortunately, it is becoming well known that sanctions against employers hiring foreign workers without legal permits to work did not happen in the past decade. Even the secretary of homeland security confirmed this in a keynote speech at the American Enterprise Institute on June 29, 2007. "In 1999, there were 24 criminal arrests for crimes related to hiring illegal migrants. In fiscal year 2004, it went up to 160, and this year so far, with the fiscal year in progress, we're up to a record 382 criminal arrests," he said. "High-impact cases, major cases with major charges against major figures" would be the new focus of employer sanctions for the Department of Homeland Security—"exactly the strategy we used against organized crime," Michael Chertoff promised.[17]

## Does Illegally Hiring Unlimited Numbers of Cheaper Foreign Workers Drive Down Wages?

The concept that an unlimited supply of anything will drive down the value of that "thing" is a precept of economics that is not a mantra. It is a fact. Still, when the concept is applied to illegal labor, this acknowledged economic theory becomes controversial. The question of whether massive numbers of unmonitored, illegal migrant labor actually drives down (or at least keeps down) wages and benefits in the fields where they dominate is fiercely debated. Ivy League economists argue on both sides of the yes-and-no spectrum.[18] Jumping to the bottom line, however, there seems to be agreement among experts on all sides of the "wage effect of illegal workers" debate that in certain job sectors—those that are experiencing increasing numbers of illegal foreign hires (who can be exploited because of their illegality and therefore their unwillingness to challenge exploitive wages and no benefits)—wages and benefits in fact have decreased. The studies confirm that as wages and benefits decline, native-born and legal immigrant workers will no longer be attracted to work in these fields. They become "jobs Americans won't do." They become jobs that networks of foreign workers—often from a single country, state, or even village—will fill with their friends and compatriots. They become jobs that mainly "illegals" do.

## Does Hiring Unlimited Numbers of Educated Foreign Workers Lower Wages in High-Skilled Jobs?

Some experts argue that the same "lowering wage effect" is happening in those skilled labor pools where increasing numbers of educated foreign workers are working illegally. After all, 45 percent of the illegal community is made up of migrants who came into the country legally on temporary visas—all with limited if any work permits. These skilled illegal workers include former tourists, business visitors, and especially foreign students who stayed on after their legal visas expired: they are the so-called visa overstayers. As with the unskilled jobs, illegal workers in skilled white-collar jobs will work for less money, fewer benefits, longer hours, and without complaint because of their illegal status. Many midlevel engineers complain in vain that they are being laid off for cheaper, more recently educated, far younger foreign engineers and tech workers eager to work more hours for fewer benefits under one-year practical training permits and so-called temporary H-1B visas.

*Does American Historical Reliance on Cheap Labor Reflect*
*a Cultural Attitude about Immigration?*

There is one last consideration to ponder about this mantra. We Americans pride ourselves on being, a nation that has always welcomed the labor of foreign workers. That is true.

To put it bluntly, throughout our country's history we have built our prosperity on the backs of cheap labor who do our dull and dirty work. For many shameful years, most of the former colonial states prospered off the backs of seemingly extremely cheap labor—slave labor. The dependency on slave labor endured until slaveholders discovered that immigrant and indentured servant labor was even cheaper because employers did not have to provide these laborers' family care from cradle to grave as they did for slaves. Immigrant labor required pay only by the hour or day, and then little of that.

Cheap immigrant labor is better for other reasons as well. American employers' consciences can be salved with two facts:

1. No matter how lowly the wages and benefits, they are still far higher than almost every illegal immigrant would earn at home; their lives are inestimably better off, especially with the availability of free schooling and medical care for their offspring and relatives.
2. Eventually, industrious immigrants who labor cheaply in the United States can become "Americans" who will assimilate into our business culture and can employ cheap foreign labor of their own to build their own prosperity.

Increasing numbers of skeptics of the myth that "(illegal) immigrants do work Americans won't do" suggest that the mantra should be rephrased to reflect the reality of illegal immigration as being an issue about cheap labor. The suggested new wording for the mantra is, "Illegal immigrants do jobs Americans won't do (or aren't doing or used to do) *for lower wages and fewer benefits.*"

## 3. ILLEGAL IMMIGRATION IS UNSTOPPABLE
## BECAUSE OF THE U.S. JOB MAGNET

The interesting thing about this often-heard mantra is that it contains commonsense truths that lead to an inherent contradiction, a false conclusion, and obvious solutions.

### What Part Makes This Mantra Seem to Be Perfectly True?

- America has better paying jobs than most countries of the world. True
- Most illegal aliens have come to the United States to work and to better their lives and those of their families by making more money; they have not come to commit crimes (other than knowingly breaking U.S. immigration and labor laws). True
- Jobs are the unquestioned immigration magnet. True
- Many foreign nationals will do anything possible to get a job that pays better in the United States than in their homelands even if it means being illegal—and so would you in their shoes. True
- It is almost impossible politically, humanely, and physically to seal the borders. True
- Illegal aliens are encouraged to come to the United States to work because of difficult economic conditions in their homelands and because large networks of their compatriots encourage them and help them to get jobs in the United States. True

### How Can We Question This Mantra That "Illegal Migration Is Unstoppable"?

The reason that this mantra can be questioned as being false is because it isn't true in any other country in the world—even in countries of Europe, where jobs often pay more than in the United States, have far better benefits than in the United States, and there are numerous neighboring nations with contiguous borders and a cheap labor force. While even the prosperous countries of Europe and Asia have increasing numbers of immigrant workers, still they do not have massive numbers of illegal workers. No country in the world has the numbers of migrants employed illegally as the does the United States of America. Why?

Massive numbers of foreign nationals work and stay illegally in the United States rather than in other First World countries for one reason—because they can. The entire world knows that U.S. immigration and labor laws are not enforced. In every other prosperous country of the world, massive numbers of migrants cannot be hired if they entered and are residing there illegally because employers cannot hire illegal migrants with impunity, as in the United States.

In a 2005 panel discussion on the immigration dilemmas facing Germany and France, experts discussed whether legal immigration should be expanded and how to handle the challenges of assimilating naturalized citizens from former colonial countries. When asked about illegal immigration in their countries, the panelists agreed that it was not a particular problem in France and Germany. They attributed the lack of a problem of illegal workers in most European countries to two basic factors:

1. National laws requiring that everyone carry official personal identity cards without which no one can be hired, go to public schools, receive social services, rent apartments, pay bills, get driver's licenses, pick up mail, and do just about any normal activity of a resident
2. The continual enforcement of very strict sanctions and penalties of an employer who hires a foreign national illegally

There is another reason as well why other First World countries do not have massive numbers of illegal migrants working in their lands. The culture of work is different in other First World countries. For instance, Europeans are adamant about protecting labor rights and benefits—the most generous in the world that are paid for by heavy taxation of citizens and monitored by strong worker/management organizations. European workers of all levels expect their governments and unions to protect them. They do not support a culture of cheap labor. "We have few jobs for non-skilled cheap immigrant workers," a German labor economist, Klaus Zimmerman, said.[19] "Most Germans do not have illegal aliens mowing their lawns and cleaning their houses," a German engineer (the author's brother-in-law who lives in a suburb outside of Stuttgart) pointed out.

In other words, there are strong cultural reasons why other prosperous countries do not have massive numbers of illegal migrants working in their lands. While they may experience waves of illegal aliens coming to their shores—such as boatloads of Albanians to Italy and recently Somalians and other African nationals to Spain—still the solution is not seen as giving them work permits. While the care of "economic migrants"—people who migrate for economic reasons (mainly to get better-paying jobs), not political ones—is a growing worldwide dilemma, every other country in the world honors their immigration and labor laws above any desire to have cheap foreign workers take their jobs. Other countries don't have millions of illegal hirees in the country because, almost universally, illegal aliens are not hired.

## Can We Stop Illegal Immigration by Closing the Job Magnet?

Many books, articles, op-eds, and legislative proposals about immigration reform include prescriptions for stopping illegal immigration. Most concentrate on closing the border. A few deal with the job magnet. Some of those suggestions are listed next. They include the two factors that have prevented Europe from having massive numbers of illegal workers—identity cards and strong employer sanctions. Many of these proposals have been incorporated into immigration and labor legislation introduced in the 109th and 110th Congresses. All can be found in immigration and labor laws of many other "nations of immigrants." All require political will and resource investment. Here is a brief look at the proposals that get the most attention:

1. Require all foreign nationals to carry tamperproof digital biometric identity cards with which the person's U.S. work permit status can be checked as easily and quickly as charging a credit card.
2. Make it a felony for employers to hire those who do not have the legal right to work in the United States and enforce the laws by greatly expanding internal immigration enforcement resources.
3. Encourage industries that utilize unskilled human labor to invest in research to mechanize their labor tasks and to support national research grants for agricultural, engineering, and business colleges to develop innovations for products and manufacturing processes.

4. Require foreign student advisers—who officially are given authority by the U.S. State Department to grant foreign student visas—to verify that all their foreign students comply with time and work limitations of that visa, or the college will lose its right to participate in the lucrative foreign student industry. If their foreign student officers are unable—or unwilling—to trace their disappeared foreign national alumni, they could pay their development and fund-raising offices to use their extraordinary alumni tracking processes and databases to do it.

5. Leverage military and other nonessential aid to large illegal-labor-source countries (such as Mexico) with conditions that they curb corruption and take care of their own poor, or forfeit the goodies their leaders get from the United States.

### Don't These Proposals Go against Americans' Core Beliefs?

To pass legislation including some of the previously mentioned proposals may mean confronting and rethinking some core beliefs of many Americans:

- Our unique perception about privacy protecting everyone from any kind of collective government information gathering; this view has caused politicians on all sides of the political spectrum to resist the introduction of government-issued "identity cards" or even Social Security cards that can't be counterfeited and that can be tracked on a national database (in our consumption-obsessed culture, however, this perception of privacy protection does not seem to include businesses or corporate-issued credit cards or college development office questionnaires that collect far more private information than any ID card would).

- The right of student privacy that even excludes parents from opening student grade cards or any other communication from their children's colleges (except tuition bills).

- The ideals of globalization that seem to consider the right to move and work globally—anywhere in the world that one wishes—as a basic human right. The word "globalization" obviously excludes the concept of "national sovereignty," which is inherent in the word "international."

- The basic sovereignty rights of a nation to control its border and who comes in and stays versus the ideal of world citizenship or a "global" citizen.
- The role of government in protecting the security of U.S. citizens— for many Americans that means security not only against international threats such as terrorism but also against unfair trade and labor practices and massive lawbreakers; for many it also means security for the American Way of Life and the American Dream— opportunity and prosperity under the rule of law. "Protecting the security of Americans" does not mean "xenophobic, racist, nativist, isolationist protectionism," as some open-border libertarians advocates might try to frame it.

## 4. THE STATUE OF LIBERTY WAS BUILT TO WELCOME THE WORLD'S TIRED AND HUDDLED MASSES TO THE UNITED STATES

It is interesting to note how early in any conversation or presentation about immigration this mantra is evoked. It usually comes up in the first few sentences.

Perhaps the Statue of Liberty mantra should be treated as suspect from the beginning. After all, it concerns history, and most Americans are known not to pay much attention to history since we tend to live in the present and the future, not in the past, as most people from other countries (particularly developing countries) do. Our generally weak sense of and interest in the facts of history is said to be one of the most distinguishing characteristics about Americans—for better and for worse.

### Was the Statue of Liberty Built to Welcome Immigrants to America?

The statue was *not* built to welcome all the world's huddled masses to the United States.[20] It was built in the 1870s by French Republic patriots and placed in New York Harbor by Americans to symbolize French–American friendship—with the "hidden" political message that Americans supported the emerging Third Republic of France, which was being established on the American ideals of liberty for all classes of men.

Clearly, the history of the Statue of Liberty has nothing to do with an open immigration policy to the United States. The belief that it does is a romantic poetic idea, a pure myth, that has been developed into a mantra with a political agenda that does not equate with U.S. immigration facts or consequences. The mantra, however, represents what the Statue of Liberty has come to symbolize.

## 5. LATINOS ARE THE FASTEST-GROWING POLITICAL BLOC IN THE UNITED STATES

This mantra is growing legs every day as the immigration debate melds into the growing media focus on electoral politics. "The Latino vote" is often cited as one that will be "deciding" or "crucial" or "will make or break a party, a candidate, or an issue." The mantra assumes a continuance of mass migration of people from South and Central America, especially from Mexico, and continued high birthrates of Latinos who reside in the United States. It implies that *all* Latinos think the same way politically and will vote as a (often-assumed Democratic) bloc.

The mantra seems to be based on a lack of knowledge about the diversity of Central and South American society and the people who come from there as well as the diversity of the Hispanic heritage community in the United States, some of whom have been citizens for many generations. It also seems to assume a very simplistic view of the process of becoming a voting citizen.

Before addressing some of the obvious and less obvious questions about this mantra, some terms should be defined.

### Who Is a Latino, a Hispanic, and a Chicano?

Various terms are used, often interchangeably, to describe a large group of people whose family origins for the most part originated in Latin America and Spain. They are often referred to as "Latinos,"[21] "Hispanics,"[22] and, particularly in southern California, "Chicanos."[23] Some are called "Espagnoles."[24]

The language about "Latinos" often takes on the rhetoric and tone of civil rights politics. "The Latino bloc" is often referred to as if they are a "racial" group or an "ethnic" group, an "immigrant" group and "minorities." But they really are none of these things per se.

## Race

Latino/Hispanics are considered by the U.S. Census to be whites (often you will see references to "non-Hispanic whites" in census reports to distinguish between Latinos and other racially white people in the population).

## Ethnicity

There really is no Latino/Hispanic ethnicity, as can be seen from the previously mentioned definitions. Latinos are made up of people from every ethnic and racial group, socioeconomic class, and any other identity known to man. Being Latino is a language cultural heritage, not an ethnicity.

## Immigrant Community

In many communities, a majority of Latinos are no more immigrants than most U.S. citizens whose families emigrated from somewhere in the recent or far distant past—most Latinos/Hispanics are U.S. citizens, not immigrants. In fact, Chicanos have a very strong opinion about this: most do not believe they ever were immigrants. Many say that "we didn't cross the border; the border crossed us. It's everyone else who are immigrants, not us."

## Minority

Finally, in increasing numbers of neighborhoods, cities, regions, and (soon) some states in the United States, Hispanics/Latinos are not the minority population but the majority. It is increasingly rare to hear Latinos refer to themselves as minorities except on university campuses and in Congress, where the (illegal) immigration rights movement uses the rhetoric of civil rights.

## Are Latinos (Hispanics) the Largest Heritage Group in the United States?

According to a 2005 report of the U.S. Census Bureau, the "Hispanic or Latino" population made up 14.4 percent of the total U.S. population;[25] in the 2002 census, Latinos made up 12.5 percent of the total. In

October 2006, the total U.S. population reached 300 million—mainly because of increases in immigration. By 2050, it is estimated that Latinos will make up 24 percent of the total U.S. population.

There are numerous statistics, graphs, and pie charts that count the numbers of legal and illegal immigrants in the United States. All are easily accessed on the Internet. Their numbers are not all exactly the same, but they all agree to some degree that Mexican nationals account for over half of the some 12 million illegal migrants in the United States and that "other Latin Americans" account for another 10 to 20 percent—about 8 million people, or about 22 percent of the total Hispanic population (and about 65 percent of the total illegal resident population and 3 percent of the total U.S. population).

As for legal immigrants, the Pew Hispanic Center reports that their distribution by region in the world has remained fairly constant since 1990. Mexico always provides the most, followed by Asia, the "other" Latin American countries, and then Europe and Canada. Within that pattern, there have been differences. Between 1998 and 2002, an immigration percentage spurt from India was higher than Mexico's—reflecting that India was one of the major beneficiaries of the increased number of visas made available to high-tech workers in the peak period.[26] Latino countries account for half of the legal immigrants to the United States, or a total of about 200,000 people.

These figures show that currently Latinos make up the largest heritage population among immigrants to the United States. Activists constantly point out that Latinos are the fastest-growing demographic in the United States—surpassing the black population in 2002 and the "non-Hispanic white" population in around 2050 if present trends continue. But is this growing Latino population in the United States a potentially powerful political and voting bloc?

### How Many Latino Residents in the United States Who Have the Right to Vote Actually Do Vote and Vote as a Bloc?

By law at this time, only people who are U.S. citizens and who have registered to vote are allowed to cast ballots. In the 2004 presidential election, the total numbers of Hispanics who were reported to be citizens was about 16 million (out of a total Latino population of some 40 million). Of those, 57.8 percent were registered to vote, and 47.2

percent were reported to vote—almost 8 million people (out of roughly 100 million citizens who voted). The turnout for non-Hispanic white voters increased by five percentage points in 2004 to 67 percent, while the gain for black voters was three percentage points to 60 percent. The voting rates did not change for Hispanics from the 2000 election, who came in at 47 percent—nor for Asian Americans, who voted at a 44 percent rate, according to the U.S. Census Bureau.[27]

## Is the Latino Vote a Significant Political Force Now and/or in the Future?

At present, the Latino voting bloc nationally is small, although it is obviously larger in states where Latinos have higher proportions of the population (particularly in California and Arizona). But it can be questioned if in the foreseeable future the large and growing Latino population will be a significant voting force in the next election. Here are some facts to consider.

First, a large proportion of the Latino population in the United States came in as migrants—both legal and illegal—in the past five years. Obviously these millions of individuals cannot vote now, nor will they be able to in the coming elections of the next 5 to 10 years.

The right to vote is only for U.S. citizens and one of the very few rights denied even to a permanent legal immigrant resident green card holder. Chapter 2 points out that the only category of migrant that can become a U.S. citizen is a permanent resident. But to become a citizen is a choice of the immigrant. Citizenship is never conferred automatically to any immigrant, nor is it in any way required. And while the act of voting is a serious obligation, a right, and a duty of every citizen, it also is not required.

Many permanent immigrant green card holders never become citizens by choice. To become a citizen is a multiyear process (usually three or more) requiring the applicant to learn English and to have been a law-abiding legal resident for a certain number of years.

To move from the status of being an illegal alien to that of a citizen—even for those who get "amnesty" and can "earn a pathway to citizenship"—takes still more years (one stalled legislative package proposed an 11-year waiting period). Every expert agrees that the vast majority of Mexican and Latino migrants flooding into the United States today come to work to give their families a better life and to send money back home. Few come with the intention of becoming a citizen.

Second, nationally, citizens of Latino heritage are extremely diverse. The likelihood that they even think as a "bloc" of like-minded people makes little common sense. The only real thing the various Latino communities in the United States share is the culture of the Spanish language. The Latin American population is as diverse as the "American" tradition.

The "Latino" people in the United States come from the countries of Central and South America, all of which have widely different national histories, geographies, and demographics. Many of these Latinos have previously been exposed to a rich diversity of national heritages— European, Chinese, Japanese, Malaysian, Middle Eastern, Jewish, Muslim, Buddhist, and Christian. For example, the large German heritage communities in Latin America are often divided themselves between early German settlers who came in the 1900s, German Jewish refugees who came in the 1930s, German war refugees including former Nazis who came in the 1940s and 1950s, and German Latin Americans of the late 1990s.

In addition, there are wide differences in the Latino countries between various socioeconomic classes, a factor affecting the politics of those countries. Some socioeconomic Latino groups are more conservatively Catholic than North American Catholics—especially about "values" issues such as abortion, gay marriage, and worshipping saints—while a large proportion of highly educated and intellectual Latinos can be more secular and politically leftist (former active Trotskyites, Communists, and the like) than their North American counterparts.

Third, it is ill informed to believe that such a mass of people with such diverse national heritages will vote in any uniform and disciplined way. Chapter 8 details more specifically the political diversity of various Latino groups. There also is growing evidence that in large states like California, where Latinos are becoming prosperous, as they prosper they become more business oriented and vote Republican.

Fourth, there are many Latino Americans (or American Latinos as some prefer to put it) who are first-, second-, and third-generation U.S. citizens and who oppose the political stands of many of the "wedge issues" immigrant advocates—especially the issue of supporting illegal immigration.

- "You Don't Speak for Me," founded by Al Rodriquez, a decorated Korean and Vietnam War veteran, is a group representing such "dissidents." "It is a Hispanic American coalition that soundly rejects the media myth that the vast majority of Hispanics support the protests and calls for immigration laws to be properly enforced," according to the colonel.
- In many areas of the Southwest and southern California, where there were large pre–U.S.-federation estancias and ranches, the heritage of the Hispanic community is just that—Spanish and even Basque, not Mexican. In fact, many early "Espagnoles" make a point of the fact that Mexico ruled the Southwest territories for less than 25 years between the breakup of the Spanish holdings and the Mexican-American War.

Whatever the background of the large and growing Latino heritage peoples of the United States is, it is clear that as American Latinos increasingly become educated, assimilated, find a voice, and become prosperous, there is not now nor will there be in the future a united and unified "Latino voting bloc." Hispanics in America and throughout the world share their Spanish-speaking heritage, and that binds them in a cultural way. But the fact is that the Latino voting bloc doesn't exist except as a mantra.

## 6. FOREIGN STUDENTS COME TO THE UNITED STATES TO STUDY TO LEARN ABOUT AMERICA AND TO RETURN HOME AS PRO-AMERICAN ADVOCATES

Most Americans, generally, do not see foreign students as part of the *immigration* issue. But there is concern about the foreign student visa.[28] The worry is that since 9/11, foreign students won't come in ever-increasing numbers as before. This concern has created new mantras, now heard almost any time the subject comes up at the time of this writing:

- Since 9/11, foreign students no longer feel welcome to study in the United States.
- The numbers of foreign students have dropped massively because of visa restrictions.

- The massive drop in the numbers of foreign students is a crisis for the intellectual progress and international standing of the United States.
- Many college science and engineering programs depend on foreign students and would close without them.
- As American kids lose interest in math and science, we depend on foreign students to take those jobs.

The implications of these mantras deal directly with issues in the immigration debate—especially those concerning granting more permanent visas and the stricter enforcement of work and time limits of temporary visas.

## Are Foreign Students in the United States the World's Best and Brightest?

In the first decade or so of the foreign student visa's history, this statement was probably true. The foreign student visa was issued selectively to elite foreign students from war-torn countries to study at our best universities. Many came on government-sponsored scholarships—theirs and ours. But that was long ago.

There are now some 600,000 foreign nationals who are registered as foreign students at every level of postsecondary educational institution in the country. The qualifications of accepted foreign students to America's wide variety of higher-education institutions obviously vary widely. The majority of these students are graduate students earning advanced degrees in the science, technology, engineering, and math fields.

Most are no brighter than the average American high school graduate—although most foreign secondary school graduates have had more specialized, disciplined, and comprehensive courses in math and science than their American peers, often graduating from 13-year specialty high school programs (not 12-year comprehensive high schools as Americans students do).

## Do Foreign Students Come to the United States because We Have the Best Colleges in the World?

It is a fact that the American postsecondary education system is truly unique in its diversity. There is no country in the world that has the number and diversity of institutions of higher education.[29] It reflects the unique American core belief that everyone should and can be educated for life at any time, at any age or stage, regardless of background or past educational achievements.

Most foreign nationals come from countries that support only a few universities for their most elite students to attend for free, while everyone else goes to work after high school. Despite the relatively high cost of higher education in America,[30] coming to the United States is the one chance many foreign nationals have to go to college at all. Foreign students flock here to study because here, more than anywhere in the world, they can go to college no matter what their qualifications.

### Do Foreign Students Return Home to Be Pro-American Leaders?

There is no doubt that a good number of the world's leaders have studied in the United States. And most—in fact probably almost all of them—remain personally sympathetic and understanding of the American people and our way of life long after they return home. Still, having been a foreign student in the United States does not guarantee that a person will be loyal and support every American governmental policy once they become their nation's leaders. A number of America's strongest opponents as well as our closest allies studied and graduated from U.S. postsecondary institutions. It is silly and naive to think otherwise. In addition, these former foreign students who are now national leaders make up only a small proportion of the millions of foreign nationals who entered the United States on the foreign student visa and who actually even returned home. Research shows that the majority of all foreign students (and almost 70 percent of graduate students) do not return to their homelands after their studies, even though that is a specific requirement of the visa.[31]

### How Can So Many Foreign Students Violate Visa Requirements?

Section 12B of the Immigration Code reads that foreign students must prove that they will return home before being issued the foreign student visa. But for the past decade this provision was increasingly ignored. Especially in the 1990s, foreign student applicants were seldom interviewed by a U.S. official. There was even a "fast-track program" for preferred countries such as Saudi Arabia that at times allowed a foreign student to pick up their student visa at a designated travel agent at the same time they picked up their flight ticket.

Vetted postsecondary education institutions designated to host foreign students by the State Department have no obligation to track or in any way monitor their former students to determine if they have complied with the must-return-home provision of the visas they have issued. "We are not policemen," most foreign student advisers claim.

While hundreds of thousands of foreign students manage to stay on legally, hundreds of thousands more simply overstay their visas. They become part of the over 5 million foreign nationals presently living and working in the United States illegally—often for decades. They work in industries that are rarely, if ever, monitored by immigration officers on long-expired visas that company personnel offices simply forget about. Other abuses such as working full time and studying one or two courses a semester for decades or dropping out of college for a year or two to work and then starting up again are overlooked by the immigration enforcement system. A foreign student has almost a free pass to stay in the country for decades, waiting for the next federal amnesty legislation to make him or her legal and give him or her a pathway to citizenship.

Foreign students staying on in the United States is almost a given. Even Secretary of Commerce Carlos M. Gutierrez has said that the United States "needs more foreign students to come study and work." (Obviously no one had reminded the secretary that the foreign student visa is not an immigration permit and has stringent work limitations.)

### Is There a Precipitous Decline in the Number of Foreign Students Attending American Colleges?

Reports of a decline have made headlines since 2003. But the numbers appear to have been greatly exaggerated. In fact, the total numbers have hardly changed at all.[32]

There are several reasons why the numbers may be spun by the foreign student industry lobby and the mantras (about a decline in foreign students and that foreign students don't feel welcome) repeated incessantly in the halls of Congress. Many educators in the foreign student industry fear a future where foreign students may no longer come. Many of their institutions depend on foreign student revenue and fear losing

it. There are some trends that are disturbing to the university administrators and the National Association of Foreign Student Advisers, the
foreign student industry's major lobbyist.

## Stricter Visa Vigilance since 9/11

One of the attractions of recruiting foreign students in the past has
been the relative ease for just about any foreign national to get a foreign student visa. Our diplomatic officers (with an appreciation of the
value of "soft power") were told not to interview prospective students
even though immigration law required it. Fast track was instituted for
preferred countries. Foreign nationals visiting the United States even as
tourists could easily convert their tourist visa to a student visa simply by
being accepted to college and waiting for the visa to arrive in the mail.
Until 9/11 there were no visa delays because few if any accepted foreign
students were monitored in any way.

Then came 9/11. All the attackers were foreign nationals who had
various immigration statuses. Several came in on foreign student visas,
some of which had expired and two for which the approvals came in
months after the deaths of the terrorists. Suddenly, the foreign student
visa was on the radar and regulations began to be enforced and tightened up:

- In the 2005 intelligence bill, all temporary visa applicants—including
  foreign students—were required to be interviewed by a consular officer who is an American citizen. That meant that all applicants had
  to go to a consular office, perhaps one far from home.
- At first, long delays occurred. But by 2006, many new regional consular offices were opened, and delays were down to three weeks.
- Stricter visa entrance requirements have caught some foreign students when they tried to renew long-expired visas and were denied
  reentry. Some students, scholars, and even professors who had
  been on foreign student visas for years were suddenly denied, while
  others were not given even initial visas. Consular officers said that
  95 percent of these denials were due to perceived or even openly
  stated violations of the visa regarding the intent to immigrate.
- Also legislated in this intelligence bill were two new student tracking systems: SEVIS to monitor the number of foreign student visas

issued by a postsecondary educational institution tracking how many of those students actually registered and graduated, and MANTIS, which restricted students from certain countries to pursue research in certain "sensitive" fields (such as nuclear engineering).

These systems track foreign students only when they are registered in a university, however.

### Possible Increase in Internal Immigration Enforcement

It is well known that "internal" (inside the United States) monitoring of visas is virtually nonexistent, unless a criminal act has been committed. In truth, once a foreign student is in the country, internal immigration enforcement has hardly changed at all in the past decade. Foreign students now may be more aware of the laws against staying on and working, but, in practice, it is no harder for a former foreign student to stay on and work than it was before 9/11. Immigration and labor laws are rarely enforced. No foreign student "visa overstayer" has ever been arrested. Increased sanctions on a few hundred employers who hire "illegals" has begun only for those hiring masses of subwage Latinos at meatpacking plants and the like. It is unlikely that a high-tech company or medical lab will be raided in the near future.

# II

## THE NEWS STORY

# 6

## The Issues Impacting Immigration: The Hottest Ones on the Hill, on K Street, and around Massachusetts Avenue

People are always talking about immigration issues. But what are they? Aren't they just facts by another name? Not really. Issues are the meat of public policy; they are how public leaders and opinion makers view what are the most important impacts of immigration. These views are what drive how policies and laws are formulated. Issues are what most of the politicking is all about. But issue beliefs are grounded on perception, not necessarily inarguable facts. And those perceptions are relative.

In this chapter and the next are the top eight immigration issues that are making news in our nation and that I consider to be the most significant—those that continuously come up in the policy discussions and legislative initiatives. The four most significant issues *impacting immigrants* as covered in this chapter are globalization, trade agreements, demographics, and integration/assimilation.

### GLOBALIZATION

In the early 1990s, globalization was greeted euphorically as the unstoppable force that would bring unprecedented prosperity to all in the future. The concept of "globalization" encompasses the international flow of ideas and knowledge, the sharing of cultures, global civil society, and world stewardships of the environment, health care, and other social issues, according to Joseph E. Stiglitz, a former World Bank economist.[1] But most of the focus is on economic globalization:

> Economic globalization entails closer economic integration of the countries of the world though the increased flow of goods and services, capital and even labor. The great hope of globalization is that it will raise living standards throughout the world; give poor countries access to overseas markets so that they can sell their goods, allow in foreign investment that will make new products at cheaper prices and open borders so that people can travel [in this case, emigrate] abroad to be educated, work and send home earnings to help their families and to fund new businesses.[2]

"There can be little question that globalization can contribute to the economic well-being of much of the world's population, at least in the long run," wrote Ralph E. Gomory and William J. Baumol.[3] But it is also clear that "in the short run, globalization can bring much pain and suffering in both the affluent and the developing countries. While the benefits can be great, there is no guarantee that they will be equally distributed. The future benefits may not be worth the price."

"Unchecked by competition to 'win the hearts and minds' of those in the Third World, the advanced industrialized countries actually created a global trade regime that helped their special corporate and financial interests, and hurt the poorest countries and some groups (such as workers)," writes Stiglitz.[4]

There is no doubt that globalization has increased the pressure for workers in some countries to emigrate in order to earn more money working elsewhere. "The developed countries are rich in capital . . . and the developing countries have an abundance of unskilled workers who want to move around the world in search of better jobs," writes Stiglitz.[5]

In 2004, a survey of 73 countries around the world found that global unemployment had reached a new high of 185.9 million workers. The report also found that 59 percent of the world's people were living in countries with growing inequality, with only 5 percent in countries with declining inequality.[6]

In June 2006, UN Secretary-General Kofi Annan reported happily that nations and immigrants' families benefited from migration brought on by globalization. "While migration sometimes reduced the wages of low-skilled workers in advanced economies, it more often freed citizens to perform high paying jobs," Annan was reported to have said.[7] Shortly after Annan's statement, AFL-CIO President John J. Sweeney had a different take on globalization's impact on immigrant workers. "Globalization causes exploitation of immigrant workers especially because so many of the jobs they take are part-time and temporary," he said. "So many of these jobs do not provide health and other benefits and no security. And [because of] the presence of 1.5 billion Chinese workers on the global job market since the collapse of the Communist 'command economy' model, there definitely has been a downward push on wages in the United States."[8]

In sum, there is no doubt that in the globalized economy, there are losers and winners. Stiglitz points out that the challenge of globalization is to find the balance between government and markets so that the inequities between winners and losers are not catastrophic.

## TRADE AGREEMENTS

Trade among nations is truly the world's oldest activity. "Almost everyone acknowledges that a nation is better off if it doesn't try to tell its citizens what they are allowed to buy from or sell to foreigners," wrote Michael Kinsley.[9] Some politicians and economists tell us that free trade will "lift all boats." Historically, the United States has been open to free trade. In 1985, President Ronald Reagan said, "Our trade policy rests firmly on the foundation of free and open markets." Most Americans believed Reagan when he said that "the freer the flow of world trade, the stronger the tides of human progress and peace among nations."[10] Prosperity comes with access to expanded markets where producers can sell more goods and consumers can enjoy lower prices and where there will be increased competition to sift out the efficient producers from the inefficient.

The problem is that "there really is no such thing as free trade," write economists Ron and Anil Hira. "Every free-trade agreement is, in fact, a negotiated document. A free-trade agreement involves all kinds of bargaining by each nation's negotiators. When you consider the different ways countries run their economies and how those procedures affect trade—such as varying tax schedules and social spending goals—it is clear that no human being or economic model could possibly predict the exact outcome of a trade agreement over time."[11]

An op-ed by Senator Byron Dorgan (D-N.D.) and just-elected Senator Sherrod Brown (D-Ohio) makes this point clearly: "With corporations trolling the world for the cheapest labor, the fewest regulations and the governments most unfriendly to labor rights, U.S. trade agreements force U.S. employers to produce the same thing with even cheaper foreign labor."[12]

The dilemma is international and it is stalling trade talks worldwide. "The trade talks are suffering from so many disputes that like the victim in Agatha Christie's 'Murder on the Orient Express,' almost everyone could be guilty of killing them off," writes *New York Times* business columnist Steven Weisman.[13] For instance, India and Brazil are refusing to lower their tariffs out of fear of export-driven economies like China, while second-tier developing countries complain they are being shut out of competition by India and Brazil; meanwhile, the poorest of the poor countries in Africa charge that rich market economies are ignoring their needs, and everyone complains about U.S. agricultural subsidies. "This is not a classic North-South conflict; it is also South-South," writes Weisman; "70 percent of the tariffs paid by poor countries go to other poor countries."

But Kinsley, always the libertarian liberal on free trade (and probably immigration), concludes that denying free trade to the whole nation and denying opportunity to the rising middle class in developing countries only protects the incomes of a relatively few (American middle-class citizens) and is harder to justify in the flat world of today.

It will probably never happen, but what would "full liberalization" of free trade policies bring? Stiglitz writes that standard economic theory has a scenario. "With full global economic integration, the world will become like a single country and the wages of unskilled workers will be the same everywhere in the world, no matter where they live. In theory that wage will be somewhere between that received today by the Indian or Chinese unskilled worker and that received by his American or European counterpart. In practice however, given the relative size of the populations, the likelihood is that the single wage will converge closer to that of China and India."[14]

Let's look at the two most important trade agreements of the United States that also have a significant impact on the decision of foreign nationals—most particularly Latin Americans—whether to immigrate, if they haven't already.

## NAFTA: THE NORTH AMERICAN FREE TRADE AGREEMENT

First negotiated by then President George H. W. Bush, NAFTA was pushed through Congress by President Bill Clinton, who eventually signed it into law in late 1993. It is classified as a "congressional executive agreement" rather than a treaty, although under international law it is a treaty. It is essentially a trade bloc between Canada, Mexico, and the United States.

NAFTA does not (like the European Union) create a supranational governmental entity or a body of law superceding the national laws of the participating countries. To some, NAFTA did not significantly bolster the Mexican workforce. According to Lori Wallach, Public Citizens' Global Trade Watch director, "In Mexico, after ten years of NAFTA, 1.5 million *campesino* peasant farmers were displaced with their livelihoods destroyed. First they went to the border industrial zone, pushed wages down there 20 percent. Undocumented immigration increased with many people dying in the desert on their way across. Generally there was growing economic and social instability in Mexico as a result of this economic disruption."[15]

And Josh Bivens of the Economic Policy Institute reports that in 1994, about 600,000 Mexican employees were employed by maquiladoras—factories near the U.S. border making goods sold in the United States. In July 2004, those factories employed about 1.1 million workers. Before NAFTA opened the doors to labor exploitation, Mexican manufacturing for export made up 11 percent of the country's gross domestic product (GDP) in 1994. By 2003 this had doubled to 22 percent of GDP, or just over one-fifth of the overall economy.

"I don't take issue with Mexico's economic success," writes Senator Dorgan. "But their gains have largely come by exploiting labor forces and pitting them against one another—a flawed strategy and just plain wrong. It's bad for labor in both countries in the long run, but it's good for the company bottom line in the short run—whether Mexican, American or most likely, multi-national—not tied to nor loyal to any country in particular."[16]

In fact, Senator Dorgan points out that under globalization, Mexicans are now shocked to see some of their jobs migrating to China because even low-paid Mexican workers can't work cheaply enough to compete with lower-paid Chinese workers. Moreover, while many mainstream economists will argue that the overall benefits to U.S. consumers outweigh the net losses of jobs in particular sectors, this does not help the now unemployed workers. While some may find jobs in other areas, gains from trade vary by industry (i.e., losing a steel mill will affect more people than gaining a travel agency). And while free trade can provide benefits in terms of competition, that depends on what kind of free trade arrangement is negotiated.

## NAFTA and Illegal Immigration

In February 2007, the *New York Times* published an article with the headline "NAFTA Should Have Stopped Illegal Immigration, Right?" The reporter, Louis Uchitelle, summarized one of NAFTA's stated aims: "[NAFTA] enacted by Congress 14 years ago held out an alluring promise: the agreement would reduce illegal immigration from Mexico. Mexicans, the argument went, would enjoy prosperity and employment—and not feel the need to cross the border into the United States."[17]

Obviously that did not happen. Wages of Mexican production workers decreased 14 percent (from $2.91 to $2.50 an hour), factory jobs had declined 15 percent since a peak in 2000, and Mexico's GDP growth had been weak since 2001, when there was no growth at all. The Mexican government had "assured President Clinton that the investment would take place" and "it would do its part by investing billions of (its oil) dollars in roads, schools, sanitation, housing and other needs to accommodate the new factories" expected to be developed under NAFTA. It didn't happen. Absent that support, factories clustered on the northern borders, and eventually many moved to China, leaving the Mexican workers with the option to return to the undeveloped south or cross into the United States. By 2004, total manufacturing employment in Mexico had declined to 3.5 million from a high of 4.1 million in 2000, according to American University economist Robert A. Blecker.[18]

All this has created a "network effect" on immigration—webs of people from the same villages and often loosely related that help each other get jobs, live together, send money home together, and sometimes bring their families up. This network is often referred to by immigration experts including Jeffrey Passel of the Pew Hispanic Institute and Mark Krikorian of the Center for Immigration Studies (CIS). "The unregulated flow of Mexican workers to the United States has become a momentum of its own," Passel was quoted by the *New York Times* as saying on February 18, 2007. "Since NAFTA, Mexican immigration has risen to over 500,000 a year from less than 400,00; 80 to 85 percent of the new Mexican immigrants are illegal," Passel estimates.

Ironically, many who come find themselves struggling. Many find that after immigrating to the states to take low-wage jobs, especially in American textile factories, those jobs are shipped abroad—back to their homelands or to China.

## CAFTA: The Central American Free Trade Agreement

A dozen years after passing NAFTA, CAFTA was passed (in the Senate by a 54-to-45 party-line vote and by a slim two-vote difference in the House) in the summer of 2005. Democrats (including members of the Hispanic Caucus) in both houses opposed the agreement.

The controversial trade deal was considered by many to be merely an extension of NAFTA, this time involving five Central American countries: Honduras, Nicaragua, El Salvador, Costa Rica, Guatemala, and the Dominican Republic. These nations make up a relatively small percentage of American trade. CAFTA removes or reduces tariffs on certain consumer, industrial, and agricultural goods and lifts restrictions on investment. Unlike NAFTA there are also provisions that added $40 million a year from fiscal year 2006 through fiscal year 2009 to aid CAFTA countries in monitoring and enforcing intellectual property and environmental protections and requiring that all member states uphold their national labor laws.

Mainly trade and business organizations supported it. In an interview with broadcast journalist Ray Suarez of PBS's *NewsHour with Jim Lehrer*, the vice president of Western Hemisphere affairs at the U.S. Chamber of Commerce, John Murphy, said that they had two reasons for supporting it:

1. First of all, we already have free trade with Central America, but it's one way: coming in. About 20 years ago, the Congress voted with nearly 400 votes in the House of Representatives to eliminate most tariffs on imports from Central America and the Dominican Republic. That's why today 99 percent of foreign goods come in duty-free from these countries and 80 percent of manufactured goods. By contrast when

American companies are selling into this large and growing market, we face tariffs that are in the 7–11 percent range. That's like going into a basketball game 11 points down from the tip-off.

2. The second reason why we're strongly advocating this agreement is because it's a helping hand to some emerging democracies that are some of our closest neighbors, our staunchest allies, and our best economic partners. Remember the last time that Washington debated Central America; it was in the 1980s when wars were raging in the region. They've come a long way. CAFTA will help them generate jobs and growth so that they can stay on the right path.[19]

By 2007, all countries involved with CAFTA had ratified the agreement—except for Costa Rica. Otton Solis, a local Costa Rican politician, explained the reluctance to ratify the Agreement:

Costa Rica is already benefiting from trade (its exports last year grew four times faster than in 2005, far better than neighboring countries who had implemented CAFTA). Joining CAFTA would only undermine "precisely . . . some of those institutions that you and I are praising": The universal health care system would be bankrupted by new rules favoring pharmaceutical companies, environmental laws could be challenged in closed-door trade tribunals, and the government-run electric and telephone companies, losing their monopoly, would no longer be able to offer the low prices and wide coverage that are "basic for social mobility."[20]

At a conference before the Economic Policy Institute in August 2007, Solis complained that the media both in the United States and in his country offered only pro-CAFTA points of view.

## The Security and Prosperity Partnership (aka The North American Union)

In March 2005, President George W. Bush, Mexican President Vicente Fox, and Canadian Prime Minister Paul Martin unveiled a blueprint for a safer and more prosperous North America. The leaders agreed on an ambitious security and prosperity agenda that would purportedly keep the mutual borders closed to terrorists but open to trade.

The Council on Foreign Relations lauded the Security and Prosperity Partnership (SPP) and urged its expansion into more open labor access between the three countries.[21] Specifically it states, "The Task Force establishes a blueprint for a powerhouse North American trading area that allows for the seamless movement of goods, increased labor mobility, and energy security." It was also proposed that the SPP expand the number of scholarships going between the three countries. This seemed to have an immediate effect. In 2005, Mexico was reported by the International Institute of Education (in its annual "Open Doors" report) to be the fifth-largest source country of foreign students to the United States—the first non-Asian country to be in the top five in almost a decade. Dr. Armand Porschard Sverdrup, director of the Mexico Project at the Center for Strategic and International Studies in Washington, D.C., told the author that it probably had to do with the number of government scholarships that were being made available to Mexican college students to study in the United States. To date, that seems to be the biggest impact of the SPP for Mexican citizens. The annual meetings of 2006 and 2007 were distracted by immigration and the war-on-terrorism issues with little substantive proposals outside of increased border security.

## DEMOGRAPHICS

On October 17, 2006, almost every newspaper in America displayed a population clock to mark a historic turning point in the country—the day the U.S. population reached 300 million. By 2040 it is expected that the population will be 400 million—an unprecedented growth in 34 years. How did this young country get so big so quickly? "There is no way that you can talk about our arrival at 300 million without pointing to the fact that immigration is such a heavy component of the annual growth," says Jacob Siegel, a retired census statistician who worked for the agency in 1967. "There's no political advantage in getting in this hot issue," he was quoted as saying in USA Today.[22] In fact, immigration, longevity, a relatively high birthrate, and economic stability all have propelled the phenomenal growth. The nation added 100 million people since 1967 to become the world's third most populous country after China and India. It is growing faster than any other industrialized nation.

About 53 percent of the 100 million extra Americans are recent immigrants or their descendants, according to Jeffrey Passel, demographer at the Pew Hispanic Center.[23] A number of diverse factors determined the rate of growth, ranging from changes in U.S. immigration law in 1965, 1986, and 1990 to steady improvements in life expectancy to decreasing fertility levels. According to the Pew Hispanic Center's population estimates and projections, the Hispanic population increased from 8.5 million in 1966–1967 to 44.7 million today. Latinos accounted for 36 percent of the 100 million added to the population in the past four decades, the most of any racial or ethnic group. Immigration from Latin America and relatively high fertility rates among Latinos were major factors in this increase. The white population grew from 167.2 million in 1966–1967 to 201.0 million today. That represented 34 percent of the 100 million added since 1966–1967.[24] Experts agree that in 2006, about 12 percent of the current U.S. population was foreign born.

### Increasing Diversity of the United States

It is obvious that immigration is contributing to the increasing racial and ethnic diversity of the U.S. population. The share of the population who will be Asian and the share who will be Hispanic is projected to double between 2000 and 2050.

Dispersement is important "as far as the implications for social integration," said Linda A. Jacobsen, director of domestic programs at the Population Reference Bureau.[25] "Population growth in the U.S. since 1970 has been more heavily concentrated in the South and West than in the Midwest and the Northeast. In fact, the West surpassed the Northeast in total population back in 2000, and is projected to overtake the Midwest region before 2030. The South will continue to have the largest population of any region through 2030. The population is also becoming more concentrated in metropolitan areas, especially in the suburbs. Fifty percent of all Americans currently reside in the suburbs of metropolitan areas."

### An Aging Population

"Because of gains in life expectancy coupled with the decline in fertility, the U.S. population, like all modern societies, is growing older. Many observers worry that there will not be enough workers to support the government and economy in the future," reports Steve Camarota of the CIS.[26] "The aging of the U.S. population creates serious challenges for Social Security, the nation's public retirement system," according to a Stanford University Social Security report.[27]

The common perception is that immigrants drive up the birthrate in the United States and that without immigrant growth, the economic stability and quality of life of Americans will shrink. Retirees depend on the number of people of working age to support them, and that percentage is going down. According to the CIS study, net immigration in the United States currently is 1.25 million individuals; 67.3 percent are of working age, 15 to 64 years old. If the immigrant population continued to increase at the same rate as today, by 2040 (when the population hits 400 million) the share of working-age population would be 59.8 percent.

The data seems to confirm the urgent need for continued immigration growth in the United States. But strange to say, dependency on immigration growth to support our aging population *is not really true.*

Both Jacobsen and Camarota agree on a surprising fact: "Even if no additional immigrants came across the border in the next few years, population would continue to grow in the U.S. because of the built-in momentum of higher fertility among the Hispanic population already in the United States."[28] If net immigration were doubled to 2.5 million a year, it would raise the working-age (15 to 64 years old) share of the population by less than one percentage point, to 60.5 percent by 2040, according to the CIS study.

"While immigration (growth) has a very large impact on the size of the nation's population, it has only a small effect on slowing the aging of American society and on the dependency ratio," concludes Camarota. The factor that would have the most significant impact on the dependency ratio is simply to raise the age of retirement—and consequently the age that Social Security would be paid out.[29]

"Increases in population are one factor that could potentially help to mitigate the economic and fiscal strains of a burgeoning elderly population. However, the extent to which this happens will depend to some extent on whether future cohorts of children are enabled to develop to their full potential," says Jacobsen. "If the U.S. increases opportunities for minority children and reduces disparities in well-being then these future generations may be more productive workers and better able to support the growing elderly population. The U.S. is in a better position

than the rest of the developed countries if the U.S. invests appropriately
to develop the full potential of all members of the population."

## INTEGRATION, ASSIMILATION, AND FITTING IN

The feeling of "fitting in" to the country where an immigrant has moved,
lives one's life, works, and is involved with family and friends can make
the crucial difference between an immigrant's success or failure in the
present and in the future. Fitting in used to be called assimilation or
integration. I use the terms interchangeably.

According to John Fonte, director of the Center for American Common
Culture at the Hudson Institute, there are different types of assimilation:

- Linguistic: the immigrant learns the dominant language
- Economic: the immigrant does well materially and perhaps joins
  the middle class
- Cultural: the immigrant acculturates to the nation's popular cultural norms (both good and ill) including intermarriage with U.S.
  natives and immigrant nationals with different backgrounds (some
  say that intermarriage is the key indicator of integration)
- Civic: the immigrant is integrated into the political system, votes,
  pays taxes, obeys the laws, and participates in public life in some
  fashion
- Patriotic: refers to political loyalty and emotional attachment to
  the United States; does not mean giving up all ethnic traditions,
  customs, cuisine, and birth languages[30]

Most experts agree with Fonte that immigration integration has nothing
to do with the food one eats, the religion one practices, the affection
that one feels for one's birth country, and the number of languages
that one speaks. "Multi-ethnicity and ethnic sub-cultures have enriched
America and have always been part of our past since colonial days,"
Fonte said. "But historically, the immigration saga has involved some
'give and take' between immigrants and the native-born. That is to say,
immigrants have helped shape America even as this nation has Ameri-
canized them. On the other hand, this 'two way street' is not a fifty-fifty

arrangement. Thus, on the issue of 'who accommodates to whom,' obviously most of the accommodating should come from the newcomers, not from the hosts."

According to Gary Gerstle, a professor of history at Vanderbilt University, "Immigrant integration does not happen overnight. Typically it takes two generations and requires both engagement on the part of immigrants with American democracy and an opportunity for them to achieve economic security for themselves and their families."[31]

This point is sometimes missed by overly enthusiastic immigration advocates like perhaps Celinda Lake, a well-known Democratic Party strategist, who claimed at a summer 2007 event at the Brookings Institution that "immigrants work hard and pay taxes—how much more American can they be?"[32] (She confirmed in an interview afterward that she really felt this is all it takes to be an American.)

### Kindness of Strangers

For all the challenges of integration, illegal immigrants also face a dilemma, identified by Victor Davis Hanson. "For all the brutality of America, the immigrant senses a weird sort of kindness here. It's present in the select and liberal group of Americans in health care, law, education, and government who feel it is their duty to help him of all people—the lowly immigrant. They deliver to the illegal immigrant, housing, medicine, and food at a level beyond almost anything found even among the well-off in Mexico City; they give college scholarships and mental health counseling."[33]

Examples of this kindness toward illegal immigrants is everywhere in America. In some areas they are offered identity cards and discounts at local stores, driver's licenses, loans, and even sanctuary if they commit a crime and are threatened with deportation. In many communities, illegal immigrants are offered free legal clinics to help them deal with the "intimate, sometimes desperate dilemmas faced by thousands of immigrant families whose households often include a confusing mix of legal U.S. residents or citizens, illegal immigrants and others with temporary permits or pending immigration cases."[34]

It is often confusing to many illegal immigrants to be told that a test of their rights as (illegal) immigrants is whether they can get help from publicly funded agencies without reprisal.[35] This often refers to cooperating with the police investigating crimes involving other illegal immigrants. Many new illegal residents are reluctant to "reach out" to public agencies not only because of the typically harsh reprisals toward illegal residents in their homelands (in Mexico, for instance, an illegal immigrant is *considered to be and is treated as* a felon) but also because, in the United States, the illegal Mexican immigrant finds it difficult to believe activists who tell them that if they cooperate with the police in reporting crimes, they will not be deported.

### Intermarriage and Naturalization Rates

Intermarriage between native Americans and immigrants has long been considered a key factor in integration throughout the history of the United States. But the rate of intermarriage has been decreasing in the United States over the past 10 years. One study found that immigration has played a key role in this decline.[36]

As for naturalization rates, as seen before, the number of permanent legal residents who naturalized to U.S. citizens reached an all-time high in 2005—over 52 percent of the estimated 24 million legal immigrants (compared to 35 percent of the total in 1995), according to the Pew Hispanic Center.[37] The reasons why the naturalization rate rose is partly due to growth in the total number of legal immigrants in the country and to growing interest (or pressure among immigration advocates) for them to naturalize.[38] Advocates also have an interest in greater numbers of former immigrants voting (presumably on the assumption they might vote for an immigration expansion and legalization of the illegals) as well as other benefits of citizenship, including the right to bring in relatives abroad as legal immigrants.

It is disappointing to many that some immigrants take the step to become citizens out of fear and for a political agenda that might be in the interest of more immigrants from their homelands but not in the interests of the United States. "It would be ideal if people were making the decision to become an American as an expression of full-fledged commitment to this country, not as a defensive measure," said Ira Mehlman, a spokesman for the Federation for American Immigration Reform, which favors limits on immigration.[39] "I hope people are feeling they want to belong. We want a democracy where everyone participates," said Tamar Jacoby, a senior fellow with the Manhattan Institute.[40]

## Growing Fear among Illegal Aliens

Since the failure of the Comprehensive Immigration Reform bill in June 2007, the fear of those immigrants living and working in the United States illegally has increased. Many employers "who rely on low-cost temporary workers . . . have been spooked by a recent immigration crackdown, including stepped-up workplace raids and enforcement of laws making employers liable for fines if they hire illegal workers."[41] The fear encompasses two dreaded consequences for the illegal immigrant:

1. To be deported involuntarily—thus becoming a felon alien and face increasingly hardship to cross the border illegally and the chance of being deported again
2. That employers will no longer hire day laborers and other immigrants without checking documentation in a federal database

Of the two threats, the second one is the greatest. If employers decide they can no longer hire illegal workers, there really is no point for an illegal immigrant risking life and limb to come. "We should not underestimate the importance of economic security in persuading immigrants to cast their lot with America," said Gary Gerstle at a May 2007 congressional hearing.[42]

This fear of being caught or not getting a job because of illegal status is not solely about immigrants from Latin America. As has been pointed out many times, almost half of illegal immigrants in the country are not Latinos but people from every country in the world who came in legally. That said, there is no doubt that the most visible illegal aliens are Latino day laborers—large numbers of low-wage workers employed in agricultural, food preparation, construction, and hospitality jobs who use false documents and whose Social Security numbers do not match their identities. They are the easiest group to target. It will be a long time before high-tech firms employing former foreign students who have overstayed their student visas will be raided. And it is likely if these more educated workers are threatened, either their employers or the employees will do something about it to get themselves legalized or choose voluntary deportation with the chance of applying legally for the jobs they've established themselves in.

No doubt this "climate of fear" is a terrible thing to have to live with. Certainly for anyone who has broken the law or lied their way into a job (with false résumés and degrees) or done anything illegal that gave them a heads-up for a job or a prime spot in a training program and gotten away with it, fear of being found out must be a daily companion no matter how entitled they feel they were to do it. But "fear" is also a drumbeat that ethnic immigrant advocates love to beat to advance their agendas. Headlines proclaiming "A Climate of Fear for Illegal Immigrants" and "Fear and Hopes in Immigrants' Furtive Existence" and "Sorrowful Barriers" are typical. They seem to ignore the fact that "fear" is a consequence of the choice of doing something illegally or fraudulently, no matter what the reason and no matter how many times compassionate people tell the lawbreaker that it is okay and not their fault.

Being honest about our mistakes and taking responsibility for one's choices are American values, however. Perhaps some may think it's unsophisticated and naive to believe this, but these values are part of the American Dream. Being in the country legally and following the rule of law should be the first priority for advocates who want immigrants to America to feel comfortable in the American culture, to find inclusion, and to integrate, assimilate, and fit in.

# 7

# The Impact of Immigration on the Host State

## IMPACT ON THE ECONOMY AND AMERICAN WORKERS

At the time of this writing, by every basic economic indicator, the U.S. economy is strong. Nationally, the unemployment rate is low, productivity is high, wages are stable, and the government recently passed its first minimum-wage increase in many years. Stock market values, while experiencing the so-called normal summer bumps in 2007, were still in the 13,000s. Even the credit crunch on mortgages was seen as a "welcome adjustment" by many economists who felt housing prices were too high and the risk of any inflation too dangerous. To the business and their political communities, "immigrants (they never distinguish between legal and illegal) are doing jobs Americans do not do" and Americans' "future social security depend on the growth of immigrant labor to make up for the low birthrates of baby boomer Americans about to retire."[1]

Recently, however, more and more American workers are anxious about the American Dream. They are concerned about their job security and maintaining their American quality of life. They feel less secure—economically, safetywise, and even culturally. Many feel the government is not helping them. In worrying about keeping their jobs and/or getting a new one, a big concern is about the competition from foreign labor willing to work for less. They worry about their jobs being outsourced to foreign workers—both outside the country and inside. They also are worried about the quality of their schools and hospitals and parks and public services. Particularly they are concerned about the impact on these public services and facilities by massively growing numbers of illegal immigrants who cost their communities far more than they give back to it (despite what national statistics might show).

Of course these concerns come from perceptions of threat, from judgments, and from personal values and experiences. Experts are split about the big economic questions: Do illegal immigrants take jobs from Americans? Expand the economy? Drag down wages? Create opportunity? "The idea that the more job seekers from abroad means fewer opportunities or lower wages for native workers, is one of the most controversial ideas in labor economics," writes journalist Roger Lowenstein.[2] But the consensus of economists seem to be in a middle ground. "On balance immigration is good for the country. Immigrants provide scarce labor, which lowers prices in much the same way global trade does. And overall, the newcomers modestly raise Americans' per capita income. But the impact is unevenly distributed." Lowenstein does not distinguish between legal and illegal immigrants, and the "scarcity" of labor that, he writes, immigrants provide is in many cases (except for perhaps bend-over agricultural work) a perceived "scarcity" by employers who find a scarcity of willing labor to work for minimum wages and benefits—a scarcity of ever cheaper labor costs. This question "lies at the heart of the national debate"—the decision about "whom should the United States let in," Lowenstein concludes. It seems that it lies at the basis of capitalism as well.

## Outsourcing

Many American workers are concerned that their jobs will be outsourced—that is, that they will be fired or replaced by foreign workers who will gladly work for less wages and lower benefits—outside the country as well as inside. Many people believe that Lou Dobbs, the economic and business pundit, was the man who put "outsourcing" into everyday Americans' vocabulary. His book *Exporting America* put into print the multitude of anecdotes and reports about Americans losing their jobs to cheap foreign labor that have become popular daily fare on his prime-time CNN television show.[3] His book was quickly followed by others.[4]

These books are full of compelling stories, facts, graphs, and solutions about Americans' job losses, wage depression, and growing inequality. The thesis that is common in all these books: it is the fault of greedy corporate chief executive officers. They detail how American corporate managers do not care about American workers per se; their priority is making as much profit as possible for their stockholders by keeping costs low. And one of those biggest costs is wages and benefits. In the corporate world, labor is seen as a cost, not an asset, not an investment. And labor and benefits are cheaper in developing countries. So American corporate bosses are unapologetic about their "need" to close their doors in the American communities they may have been located in, contributed to, and provided jobs and security for decades to local workers and move to countries where the native workers often make less in a day than an American worker would make in an hour and the foreign government supplies the benefits, if any.

Global labor advocates say outsourcing actually benefits everyone: the immigrant worker who gets a better job, the displaced American worker who can retrain and get a more modern job, and everyone in America who benefits from the cheaper consumer goods and services that come from cheaper labor.

Certainly the two sides are correct to some degree. What is clear is that massive immigration—legal and illegal—impacts Americans and their anxieties about the American Dream's work opportunity and job security. Especially Americans are becoming increasingly outraged about rising inequality and the greed of corporate and mortgage bankers.

## Middle-Class Americans

Many economists concede that massive immigration into particular geographic areas and work occupations (usually the low-wage jobs) does impact negatively on American workers in those areas. But the rising support for immigration enforcement against illegal immigrants is coming from America's middle-class communities throughout the nation. Why are they so upset?[5]

"Immigration seems to adversely impact native employment. Only 9 percent of the net increase in jobs for adults (18–64) went to natives between 2000 and 2005, even though adult natives accounted for 61

percent of the increase in the overall size of the 16-to-64 year old population," reported immigration expert Steve Camarota.[6]

Congressman Lamar Smith (R-Tex.) has stated that virtually all credible studies show that competition from cheap foreign labor displaces
American workers—including legal immigrants—or depresses their
wages.[7] Add to that the depression of wages in solid middle-class professions such as computer technology and engineering due to the aggressive recruitment by some major tech companies for immigrants who
obtained degrees at U.S. colleges. These former foreign students are encouraged by immigration expansion advocates to "adjust" their temporary foreign student visas to a longer-term J visa or an H-1B, from which,
they are told, there is a great possibility to convert them eventually
(after some investment in time, money, and energy) to the permanent
green card. The price they pay is to quietly accept lower-than-prevailing
wages and never blow the whistle about it. What they're not told? Probable layoffs for newer, cheaper H-1B visa holders in their future.

### African Americans

"Almost 20 percent of all black Americans and 40 percent of legal
Hispanic workers don't have a high school degree. These low-skilled
workers are the ones who disproportionately must compete with foreign workers. They are the real victims of America's failed immigration
policy," said Representative Smith at the House committee hearing.

"It's not that African Americans won't work in every occupation
where there are jobs," he said. "After worksite enforcement actions by
the Bureau of Immigration and Customs Enforcement, Georgia's Crider
Inc. lost over 600 Illegal workers." The *Wall Street Journal* reported what
happened next: "For the first time since significant numbers of Latinos
began arriving in Stillmore, Georgia in the late 1990s, the plant's processing lines were made up predominantly of African Americans. Crider
continues to fill positions now with legal workers."[8]

Robert J. Samuelson, economist and columnist, pointed out that
the importation of poor unskilled, low-wage Hispanic workers into
the United States hurts low-skilled black in competing for low-skilled
jobs—"although some economists disagree."[9]

In 1965, Senator Edward Kennedy (then as now the chairman of
the Senate Immigration Subcommittee) said the new immigration law

(based on extended family unification) "will not flood our cities with immigrants; it will not cause American workers to lose their jobs."[10] "Well, so much for predictions," said president and chief executive officer of the Urban League of Greater Miami T. Willard Fair.[11] "Since 1965, 30 million legal immigrants plus millions of illegal aliens have come here. The results have been devastating for those Americans—black or white—who compete for jobs with this immigrant tide. While no individual immigrant or particular immigrant group can be blamed for the difficulties facing black men's unemployment, still immigration is the largest single reason, though certainly not the only reason."

### Poverty

You don't hear much about poverty in America these days. The "War on Poverty," which was a major policy of President Lyndon Johnson's administration with the aim to give massive government help to the nation's poor, was not very successful and is long gone with successive centrist Democratic and conservative Republican administrations. The War on Poverty was replaced by new policies, such as "faith-based initiatives" that give government money to religious organizations such as Rescue Missions with highly successful poverty programs without regard to their religious conversion and restriction requirements, and "welfare reform programs" that provide low-income recipients with job training and require that they get a job within a certain period or they're off the welfare rolls (a policy that has indeed lowered the number of people on welfare significantly).

Most people believe that the U.S. poverty rate (measured by household income under the official "poverty line," currently $20,614 annual income for a family of four) had flattened out, persisting among a stubborn few who had bad luck and made bad choices. But a 2007 government report[12] found the following:

- 12.3 percent of the population, or 36.5 million people, lived below the poverty line in 2006.
- The rate was slightly lower than in 2005 (12.6 percent) and 1990 (13.5 percent), but the populations were smaller then (in 2005, 33.6 million people lived below the poverty line in the United States).

- Hispanics accounted for the entire increase of people in poverty from 1990 to 2006—2.9 million people: the number of poor Hispanics increased 3.2 million from 1990 to a total of 9.2 million in 2006. In comparison, non-Hispanic whites in poverty fell from 8.8 percent of the population in 1990 (16.6 million) to 8.2 percent of the population in 2006 (16 million); the number of blacks in poverty declined from 9.8 million in 1990 (31.9 percent) to 9 million in 2006 (24.3 percent).

Economist Robert J. Samuelson states that "[poor] Hispanics [many of them immigrants or dependents on immigrants, a majority of them illegally in the country] accounted for all of the gain" in the population living under the line of poverty.[13] They accounted for 41 percent of the increase of people in the country without health insurance. "This imposes a strain on local schools, public services and health care." Most of all, assimilation—which should be our goal—will be frustrated if we keep adding to the pool of poor.

"Only an act of willful denial can separate immigration and poverty," writes Samuelson, in pointing out these statistics. There is no dispute that the vast majority of Hispanic immigrants, especially those who sneak across the Mexican border, are low-income, uneducated, low-skilled, and low-wage workers and their families. Allowing massive illegal immigration (and, many argue, extended family immigration as well) of this poor population is *importing poverty* into the United States, Samuelson concludes. "Yet the link between poverty and immigration is rarely if ever addressed by journalists in public forums."

## Job Protection

Witnesses representing labor unions and labor economists before a House subcommittee hearing seemed to agree that the labor movement had come to rely on immigrant labor. They acknowledged indirectly that many of their members did not have legal permits to work. The union hearing witnesses agreed that there was a need for many more legal work permits for immigrants. "Immigration reform must reflect U.S. labor needs," said Fred Feinstein, who was representing the Service Employees International Union.[14] He obviously implied that all illegal immigrants should be legalized and given amnesty and a pathway to citizenship.

The witnesses also seemed to favor new permits that would be permanent rather than temporary. "Temporary work permits might discourage native workers—particularly in high tech jobs," said Michael J. Wilson, director of the United Food and Commercial Workers International Union legislative and political action department.[15] "Temporary status without a pathway to permanency is close to slavery!" he concluded. But Vernon Briggs Jr. of Cornell University recognized the "agony that the issue of immigration causes the American labor movement. It influences the size, skill-levels and geographic distribution of the nation's labor force, as well as the labor conditions of local to national markets."[16]

Business representatives concurred with labor leaders that foreign workers should be legal and plentiful. At the hearing on the Business Community Perspectives on Immigration Reform, Google Inc., the National Restaurant Association, Mixon Family Farms, and the U.S. Business and Industry Council (BIC) focused on the expansion of legal work visas.[17] Witnesses in general supported expansion, but many of the subcommittee members expressed concern about the impact on native workers.

But William R. Hawkins at BIC stated that "recent immigrants are four times more likely to lack a high school degree than non-immigrants."[18] "The flood of unskilled and impoverished aliens needs to be halted before they drag down American living standards," he said. "While demographics is destiny, I am concerned about the possible hordes of [foreign] workers pressing down wages," said Representative Howard Berman (D-Calif.).[19]

But it was the vice president of Google's people operations, Laszlo Bock, who received most of the questions about the high-tech industry's request for hundreds of thousands of new H-1B visas. Representative Maxine Waters (D-Calif.) said that she was "constantly hearing about worker displacement especially having to do with the H1B visa. Why don't we look at this country first, about job training for Americans first?" she asked.[20] "I am not interested in supporting industries that simply want to hire [foreign] low wage workers with no benefits, no unions and no [continuing] education," she said. "Most of us sound very progressive about pathways to citizenship for immigrants, but we are going to look very hard at these [high-skilled] guest worker programs!"

"They took all my words right out of my mouth," said ranking member Steven King (R-Iowa). He sits next to Chairman Lofgren on her left at every hearing. "I just told Zoe that they were asking all my questions!" King told this reporter with astonishment.

## IMPACT OF GLOBALIZATION AND TRADE AGREEMENTS

The public's belief in free trade is changing and Congress has noticed. "Fewer and fewer Americans support our government's free trade policy," write Senator Byron Dorgan (D-N.D.) and then Senator-elect Sherrod Brown (D-Ohio).[21] "They see a shrinking middle class, lost jobs and exploding trade deficits."

It turns out that trade policy is also about the American Dream, according to the senators. "Americans are anxious about the American Dream. NAFTA [North American Free Trade Agreement] forces workers to accept cuts in their pay and benefits so their employers can compete with low wage foreign producers—that is, those lucky workers whose jobs have not yet been moved overseas. It's a race to the bottom for America's middle class," write the senators.

Michael Kinsley, formerly with *Slate*, disagrees. He believes (as do many liberal libertarians) that the American middle class owes it to the rest of the world to let them become middle class as well. "Denying free trade and job opportunities to the rising middle class in developing countries, is harder to justify in the flat world of today," he writes.[22]

However, one self-described "free trade skeptic," Harold Meyerson, a *Washington Post* columnist, worries about the changing attitude toward free trade. In one column he notes that "the nation's free trade policies have become threatened by growing public anxiety over our economic future. . . . The U.S. median income has flat-lined . . . corporate profits soar, individual wages stagnate . . . and voters sent to Congress a freshman class composed almost entirely of free-trade skeptics."[23] They and the middle class that put them in office are looking closely at how Congress is negotiating existing and new trade agreements (and no one even wants to talk about U.S. trade deficits, which seem to be regarded of late as a "benign" growth rather than a life-threatening cancer).

Congressman Walter B. Jones (R-N.C.) expressed concern that the executive branch was unconstitutionally trying to regulate commerce with foreign nations and in secrecy. "Since NAFTA was approved, the U.S. has lost 3.1 million manufacturing jobs. More than 10,000 illegal aliens stream across our southern border every week. The U.S. does not need its government equalizing standards and regulations that will result in more American jobs going to Mexico and more illegal aliens coming to America."[24]

## IMPACT ON STATE AND LOCAL GOVERNMENTS

The problem of uncontrolled illegal immigration has changed jurisdictions. Back in 2005, it was generally seen to be exclusively not only a concern but also a failure of the federal government. But today the impact and management of illegal immigration visibly shifted to state, county, and community jurisdictions. "We can no longer wait for the federal government to fix the problem of massively growing illegal immigration populations in our communities" was the common lament of state and local legislators throughout the country—whether they wanted to punish or protect illegal immigrants.

Increasingly, legal immigrants will let you know their status fairly early in an encounter with phrases like "when I became a citizen" or "when I came in as a refugee with my parents" or "when I came in as a foreign scholar." Those illegally in the country are less clear, referring mainly to their longtime residency in the country or their hard work here, their children in schools, or their community activism. Even mainstream newspapers increasingly distinguish between legal and illegal immigrants—forced to by events such as the arrest of identified illegal aliens, some of whom even had been deported several times, for allegedly committing violent crimes.[25]

A conflict over government's role in enforcing immigration laws hovers over the multitude of diverse legislative and legal initiatives by state and local governmental entities that have been pouring onto the desks of governors, county boards of supervisors, and city councils. They all seek to manage the impacts of out-of-control illegal immigration on their communities.

Many of these initiatives are creative and sometimes unique to particular areas. But there are some common problems involving illegal aliens that are being addressed by local entities throughout the nation:

1. The need to identify illegal aliens—especially those who are working for large companies as well as everyone arrested for crimes and in detention for a crime

2. The overwhelming use by illegal aliens of benefits and services funded by local taxpayers from hospitals, after-school programs, welfare programs, public libraries, and parks
3. A demand to provide illegal aliens with local public documents and services in languages other than English, involving translation and interpretation costs
4. Training local law enforcement officers to help (underfunded and undermanned) immigration enforcement agents
5. Community quality issues, especially housing density and multiple vehicles parked on lawns, public disturbances in neighborhoods, and public sanitation
6. School achievement levels and costs, especially for those who do not speak English

Prominent initiatives that are currently in play include day laborer centers in communities like Herndon, Virginia; court challenges of renter restrictions in Hazleton, Pennsylvania; local ID cards for illegal aliens in New Haven, Connecticut; and sanctuary actions by churches and cities to protect illegal immigrants at risk for deportation.

Individuals impacted by illegal immigration (positively and negatively) are finding their voices, unafraid to speak out and to make their public representatives know how they feel. The public scrutiny by the press that is finally waking up to the immigration issue and moving beyond knee-jerk conservative and liberal responses will ultimately expose ridiculous extremes and highlight reasonable, practical solutions. Despite the emotion of many on all sides of these issues, they do involve problems that community residents are deeply concerned—and in many cases increasingly angry—about. There will be many experiments with how to use local and state law, government agencies, regulations, court actions, nonprofit organizations, community action groups, and responsible business organizations.

### Rule of Law and Immigration Law Enforcement

When it comes to laws controlling immigration, many people in the United States have conflicting views. "We're a nation of laws but also a nation of independent people who obey laws at will," scoffed a good friend of mine, an avowed liberal Democrat and a former foreign service officer who was a political attaché for the United States in several major countries during her long career. "We don't obey traffic laws or drinking laws or drug laws. And we certainly shouldn't obey any law that goes against our tradition of inclusion and humanity."

Immigration activists who believe this see the issue fundamentally on a personal level. It is about the individual, a hardworking person who immigrated in order to have a better life. They say, There's no such thing as an illegal worker.

Those in the corporate community who believe this also seem to believe that immigration laws should be winked at. They view immigration as an issue of free labor markets, unrestricted trade, and a global labor pool, which allows them to hire the cheapest workers possible in order to maximize profits. Anything that limits their making more money is bad, and unless a rule is strictly enforced, they do not have to follow it.

But a growing number of Americans feel differently about immigration law enforcement. "Just what part of *illegal* don't you understand?" is becoming a common refrain. Many Americans point out the generous number of immigrants and visitors the United States welcomes every year. Everyone knows that immigration is complicated and that mistakes can be made. But that does not mean that the rule of law should be ignored or mocked. They see the role of government and laws as providing security—not only against crime and terrorism but also for jobs, a civilized society, and the integrity of citizenship. They view immigration policy from the point of view of the demands and needs of a successful nation-state.

When it comes to immigration laws, law enforcement agencies are stuck between these two views. They have the authority to enforce the nation's and communities' immigration laws against those who break them. But they get mixed messages from taxpayers about how much to enforce them.

Immigration enforcement really pertains to two different spheres, and it is important to distinguish between them. Each is enforced by different agencies and evokes much different support and emotion. One is enforcement of the borders. The other is enforcement of immigration laws inside the country.

## Border Security

Anyone who has ever lived in a border town knows that there is a certain looseness about the comings and goings across the, at times, invisible lines that separate one country from another. For centuries, Mexican workers easily crossed over the 1,900 miles of border with the United States to work, mainly in seasonal farm jobs, sometimes going back and forth each day on unmonitored trails, sometimes staying for a few months before returning home to their families. Everyone pretty much knew each other and worked for the same employers year after year, and the laws regarding visas were pretty much ignored. But now, some 300 million people, about 90 million cars, and 4.3 million trucks cross the manned ports of entry between Mexico and the United States each year. Since NAFTA, the number of commercial crossers each day has increased by 41 percent. In the past 15 years, the flow of workers without legal documents to work and sneaking over the southern border has increased by thousands a day, tens of thousands a week, and hundreds of thousands (some say a million) a year. Their identities are unregistered and impossible to validate.

Prior to late 2001, border officials often let those they caught sneaking into the country off with a ticket and a reprimand. After 2001, deep concern grew about the possibility of terrorists coming across. Border officials started detaining OTMs (other than Mexicans).[26] Then with the increasing public outrage over the rapidly growing number of illegal Mexican and Central American workers (doubling and tripling numbers in one year in many communities), Mexicans were included in those detained and deported.

The most controversial border control is the *fence*. In 2006, Congress passed a bill, and President George W. Bush (grudgingly) signed into law a plan to build some 700 miles of triple-layer fencing at crucial sites along the Mexican/U.S. border. It was estimated to cost about $1.5 billion and take about six months to build. Experts believed the walls would reduce illegal crossings into the United States by 90 percent. But by mid-2007, less than 20 miles had been built. Delays were caused by legal challenges brought by ethnic immigrant advocates and environmental protection groups, logistic concerns, and the belief by congressional opponents (certainly including some of President Bush's people) that a new Comprehensive Immigration Reform (CIR) bill in 2006–2007 would change the dimensions of the "fence." After the demise of the CIR, however, administration officials promised that the wall would be built and began it anew—at a turtle's pace.

## Internal Enforcement of Immigration Laws

Internal enforcement faces different challenges than border enforcement. The problem with internal enforcement starts with philosophy. It is a question of *if* laws should be enforced, not *how*. A typical example is when New York Mayor Rudy Giuliani said in a presidential campaign speech that "being in the country illegally is not a crime."[27] But as we have seen, coming into and/or staying illegally in the United States and using fraudulent documents to get a job or other benefits and knowingly hiring someone who is illegally in the United States *is* breaking U.S. laws and *is* a criminal act.

During negotiations on the Comprehensive Immigration Reform bill in the summer of 2007, proponents looking for compromises that would enable the bill to pass agreed that *not all* foreign nationals living in the country illegally should be forgiven for breaking immigration laws, given a legal visa, and rewarded with a pathway of citizenship after a few years (also known as "conditional amnesty"). Most parties agreed that legalization should not be given to criminal felons. But they quickly had to move away from that position. Proponents suddenly realized that a vast majority of the foreign nationals living illegally in the United States knowingly—those whom they usually refer to as "undocumented"—had bought and used *fraudulent* Social Security cards, green cards, driver's licenses, passports, and other identification documents, all felonies. Suddenly all their so-called undocumented immigrants became "fraudulently documented felon aliens" who would not qualify for legalization. Proponents had to go back to their original all-or-nothing legalization umbrella.

To assuage this conundrum, historically the anger and blame for illegal immigrants inside the country focused on the border—why didn't the feds keep them out in the first place? Why were they allowed in or allowed to work? Why should mere citizens, those who know the illegals, have sympathy for them and profit from them, and why should they now have to support their deportation? They just don't think those national laws should be applied to the ones they know who work for them and are their neighbors. They should be the exceptions. No wants to do tough love to those they like.

So for over a decade, immigration laws have not been enforced internally—not on illegal hires and not on their dependent extended family members (many who came in as visitors and never left). Immigration came to be seen as a human right, and millions of illegal immigrants were told that once they were here, it was their human right to stay, to settle. All they had to do was work hard and pay taxes, and then they had the right to use public services and demand the rights of citizens.

This "permissive" immigration system seemed to work well throughout the 1990s—until September 11, 2001. All the terrorists who destroyed the twin towers in New York, damaged the Pentagon, and killed thousands were foreign nationals. Several were in the country illegally, having overstayed legal visas. Some had even appeared on terrorist watch lists. With this backstory, it is reasonable to see illegal immigration as a national security issue. So now the problem is how to deal with the problems of illegal immigration inside the country. Officially, any immigration matter inside the United States is supposed to be dealt with by one of two agencies of the Department of Homeland Security: Immigration and Customs Enforcement to deal with enforcement and the U.S. Customs and Immigration Services to deal with services for legal immigrants and those attempting to adjust their status from one legal status or another.

But one only has be aware of local news throughout America today to see that many other agencies are involved with fixing the impacts of illegal immigration. Because of the failure of the feds to stop illegal immigrants, states and local governments and organizations are now intimately and intricately involved.[28]

Despite the robust—on paper—role of federal, state, and local efforts, most illegal immigrants have been little affected by the new enforcement agencies and new regulations challenging their status. Generally the main focus of all the agencies is on those relative few illegal immigrants who have been caught committing violent crimes and who are absconders who have ignored deportation orders. Public attention is focusing increasingly on the day laborers because advocacy groups have "brought them out of the shadows" so visibly. And there are some attempts to punish large and visible employers and employees who use false documentation. But most illegal immigrants (especially highly educated ones or those who are not working but who are dependents) do not reveal their immigration status and pretty much live out their illegal residencies with impunity.

This may well be changing as the voices on all sides of the illegal immigration issue become louder.

## IMPACT ON AMERICAN CULTURE AND CITIZENSHIP

The assimilation of the immigrant community into the American way of doing things, its values, and its lifestyle is as important to the nation of immigrants as it is to the immigrant. One of the greatest concerns about our present minimally enforced immigration system is that rapidly multiplying numbers of immigrant families concentrated into ethnic enclaves won't value, take on, be interested in, or even be exposed to the American way of life. Most Americans don't want immigrants to come here merely to make more money than they could in their homelands. We want them to come because they love America, our values, and our ideals and because they want to raise their children to become good Americans.

### Defining Characteristics of the American National Identity

Professor Samuel P. Huntington is concerned that American national identity and assimilation of immigrants has greatly weakened in the United States because of multiculturalism and "the weakness or absence of various immigration assimilation factors including immigrant ghettoization."[29] I don't agree. Americans have a definable culture and identity that one really appreciates only when you compare us to other nationalities.

Obviously the United States today is a country comprised of citizens of every race and ethnic background that exists in the world. We have intermarried and had such mixed-race, mixed-nationality, and mixed-ethnic children that the honest "ascriptive" identification of a defining American race and ethnicity today I believe is honestly none—there is truly no single race or ethnicity that today can be ascribed as American. It is almost impossible to tell who is an American citizen from appearance alone.

The United States has a well-defined and well-documented history as a nation-state, but many visitors from abroad are astounded by the paradox they see in our historical memories. On the one hand, they see that surely the United States has more museums to commemorate our national history (including museums for every cultural memorabilia of America from baseball to barbed wire), and we publish and buy more biographies about our historical characters than any other country in the world. On the other hand, Americans are famous for being historically illiterate—even about our own history as well about other countries' histories. In fact, a defining characteristic about Americans is that we are a people who live almost exclusively in the future. Reliving the past is not the American way. It is something we expect assimilated immigrants to eschew as well.

Professor Huntington writes strongly about America's defining religious identity.[30] He asserts that "throughout our history people who were not white Anglo-Saxon Protestants have become Americans by adopting America's Anglo-Protestant culture and political values."

On the other hand, sociologist Peggy Levitt makes another point about religion's influence on new Americans and vice versa: immigrants stay attached to their homelands by participating in their native religious institutions, made possible by technology and the ease of travel. These religious institutions are a powerful but little-known force in today's world. Immigrants are changing the face of religious diversity in the United States and making American religion just as global as U.S. corporations, subtly challenging the very definition of what it means to be an American.[31] Levitt implies that the religious identity from the homeland supersedes the forces of national identity and assimilation. As far as American national identity, I have to stand with Huntington on this point.

There is no doubt that one of the strongest elements that defines the national identity of the United States is that it is monolingual and dominant-English speaking. This monolingual and English-dominant identity is also perhaps our greatest advantage among all the nations of immigrants.

To state the obvious, different languages are different from one another because of the different cultures they reflect. When you speak a language, you use grammar and terms that have been determined by the culture—the history, values, and beliefs of the people who speak it. Language reflects the linguistic and national culture of the speakers. When you learn another language, you learn about the culture and national identity behind that language.

It is possible to be an assimilated American citizen without knowing English? To my mind, the answer to this question is a quick and definitive "of course not." But Representative Keith Ellison (D-Minn.), the first Muslim in Congress, disagrees with me. In a 2007 congressional hearing on integration, he remarked, "We are the only country that I know of that is bound together by a Constitution as opposed to long tradition, history, and culture. And maybe that is what we need to be focusing on, and maybe you don't need to speak English to do that."[32]

## ON CITIZENSHIP

Citizenship is one of the oldest relationships between an individual and a nation-state and its government. In its barest terms citizenship confers official membership on an individual within the nation-state. But it implies much more. Citizenship by various definitions implies the following:

- Allegiance
- Duty
- Participation
- Loyalty
- Rights—particularly the right to vote
- Contribution
- Union
- Integration
- Attachment—including attachment to the history of the country
- Shared values (of enlightenment and of America)
- Comfort with the national identity traits, especially the national language
- Privileges and special benefits

One central idea has always maintained the concept of citizenship, according to Samuel Huntington: "The American and French revolutions replaced subjecthood with citizenship . . . which is a distinctive political identity—a set of public values about governance and law that are widely shared by those within it."[33]

Citizenship in an integral issue in immigration. Many people assume (and many immigrant activists would like to perpetuate the belief) that all immigrants come to the United States with the dream of becoming citizens. One survey found that 93 percent planned to pursue citizenship. Immigrants were asked how best to describe what becoming a U.S. citizen meant to them. Fifty-six percent stated it was a necessary and practical matter, 34 percent a dream come true, and 8 percent something not so important, and 2 percent had no response.[34] But this, of course, is not entirely true. While naturalization is a choice, we have seen from the facts and issues presented in this book that barely one half of the millions of foreign-born individuals in the United States have been naturalized. Less than 20 percent of the foreign born are qualified to be so and choose not to, many for their lifetimes.

"The Balkanization of America has changed citizenship in the U.S. drastically and for the worse," wrote columnist Georgie Ann Geyer.[35] She cites the failure of new citizens to put down roots beyond the economic and records even in the early 1990s the growing anxiety of Americans about illegal immigration, noncitizen voting, and bilingualism.

Huntington echoes her concerns in his book nearly a decade later. But to him a new huge threat to the American identity is dual citizenship. "Citizenship is exclusive; individuals can change their citizenship, but they cannot have more than one at a time. It is a distinctive status conferred by government, involving rights and obligations that distinguish citizens from non-citizens."[36] But today, an increasing number of people from an increasing number of countries are permitted by their national governments to continue being citizens of their country even after swearing allegiance to the United States and gaining U.S. citizenship.

The excuse is often that everybody has multiple identities and that nationality is just another one to add to the list. But there is a legitimate and innate question of priorities of loyalty. If your heritage country and the United States were in conflict (or, in a worst-case scenario, at war), which one would you defend? If citizenship does not mean loyalty and even sacrifice, would the dual citizen of a warring country even consider sabotage?

Of equal concern to many is dual-citizen voting. There are now cases of citizens of Mexico also serving on governing boards in the United States, campaigning for Mexican candidates in the states, and representing Mexican interests while serving on a governing body open only to American citizens who supposedly hold the interest of the United States first.

There is no doubt that, ultimately, the goal of assimilation into an American identity can be best fostered by immigrants becoming U.S. citizens. This goal should be valued with a drumming up of the requirements and the exclusive benefits of citizens, not dumbing them down into a meaningless one-more-group-whatever identity. More than ever, the United States needs citizens committed to the ideals of the American Dream—fostering opportunities to live, work, and participate in the American way of life under fair and enforced laws that provide security for U.S. citizens and their invited guests.

# 8

# Immigration Politics

Many Americans enjoy the competitive excitement of politics, especially around presidential election times, but most could not care less about the endless nattering details. Most want to keep the choices simple—and politicians and the media happily oblige. For every big political issue, the politicians and lobbyists and opinion leaders try to make it easy for American voters by framing the legislative debate as if there are only two opposing sides. There are two political parties (Democratic vs. Republican), two points of view (liberal vs. conservative), two sides to every conflict (left vs. right), and two kinds of culture (secular vs. religious).

But the immigration issue has utterly defied this two-sided spectrum. And the politics of immigration confound even the most popular pundits. If every political issue is parsed along a horizontal line running from liberal Democrat on the left to conservative Republican on the right, then how can the partnership for comprehensive immigration reform (CIR) by the most liberal and senior Democratic leader, Senator Ted Kennedy (Mass.), and the most conservative (and detested by many Democrats) President Bush be explained? And just how can the double defeat of the Senate CIR bill (which contained strict border and interior enforcement measures and gave a heavily conditioned amnesty to illegal immigrants in the country) in June 2007 be explained when Senate leaders from both parties lobbied heavily for it?

# THE POLITICAL PLAYERS

## President George W. Bush

We have to start at the top with the sitting president of the United States. This president is extremely relevant in the immigration legislation politics of this century because he is the major political driver of immigration reform. President Bush came into office in 2001 declaring that immigration reform was going to be one of his signature, if not his major signature, issues. He was no less sure in the summer of 2007 when he returned from a European Security Summit meeting in early June and demanded that the just-failed CIR bill be revived.

From the beginning of his presidency, Bush enthusiastically supported former Mexican President Vicente Fox's demands that the borders between Mexico and the United States be opened wide to workers, without restrictions. He supported expanding the North American Free Trade Agreement (NAFTA) and the formation of a North American Union. By September 2007, President Bush personally had visited Latin America eight times and had sponsored a White House conference on Latin American trade. As for immigration reform, Bush strongly supports the legalization of illegal aliens presently in the country—though not in so many words.

"Resolving the status of illegal immigrants" became yet another buzzword for "amnesty." It was soon the way the president's men from Tony Snow to Secretary of Commerce Carlos Gutierrez and Homeland Security Secretary Michael Chertoff referred to amnesty. President Bush reacts with visible annoyance when the word "amnesty" is used.

But "resolving the status of" illegal immigrants by immediately legalizing them and giving them a chance to get green cards and citizenship (as Bush's CIR bill would have done) is the absolute dividing line issue between President Bush and the majority of his conservative base. Millions of his former supporters see any form of forgiveness and a chance at citizenship—no matter how many conditions are required and how long they have to wait—as amnesty.

## Republicans Split over Immigration

Since the 2006 election when the Republicans lost both the House and the Senate majorities to Democrats, many in the press, political pundits, and inside-the-Beltway think tanks have been blaming the conservative ethos itself for all the losses. "Conservatism itself caused the Republican debacle. It is existing conservatism itself. Conservatives get the world wrong," wrote Robert Borosage.[1] He is undoubtedly a bit over the top in his hubris. But his mantra is typical: Republican conservatism and conservatives themselves are dead.

But this ignores the success of Republican conservatives in killing the Senate CIR bills of 2006 and 2007. Bush's conservative Republican Party has been split over immigration from the beginning. While Bush favored opening the borders with Mexico and expanding NAFTA into a North American Union, many of the conservative (not necessarily evangelical) base wanted stricter enforcement of the borders, restrictions of visas, and the end to the flows of millions of illegal immigrants who were flooding into their communities from Georgia to Iowa. Grassroots organizations that advocated for enforcement of immigration laws first became so organized that they managed to defeat Senate immigration reform bills that included amnesty and had strong support from party leaders. In June 2007, these conservative Republican grassroots enforcement-only advocates were able to shut down the Senate communications system with over a million faxes and phone calls against the CIR.

But Borosage lumps all things Republican into one label: conservatives. Despite the various focuses of Republican conservatives, he fails to see them as different constituencies in the Republican Party. And without that, he cannot, like most Democratic pundits and analysts, understand the political significance of the split in the party over immigration. Nor can he see that the same thing exists in the Democratic Party.

There are three distinct Republican groups when it comes to the immigration issue. The first group consists of corporate libertarians who include some of the most powerful lobbying groups in the United States.[2] Many businesses that these lobbyists represent hire large numbers of immigrants, many of them illegal. They have a strong voice in the immigration debate and support Bush's plan to expand visas, to legalize all illegal aliens in the United States, and to oppose strict sanctions of employers who hire illegal immigrants. The libertarian presidential candidate Ron Paul has raised record amounts of money and is wildly popular among some young Republicans.

The second group is the neoconservatives. On immigration, neocons have been rather "in the shadows." Their major publication, *The Weekly*

*Standard,* has had few articles or cover stories about immigration outside those dealing with terrorists and one (mine)[3] on the foreign student visa loophole. Neocon pundits such as editor Fred Barnes and columnist Charles Krauthammer usually take a scornful attitude toward attempts to enforce immigration laws that will impose on American enterprise, however, and seem to bow to President Bush's immigration policy. Ramesh Ponnuru, of the neocon-leaning magazine *National Review,* warns Republicans about "making a fetish out of toughness on immigration," especially when it comes to issues dealing with the children of illegal immigrants (such as birthright citizenship and the DREAM Act, the latter discussed in chapter 9).

The third group consists of traditional conservatives—the true base of the Republican Party. On immigration they generally agree with Pat Buchanan and the position on immigration of his magazine the *American Conservative.* They are aghast, furious, and increasingly enraged at President Bush's stance on immigration.[4] Their views are widely represented in the broadcast media—especially local talk radio and cable television throughout the country and CNN's Lou Dobbs.[5] They have been activated effectively by numerous local, state, and national grassroots immigration reform groups (such as CAPPS in California and Numbers-USA in Virginia) that advocate especially against giving amnesty of any kind to illegal aliens in the country.

### Senator Ted Kennedy

Again we start at the top of the party leadership—with the venerated Senator Ted Kennedy. When it comes to the immigration issue, it is relevant to start with Kennedy, the crown head of the Democratic Party, because, like President Bush, he is the face of his party in immigration legislation—since the 1960s up to today.

The failure of the Senate CIR bill in June 2007 was a shock to Kennedy. How could this political warrior—who is so famously bipartisan, so famously open to all opinions, and so politically astute—be deaf to the majority of middle-class Americans' anxieties about the American Dream and their growing concern that illegal immigrants were being favored and given benefits over American citizens?

It seems that just as President Bush could be said to be our first "Latino president," Senator Kennedy is perhaps the most passionate immigrant (especially illegal immigrant) sympathizer on Capitol Hill.

One of his signature issues is civil rights, and this includes passage of his 1965 Immigration Reform Act. That act did away with the totally unacceptable bias toward preferred nationalities—the nationality quota for permanent visas that had been in place since the 1920s was eliminated. The measure not only threw out nationality preferences but also replaced the preference for immigrants with desired work skills with a preference for extended family members of new citizens.

In the 1986 legislation, which Kennedy also led, a "one-time" amnesty was given to all illegal immigrants who had been in the country before 1986, and the number of permanent visas was increased for extended family members of legal immigrants.

Kennedy's CIR bill of 2007 would have again given a "pathway to citizenship" for all illegal aliens in the country who met certain conditions—just as the 1986 bill did (only he denied adamantly that it was "amnesty" since the 1986 bill was supposed to be a never-again amnesty provision). It also expanded the number of so-called family unification visas. Thanks to his zeal for immigrant families, today three-quarters of green cards go to extended family members. Immigrants with needed skills are left with the choice of coming in on temporary work permits; of trying to adjust those to a permanent visa with great time, expense, and no guarantee of success; or of overstaying the temporary visas and becoming illegal workers. Kennedy believes there is need for more foreign workers—especially high-tech workers that Bill Gates claims are needed in the hundreds of thousands. But Kennedy also believes that illegal immigration is exacerbated because there are not enough visas for extended family members who want to come in to be "reunified" and who are forced to just do it illegally. Kennedy's passionate belief that immigration is about human rights, social justice, family unification, and "want" seems to put no limit on new visas to the United States.

On immigration, both President Bush and Senator Kennedy are libertarians. On immigration legislation, they obviously believe in the same thing—"open borders" and permissive immigration laws. But they believe in it for entirely different reasons. Kennedy is a liberal libertarian—he believes in open borders for humanitarian and social justice reasons.

### Democratic Party

When I asked former Democratic Congressional Campaign Committee Chairman Rahm Emanuel (D-Ill.) why he did not include immigration in his recent book on Democratic Party issue priorities, he said, "I didn't include it in the book because we don't want to talk about it; the Democrats are completely split over immigration."[6]

"Like the Republicans?" I asked him.

"Yes, like the Republicans," he answered.

In the summer of 2007, Emanuel was widely quoted as saying that he doesn't want Democrats to address the immigration issue until the second term of a Democratic presidency. The next month, the Democratic leader warned his party that "immigration is the third rail of politics."[7] "Democrats display nervousness over immigration, because the issue could split the party much as it has the GOP," said Brent Wilkes, executive director of the League of United Latin American Citizens (a prominent national Latino lobbyist organization).

I hear confirmation of Emanuel's comment about the Democratic split over immigration every week when I talk to Democrats at the National Press Club or at the Women's National Democratic Club in Washington. "I don't know what to think about immigration," they say. "It's very confusing."

Immigration is particularly perplexing to Democrats because it seems to place two of the core Democratic principles in contention: inclusion of minorities and the poor and the protection of American labor. Even more than the Republicans, the immigration issue splits the Democrats into such distinct ideological positions that they can scarcely talk about it among themselves. And most pundits seem to have missed the dilemma altogether, which doesn't help the Democrats to talk about it. Like the Republicans, the Democrats seem to be split into three different ideological groups that can be seen plainly in their different attitudes toward immigration legislation.

### Civil Libertarians

These are Democrats who, like most libertarians, tend to be strongly socially liberal and economically conservative. They believe in permissive laws and freedom to behave and act within broad borders of light restraint—both socially and economically.

Civil libertarians strongly believe in social justice for all. They seem to equate human rights, civil rights, individual rights, and social justice to be all one thing, and they are extremely sensitive to the abuses of those rights, especially by government.

The core immigration stances for civil libertarians include the following:

- The rejection of the term "illegal" immigrant; they do not accept that any immigrant can be "illegal" and that illegal residency in the country is breaking any law.
- The immediate legalization of illegal immigrants in the country and the granting of citizenship as soon as possible.
- Opposing any present process of enforcement including validating identity cards, employer sanctions, fences, denial of any benefits, and any use of local law enforcement resources—while not proposing how immigration laws are to be enforced.
- Expanding family unification visas.
- Changing temporary "guest" worker visas to ones that can be easily adjusted to permanent status.

The voices of the civil libertarian philosophy include the think tanks Center for American Progress and People for the American Way; political pundits Jon Stewart at Comedy Central and Keith Olbermann at MSNBC; the political newsmagazines *The Progressive*, *The Nation*, and *In These Times*; and the American Catholic Church and some more liberal branches of Protestant churches as well as many Jewish organizations. The most prominent civil libertarian is Markos Moulitsas Zuniga, "whose blog the Daily Kos has become the official headquarters for America's liberal resistance," according to Matt Bai in his book *The Argument*. "My next book is going to be 'The Libertarian Democrat,'" Markos told Bai.[8] Brink Lindsey of the CATO Institute writes about why more liberals are becoming libertarians in his book *The Age of Abundance*.[9] Some call them neoprogressives.

### Progressives (aka Liberals)

The core ideology of the Democratic Party has been regarded as liberal—now known as Progressive. Its base is made up of "women, professionals, and minorities," write commentators John B. Judis and

Ruy Teixeira.[10] But now two new groups have been added: younger voters (those born after 1977) and independents primarily in the North, Midwest, and far West. The term "progressive" is a relatively new one. It was adopted by adherents to replace the term "liberal" that was so effectively trashed by Republicans over the past couple of decades.[11]

Progressive Democrats tend to believe the following:

- Government should guarantee every citizen enough to eat and a place to sleep.
- The minimum wage should be raised by more than $2.00.
- The government should guarantee health insurance for all citizens.
- Labor unions are necessary to protect the working person.
- Gun control laws should be toughened.
- Corporate profits are too high—the rich really are just getting richer while the poor get poorer.
- Government needs to protect the middle class and rein in business excess.
- There should be a strong separation of church and state.
- Churchgoing people should work to help promote liberal social causes for the poor such as voting rights and citizenship education.

On immigration, progressives actually divide into two camps: the centrists and the populist progressives. Centrist progressives (who ran the Democratic National Committee under the Clinton administration) favor more expanded work visas and family unification and the legalization of illegal aliens who have resided in the U.S. for a verifiable number of years. But some also favor tough border and interior enforcement of immigration laws. Senator Charles Schumer (D-N.Y.) represents centrist progressive opinion (some call them "old liberals") on immigration. He wrote about immigration reform in his book *Positively American*.[12]

Populist progressives consistently support policies that would protect American workers and American identity. Many, while very liberal on social issues, especially the government's role in helping minorities and the poor, increasingly see the unhappiness of the public (especially in the midwestern and southern states) over what they perceive as Democrats ignoring the rule of law on immigration matters and seeming to favor illegal immigrants over legal immigrants and U.S. citizens. New think tanks have emerged in the past six years that reflect the progressive centrist point of view, including the New Americas Foundation.

## Blue Dog Democrats

In 1994, House Democrats organized a new, exclusive, limited (47 members maximum) caucus called the Blue Dogs.[13] Members are basically conservative and moderate Democrats.

A majority of the Blue Dogs either favor immigration restriction (20 of them) or are for more enforcement and more expansion of immigration permits (15). The enforcement-only (no legalization for illegals) immigration proposal SAVE, which freshman Representative Heath Schuler (D-N.C.)—a Blue Dog—cosponsored on November 10, 2007, with Representative Brian Bilbray (R-Calif.), chair of the Congressional Immigration Reform Caucus, quickly gained the support of over 100 members of Congress—many of them Democrats. Libertarian Democratic immigration groups expressed concern. "We will have to keep our eye on the Schuler bill," said the director of the Immigration Policy Center of the American Immigration Law Forum. "Democrats might see this as a way to get the immigration wedge issue off the table, to show that 'they are really doing something.'"[14]

## POLITICAL WRAP-UP

These ideological "splits" within the political parties over immigration reflect what is going on in the grassroots civic and public affairs culture of the United States. Americans are becoming increasingly diverse with mixed identities. They are moving well beyond the traditional narrow classifications of political party, labor group, religious affiliation, and even ethnic and religious heritage identities. Increasingly Americans are realigning their political support behind positions on specific issues, not just a political party label. Increasingly American citizens vote for members of Congress and pressure Congress on the basis of their positions on certain issues. Unfortunately for the press and those who want every political fight to be a simple horse race between two opposing parties, today's Americans often have strong beliefs on certain issues that cross party lines. In the past five years we have seen major political "blocs" split as their constituencies divide over ideology: in labor unions, major American churches, universities, and even traditional ethnic heritage groups. None of these once monolithic associations really can offer politicians lockstep voting blocs any longer, much as their leaders market their ability to do so. Strange bedfellows on issues will become increasingly common.

                    *Chapter 8*

Many issues have become vertical ones, cutting across the traditional horizontal line that has liberal Democrats on the far left end and conservative Republicans on the far right end. I see the immigration issue as such a vertical issue, splitting the parties. To understand the various positions of the immigration issue, I think it is helpful to visualize pulling the two ends of the traditional horizontal spectrum down to form a horseshoe. It will encase a vertical bar that has corporate, globalist libertarians at the bottom open end of the horseshoe and populist, protectionist economic nationalists at the top. The various political ideologies described in this chapter can be placed along this vertical spectrum. This explains the various bipartisan alignments that are happening in immigration politics (see figure 8.1).

### THE POLITICS OF IMMIGRATION

A Typical Horizontal Political Issue

Immigration is a VERTICAL Political Issue

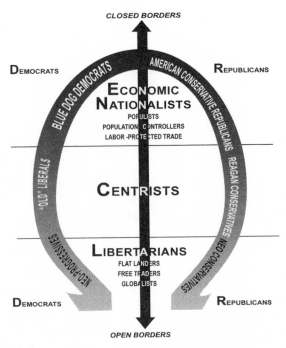

**Figure 8.1.**

The immigration horseshoe shows why the so-called liberal Democratic leaders have partnered with their political nemesis, the so-called conservative Bush Republicans and the libertarian CATO Institute, to stand behind a so-called comprehensive open-doors immigration position (greatly expanding the numbers of legal immigrants and legalizing all illegal aliens in the country). On immigration, both groups are globalist libertarians and believe in "a very big gate" (as the "flat-world" guru Tom Friedman of the *New York Times* likes to put it).[15] The horseshoe also shows why Blue Dog and other Democrats concerned about unprotected labor trade agreements and population growth line up with traditional American conservatives worried about the economy and wage inequality. On immigration, these groups are economic nationalists and are concerned about protecting jobs and the quality of life of the American middle class. They worry that our national diversity will be overwhelmed by massive uncontrolled enclaves of low-wage immigrants coming from a dominant single nation or foreign culture.

Like many major issues in America today, immigration brings together what the traditional punditry may see as strange bedfellows around beliefs that run deeper than political affiliation.

# III

## BREAKING NEWS

# 9

# The Future: What's Next?

The tabling of the comprehensive immigration reform effort in the summer of 2007 had three positive consequences. First, we now have time to examine and cool down the highly emotional name-calling, spinning, and rhetorical excesses. Public opinion leaders now have time to decontaminate the fearful intimidating labels like "anti-immigrant," "bigot," "racist," "xenophobic," "nativist," and "traitor" that had been thrown at opponents of one side or the other. "Increasingly people aren't afraid of these labels anymore; they've been said so often," one activist from the Choose Black America organization told me.[1] "I am no longer afraid to be called a 'Black Racist' because I oppose illegal immigration." There is also now time to parse out the highly complex issues. And there is time to think out the consequences of various proposed actions and solutions—from the legalization of all illegal aliens to the deportation of all of them and every option in between.

Second, immigration issues now have the full attention of a good proportion of the American public. Finally, it is increasingly clear that most Americans now have the will to do something about our unmanaged, unenforced immigration system. Political and social motivation grows daily. It is natural that since the federal government is now on hold to do anything new to change the nation's immigration laws, local legislative and governing bodies in almost every state, region, county, city, and community are stepping in to fill the breach.

By the end of 2007, thousands of legislative proposals and regulations were piling onto the desks of governors, county boards of supervisors, and mayors to be signed, enacted, and enforced without delay. Most proposed limiting and some would protect illegal immigrants who seek to obtain work, rent housing, or access public benefits other than those granted by federal law (mainly public schooling grades K–12, child vaccinations, and emergency room care for medical emergencies). In most areas, the new bills are backed by vociferous supporters and opposed by equally vocal opponents.

## THE LOCAL GRASSROOTS LEVEL

### Ethnic Immigrant Advocacy Groups

In my opinion, well into the future, most of the actions and opinions of the ethnic immigrant advocacy groups will continue to garner positive press coverage from the major newspapers of America, especially the *New York Times, Washington Post, Los Angeles Times, Boston Globe*, and the like. They are helped immeasurably by the immensely popular and influential news comedians Jon Stewart and Bill Maher, who unfortunately probably will continue to view all illegal immigrants as victims and all those who want immigration control as "anti-immigrant."

After the defeat of the Comprehensive Immigration Reform (CIR) bill in June 2007, the various ethnic immigrant advocacy groups planned various defensive and offensive actions to pass pieces of the CIR in must-pass legislation and to actively register immigrants to vote in a campaign called *"Ya es hora ciudadania"*—the U.S. citizenship campaign.

But I doubt that Cecilia Munoz, director of the National Council of La Raza (NCLR), and her colleagues in other ethnic immigrant advocacy groups actually will achieve much if any substantive success with either their defensive or their offensive actions. The immigration issue has moved far beyond the racial and civil rights platitudes of ethnic immigrant advocacy groups, who seem mired in 1970s rhetoric. No one is afraid of their labeling anymore. Most of the public has tired of ethnic immigrant advocacy groups equating illegal immigrants from the relatively well-off though corrupt countries of Latin America with black slaves of the colonial and antebellum eras.

Even the multilanguage issue is backfiring. Increasingly, Americans of all socioethnic levels say they "hate" having to choose between English and Spanish on public utilities and bank service phone calls and ATMs. The ethnic advocacy groups mistakenly shrug it off as "fear of differences" and "xenophobic racism." That kind of rhetoric only insults and makes people mad. It shows how out of touch with the American mainstream the narrowly focused ethnic immigrant advocacy groups are and with the dynamics of issue coalition building.

I have seen a huge change over the past five years in the attitude of grassroots Americans about the immigration issue. It is no longer politically incorrect to talk about and even to study illegal immigration. The immigrant advocacy groups would do well to show that they too believe in immigration law and control of illegal immigrant waves as well as in increasing the number of legal immigrants into the country.

In the next five years, it can be hoped that the ethnic immigrant advocacy grassroots groups will push forward new immigration laws that will do the following:

1. Stop illegal immigration (not encourage or enable its future growth)
2. Reflect America's commitment to diversity and growth based on immigrant ingenuity and the true needs of certain industries for foreign labor (not immigrant growth from single nation-states based mainly on extended family ties)
3. Support and enable the passage of strong legislation with clear enforcement mechanisms to ensure that there is an established decent minimum wage, work standards, benefits, and equal treatment for all legal workers in the United States

Perhaps advocacy groups and their powerful array of allies will do all this in the foreseeable future. But in late 2007, there are no signs of their willingness to expand their focus beyond the legalization and naturalization of millions of illegal immigrants currently in the United States.

## Immigrant Control and Enforcement Advocacy Groups

On the other hand, given their successes and their growing power in 2007, it would seem that the immigration enforcement advocacy groups such as NumbersUSA would have an optimistic attitude about a clear and easy path to legislative power in the future. "Our side has never been in such good shape," remarked George Fishman, the minority counsel for the House Judiciary Subcommittee on Immigration at a meeting of a local immigration reform group.[2] But the immigration enforcement advocates don't see it that way. They probably will continue to see the future in surprisingly gloomy and pessimistic light. Most seriously believe that the country probably will be taken over by illegal immigrants in the future. Some are convinced that the United States will become like a Third World Latino country within a few decades.

It is unclear whether these immigration enforcement advocates will learn, over the next few years, what they need to do in order to be ultimately successful. I'm not sure that they can move beyond state Republican politics. At this point, they are making some efforts to move beyond their easy-to-get supporters of military veterans groups and social conservatives. They are beginning to frame their positions in ways that remind listeners and viewers and Internet participants that the issues they are talking about and the solutions they are advocating are nonpartisan. Increasingly their meetings and rallies include Latino and African American supporters (although most are moderate Republicans). But in the end, there is no guarantee that they will reach out to mainstream centrist middle-income and professional Democrats. They are at heart staunch Republican partisans.

## Local Initiatives

Various local and state governments are passing regulations and creative initiatives that target illegal immigrants. Some may work only in a local region. Others may be found to be unconstitutional. Most are aimed at stopping the flow of illegal immigrants into the community, and some would protect illegal immigrants and the employers who hire them from federal immigration law—which also probably will be tested in court. The following are some of the local initiatives that have been passed to date that I believe will be successful or become a national model:

- Increased enforcement of housing density regulations in single-family-home neighborhoods

- Increased enforcement of community loitering and solicitation regulations
- Expanded use in states and communities of the 287g clause, which would allow the training and deployment of local law enforcement officers to help enforce immigration laws in the community
- Authority of prison officials to check immigration status of anyone imprisoned and consider them eligible for deportation
- Stricter sanctions against employers who employ more than 10 illegal aliens, including the denial of business licenses for those who continue to do so
- Denial of public office for any foreign national holding public office in another country from which they carry a passport as a citizen
- Official English only—that is, the use of only English for official public documents, including ballots

On the other hand, the following are some local initiatives that I believe will not be successful:

- Punitive sanctions on anyone who knowingly rents property, even a room in a private home, to an illegal alien
- Limiting public library and other open services to legal visa holders and citizens only
- Issuing no-questions-asked community identity cards to illegal aliens in a particular community for use (and even discounts) in local enterprises
- Legislating that businesses must defy homeland security enforcement activities
- Offering citywide sanctuary to any illegal immigrant, including those with felony deportation notices
- Locally funding detention centers for illegal aliens and their families that encourage voluntary deportation
- Denying in-state tuition to illegal immigrants who graduated from state high schools

These and other creative, good and bad initiatives will continue to be proposed and to make news in the next five years. Some states will propose these more than others. Virginia especially is a state where, following the midterm election in 2006, immigration became a "red hot issue," said State Senator James K. "Jay" O'Brien Jr. (R-Fairfax).[3] "Immigration is an issue everywhere in Virginia. Any candidate that speaks with confidence about [requiring immigrants to have a] legal presence will generate a terrific response." While Virginia Republican leaders see the issue as a real opportunity to mobilize their base constituency, Virginia Democrats see it as a distraction from other issues. "It's a bumper sticker issue," said Flavia Jimenez, an immigrant policy analyst for the Nation Council of La Raza, which bills itself as the largest national Hispanic civil rights and advocacy group in the United States. "Virginia's U.S. Senate race next year will no doubt include an airing of the immigration issue," warn national party leaders.[4]

In this climate of immigration awareness, it can be expected that these local and state initiatives that "do something" about immigration will continue. They will only lose momentum once federal immigration laws—old and new—are seriously implemented and, more important, enforced. Local and state initiatives will stop only when citizens regain trust in the federal government agencies to support immigration enforcement and services with the resources of money, personnel, and equipment needed to do the job.

## NATIONAL POLITICS

At the congressional level, the main focus of activities will be attempts to attach pieces of the CIR bill into "must-pass" legislation or smaller-scale stand-alone legislation.

One notable example of this tactic is the effort to revise the DREAM Act. The DREAM Act started out as a baby of Senator Orrin Hatch (R-Utah) to allow states to give in-state tuition at publicly funded colleges to illegal aliens under certain strict conditions. Those included residency of over five years in the United States, graduation from an accredited high school, and a clean police record. The students would also be eligible for state education scholarships if the state so chose, and they would be eligible for a green card once they had graduated from college. It was enthusiastically supported especially by Latino groups as the way that the children of illegal aliens who had no choice in coming to the United States illegally with their parents "could follow their dreams" to get a college education. But for years the bill did not get out of committee as a stand-alone.

Opponents pointed out that the youths who would benefit from the DREAM Act were no longer children but now young adults who know full well they are in the country illegally, had already gotten a free public school education, and were now to get a benefit not given to out-of-state American citizens or to the children of legal temporary visa holders. Moreover, they decried the apparent unfairness of favoring illegal alien students over low-income and middle-class American students who also are competing to get scholarships and to get a place in an affordable public college themselves.

After the CIR bill was defeated in June 2007, Senate Majority Whip Dick Durbin (D-Ill.) and Senator Ted Kennedy (D-Mass.) tried again to get the DREAM Act passed—but in a truncated form. In July they eliminated the in-state tuition part of the bill—which increasingly states were saying no to in local elections. They added the benefit of a green card to high school graduate illegal immigrants who completed two years of military service. They then tried to attach the rewritten DREAM Act to the Defense Authorization Act, the Student Loan Reduction Act, the intelligence funding bill, and the Higher Education Authorization Act. None succeeded. On October 24, the faithful Senator Durbin tried one more time. He offered up the DREAM Act as "stand-alone legislation" with support from the Majority Leader Senator Harry Reid (D-Nev.). On November 16, the bill failed a cloture vote by eight votes.

The defeat of the DREAM Act has seemed to discourage senators from supporting other pieces of the CIR bill, such as the AgJOBS bill—which not only expanded the number of low-skilled worker temporary visas but also gave a pathway to citizenship. A few days before the farm bill was to come up for debate on the Senate floor, Committee Chairman Tom Harkins (D-Iowa) was asked if he was expecting Senator Diane Feinstein (D-Calif.) to add an AgJOBS amendment to the bill. He said, very firmly, "She told me she would propose it, and I told her I would not support it. Even though I supported it in the immigration bill, I don't want to drag down the farm bill with a filibuster or anything like that. It is an immigration matter. It is part of comprehensive immigration reform, and we won't get to that until 2009 or after."

By the time of the Iowa caucuses, while most experts agreed that immigration had become a major issue in the 2008 election debates, the likelihood of passing any kind of immigration reform legislation that included amnesty was nil. "It is unlikely that any piece of immigration legislation with anything other than strong border and employer enforcement provisions will be passed in 2008 and maybe not even in 2009," said Frank Sharry, executive director of the National Immigration Forum. "We must keep in mind that there has been a real shift in the Senate—a decided movement to the right in terms of immigration," said Angela Kelley of the American Immigration Law Foundation. "And it's even shifting more in the House. It had been a progressive place, but they are becoming more moderate. Sadly even prominent Republican Senators who supported comprehensive immigration reform in the past have now grouped together to support enforcement-only legislation. Republican Senators such as Arlen Specter (PA), John McCain (AZ), and Lindsey Graham (SC) don't think 'comprehensive' reform (i.e. anything with legalization proposals in it) will go anywhere next year, Unfortunately some once sympathetic Democratic Senators agree such as Mary Landrieu (LA) and Mark Pryor (AR)," Kelley said.[5]

## DEMOCRATS AND THE 2008 ELECTION

The Democrats are vulnerable on the immigration issue, especially with moderate mountain and Midwest voters that are absolutely crucial for a Democratic victory in 2008. But they are also vulnerable on the issue with American blacks, many of whom feel they have lost jobs to illegal immigrants, especially in the construction and hospitality fields. Democrats will particularly confront the illegal immigrant controversy in the issue they consider their top priority: universal health care. The big question is whether foreign nationals living in the country illegally will be covered. Senator Hillary Clinton (D-N.Y.), when asked by George Stephanopoulos on the ABC television program *This Week with George Stephanopoulos* on September 23, 2007, was clear about it:

Stephanopoulos: "Will your universal health plan cover illegal immigrants?"

Clinton: "No, it will not cover illegal immigrants. My health plan of 1992 did not cover them, and neither will this one."

This is why I expect Senator Clinton (the front-runner in late 2007) to become increasingly open about the need to stop illegal immigration and to enforce immigration laws not only at the borders but inside the United States (as could be seen by her eventual strong stance against giving New York state driver's licenses to foreign nationals living in the country illegally, as proposed by Governor Eliot Spitzer (D) in the fall of 2007). I expect her to take up the cause of the American worker. I expect her to demand that employers verify the legality of their workers and to prove that their first priority is to hire American workers at American wages and working conditions first. And where the senator goes, I expect most of the others may follow. The health plan of Presidential candidate Barack Obama, the leading Democratic candidate in the primaries in early 2008, also did not include illegal immigrants. Obama also is on record for supporting driver's licenses for illegal immigrants and the DREAM Act.

Democrats will have to prove to an increasingly skeptical public in 2008 that they are not favoring illegal immigrants over Americans in almost every sphere of life. There are many ways they can do this—natural ways for Democrats.

Democrats can work closely with their liberal religious constituents who believe that helping the poor and the needy can begin with poor American citizens first. Democrats can also prove to a fearful public that they can be tough on difficult issues. Many Democratic legislators, including Senator Clinton, are showing they can be tough when it comes to protecting Americans from threats outside the borders. Democrats can also show they can be, have been, and will be tough with those who need to get off entitlements and take responsibility, as well as help, to get out of difficult life situations. It worked for welfare reform. It can work with illegal immigration.

## REPUBLICANS AND THE 2008 ELECTION

For the first time in a long time, the Republicans will not be going to their presidential nominating convention with a preordained candidate. There is no doubt that the Republican Party is discouraged about its prospects in 2008. Most Republicans (at least privately) blame President George W. Bush. Many were outraged (at least privately) with Bush's stand on immigration. It was unfathomable to many Republicans that their president hooked up with that most liberal Democrat, Senator Ted Kennedy, to push his open border immigration agenda. They were furious at the weakness of Senate Minority Leader Mitch McConnell (Ky.), who was conspicuously absent from the Senate floor during most of the vote's pre-days. This is translated into deep gloom by Republicans about their chances to take back Congress and even the presidency in 2008. "It is difficult to exaggerate the pessimism about the immediate political future voiced by Republicans in Congress when not on the record," wrote columnist Robert Novak.[6]

This gloom is probably the unadmitted reason why, by early December 2007, 19 Republicans had announced their decision not to run again, including former Speaker Dennis J. Hastert (Ill.), former Senate Majority Leader Trent Lott (Miss.), ranking member of the House Ways and Means Committee Jim McCrery (La.), and Congressional Immigration Reform Caucus founder Tom Tancredo (Colo.), who was widely responsible for immigration enforcement becoming the focus of immigration legislation. They all reflect the well-known adage that it's no fun being in the minority when it is a constant fight to even get minority bills on committee agendas and witnesses on the list of hearing testifiers. "Their hasty retreat . . . is providing multiple opportunities for Democrats to expand their majorities in next year's elections," wrote reporter Jill Zuckman.[7]

Whether the tough stance on immigration control and enforcement by many in the Republican Party who opposed their president's comprehensive (legalization) immigration plan would be more of a factor in Republican 2008 election losses than the failures of the Iraq War was controversial. Three weeks before the Iowa caucuses, all the Republican presidential candidates were talking tough on immigration control. "Immigration will be 'front and center' in the congressional, presidential, and even in local races in 2008," agreed Frank Sharry and Angela Kelley.

"Get ready," warned Kelley, "because tough immigration enforcement is coming out of the corner," with both parties embracing the anti-immigrant side of the issue. She warned that more plans to force illegal immigrants to leave (such as Republican presidential candidate and former Arkansas governor Mike Huckabee's immigration plan that would give illegal immigrants 120 days to leave voluntarily and apply for legal entry or else be deported) will be common. "Only Rudy Giuliani stuck up for earned in-country legalization at the Univision-sponsored Spanish-language candidate's debate in December [2007]," said

Kelley. We'll see if there will be a backlash." "The politics of all this will play out in 2008," Sharry concluded. "But get ready! There will be nasty and vitriolic campaign ads coming out about various candidates' stands on immigration up until the election."

## FOLLOWING THE ELECTION: 2009 AND BEYOND

We saw already how Democrats who were emboldened by the 2006 election wins suddenly became tough on trade deals, demanding that increased protections for decent worker wages and standards abroad and at home be added to the trade agreements as well as sanctions against environmental degradation. But what will happen to immigration reform if the Democrats win not only the majority of both houses of Congress but the presidency as well? Can the millions of illegal aliens in the country expect immediate legalization and a pathway to citizenship? It is not likely.

We have already seen how Democratic House leaders Speaker Nancy Pelosi (Calif.) and Rahm Emanual (Ill.) have warned Democrats that immigration is a "third-rail" issue. Comprehensive immigration reform has been taken off the table publicly by these leaders until 2009 at the earliest, despite the protests of Hispanic Congressional Caucus leader Luis Gutierrez and immigrant advocacy lobbyists like the National Council of La Raza. "After the election, even if the Democrats win the Presidency and both houses of Congress, immigration experts agree that the atmosphere will be no better to pass comprehensive immigration reform for at least one or two years, if not a full term. Democrats are terrified by this issue," said Mark Krikorian of the Center for Immigration Studies. "Because of the moderate Democrats in Congress now" (many of whom are Blue Dogs from mountain states and enabled Democrats to win "without the South" in 2006 and possibly again in 2008), "the Democrats will have to move to the right on immigration for at least the next two years."[8]

"This is especially true if Hillary wins the Presidency," said Douglas Massey, codirector of the Mexican Migration Project at Princeton University. "Many of the present problems of immigration (lack of enforcement at the border and of employers who actively hire illegal immigrants with impunity) were caused by the Clinton administration. As president, Hillary Clinton will have to be careful (show she is strong on immigration enforcement)."[9]

This is not to say that nothing will happen to the immigration situation in the next few years—especially regarding the millions of illegal immigrants currently living in the country. It is clear that at least through 2008, the borders will be tightened up with the thousands of new border agents and the completion of at least a few of the hundreds of miles of border fence whose funding has been appropriated. Homeland Security Secretary Michael Chertoff also will increase enforcement of sanctions against foreign nationals using false or stolen documents to work illegally in American companies and against the employers who knowingly have hired them. Sooner rather than later, it is expected that a digital verifiable work permit tracking system will be perfected and operationalized. In addition, many states and local governments will continue to test in court various local initiatives to discourage illegal immigrants from settling in their communities; some will pass and be enforced, and some won't (for those requiring federal interaction, such as Arizona's strict new business sanction laws, however, it is possible that a Democratic administration will drag its feet over such compliance).

The end result of all these endeavors over the next few years, however, could well be that the flow of new illegal immigrants will decrease dramatically (especially if the U.S. economy goes into a recession). It also is likely that over the next few years, the number of foreign nationals currently living in the United States illegally will find it harder to keep their jobs in the United States. Many—especially the millions who came in legally and overstayed their visas—will find they have better and friendlier employment and benefit options back home (in countries such as Brazil, Ireland, Russia, India, Venezuela, and Chile, among many others whose economies are growing). The outflow has already begun. It is possible that eventually millions of illegal aliens could decide to self-deport over the next few years, leaving the United States with a clean record and contacts for possible legal immigration in the future. It is possible that by the time Congress gets around to a comprehensive immigration reform, the numbers of illegal aliens in the country will have dropped to more manageable numbers.

Under a more international-affairs-friendly Democratic regime starting in 2009, it is probable that the number of refugees accepted into the United States and given green cards from Iraq and parts of Africa will increase dramatically. And once the American public sees that they can trust government agencies to enforce border security and employer sanctions, they will be more willing to support legislative initiatives to increase visas in certain categories where there is true need. In the future, it is hoped that the "racist" and "anti-immigrant" name-calling that is currently applied to any American concerned about immigration enforcement will eventually be given up as the tired political labeling that it is. If so, Americans of all political persuasions will be able to come together to develop new immigration laws and regulations that may give out more permanent immigrant visas to immigrants with a true diversity of nationalities, work skills, and talents.

This will enrich the lives for all in the United States—immigrants and citizens alike.

# 10

## Conclusion: "Es Su País"

There is almost universal agreement about several aspects of our immigration management system in the United States today:

1. It is a problem—for everyone.
2. It is not working in a fair, just, or legal way for immigrants and citizens alike.
3. Public anger about massive uncontrolled illegal immigration has finally caught the attention of the political and media leaders.
4. Immigration will be a major issue in the 2008 presidential election.

The good news about all the attention now paid to immigration is that most decision makers are now aware of the issues that impact both the immigrants who are wanted and needed in the United States and—often negatively—the communities, regions, states, and nation as a whole that host immigrants.

The best news is that as a result of all this attention, a wide range of serious policy recommendations are now circulating. These include the following:

- Better border enforcement—such as funding more and better-trained manpower, physical obstacles such as border walls, and technology that would act as virtual fences and unmanned border patrol surveillance resources

- Help for employers to identify, recruit, and employ more verifiably needed foreign nationals to work legally, either temporarily or permanently
- More flexible visas that would allow workers from border countries to easily cross back and forth over the border when employed in certified seasonal work sites
- Valid ways of ascertaining the minimum and maximum numbers of immigrants needed as foreign workers and permanent residents that should be allowed into the U.S. each year
- Dealing with the millions of illegal immigrants currently in the country through a variety of processes including the immediate deportation of illegal felons, encouraging voluntary deportation (perhaps with incentives such as exit business development grants), statutes of limitation for the deportation of immigrants who had been in the country more than a set period of time, legalization for those with American-born children over a certain age, and an "official" process of allowing "natural" attrition of illegal immigrants through the "drying up" of the job magnet by employer enforcement actions
- Organizing immigration management and oversight within the national and state governments
- Coordination with international migration and labor organization projects dealing with global migration forces and challenges
- New foreign aid policies, from the Peace Corps to small, direct business incentive grants, that would directly impact the economic development of large emigrant source countries to help them keep their own labor at home and to develop their own economies

Many serious and prominent organizations, think tanks, academic centers, and governmental advisers are developing immigration reform plans that can be discussed in the public sphere. It is an exciting time for those concerned about immigration reform. The choices are many. The process will be dynamic. The decisions will be significant. They will tell us much about how we view the role of government, nationhood, citizenship, and the American identity.

How we decide as a country, through our democratic political system, exactly the way we are going to manage immigration to the United States will, in the end, tell much about how we as a country (or at least those citizens who influence the public policy process) view the role of government. It will also show how we view nationhood, citizenship, and the American identity.

## ROLE OF GOVERNMENT

A majority of Americans think government should have a significant role (and a bigger role than at present) in providing for the safety and security of the population, not only from outside terrorist and military threats but also from forces that threaten American economic and educational opportunities and the middle-class quality of life. Americans who believe that government has a strong role in protecting them would expect government officials not only to make rules and regulations that will authorize them to protect the citizenry but also to enforce them vigorously.

On immigration matters, Americans are disappointed that the federal government has failed to enforce immigration laws. These include most Americans who are concerned about flattening wages, job outsourcing, and whether the American Dream of going to college, owning a home, and living in a secure and clean environment will be available to their children in the future. They are deeply disturbed by the appearance of wealthy elites who seem to prefer illegal immigrants over Americans by giving them jobs to build their mansions and maintain their landscaping and households, and even wanting to give discounted tuition in public colleges to the adult children of illegal aliens when working middle-class American children have to pay more.

## NATIONHOOD AND CITIZENSHIP

With the concept of globalization so dominant in the discussion of immigration management, the idea of the nation-state seems to be under question. There are different views.

Do we see America as an open, inclusive, multicultural nation with the longest borders in the world contiguous to another single country (Canada) that should not be defined, identifiable, or wholly blocked? Do we believe those borders should remain open to anyone in the world who only wants to come into the country to get a job at any price the employee will accept? Do we cringe at the idea of an American core culture or identity? Do we find it impossible or uncomfortable to define what are American national characteristics, what is an American identity, and what makes Americans culturally different from people of other nationalities? Do we see English as a language that only the Founding Fathers spoke and that has nothing to do with our American culture today? Do we believe that one can be an integrated American (citizen) without knowing any English? Do we see the nation-state as an old and dying institution, trumped by more lucrative global or regional or even continental entities? Do we advocate for global citizenship?

Or do we believe that we Americans live in a sovereign nation-state with defined borders, a core culture, and a readily identifiable identity, including American English?

Closely connected to the idea is also the concept of citizenship. Historically, Americans have always had a slightly different view of citizenship than in most countries of the world—or at least we did. In the past, up until the 1990s, many assumed that it was the dream of every immigrant who was lucky enough to get into the United States to become an American citizen. Some considered it an insult if the immigrant did not become a citizen.

So it used to be a great surprise even to many European immigrants to the United States that Americans not only were eager for but also expected them to become American citizens. For us Americans, it was all part of getting the American Dream. At least it was. But over the past decade or so, it seems this expectation has changed. Now it seems that for many young Americans—especially highly educated, well-traveled, professional Americans with big jobs in big cities—getting the American Dream means getting a job in America, working hard, and making money.

New "global" entitledments include the right to dual or more passports and citizenships, the right to vote in multiple countries' elections, the right to serve in public elected office while a citizen of another country (perhaps the most famous example being California Governor Arnold Schwarzenegger [R], who is still a citizen of Austria), and the right to language services and U.S. government documents in other languages. All these global rights have been pointed to as having contributed to diminishing the importance of assimilation into the American English-speaking culture. Ethnic immigrant advocacy activists argue that these new multicultural rights "help the immigrant to feel at home in the United States" and hence aid their eventual integration. Even multilingual ballots (really monolingual in another language, as most "bilingual" things are) are said by proponents to help immigrants be better voters, while opponents point out that to be a citizen and gain the privilege to vote, the immigrant is supposed to know English. While I certainly believe in the enriching life experience of speaking numerous languages fluently, I firmly believe that not learning the language of the country to which an immigrant has committed him- or herself absolutely discourages successful assimilation, if not making it impossible.

## AMERICAN IDENTITY

But my concern for American identity goes deeper than the assimilation of immigrants into it. Sometimes I wonder how assimilated (committed, perhaps, is a better word) many Americans themselves are into our core values and identity. It seems that today it is politically incorrect to talk about having an American identity—especially among Democrats. But national identity and the obligations of citizenship and loyalty are legitimate, not bigoted, questions to discuss. And they are intricately involved in the immigration debate.

### Responsible Capitalism and Consumerism

Up until recently, the United States has been the ideal, the unique model of a large democratic and capitalistic country that has successfully attracted and integrated throughout its history waves of immigrants from every cultural, religious, ethnic, and racial background in the world into a thriving and prospering American middle class. We have encouraged the creative and open acquisition of wealth by all, based on hard work and merit, no matter what a person's background. We have shown up until now that a national identity can be comprised of a very pluralistic *we*.

But it seems to me that this ideal is now being threatened by overzealous profit making and the encouragement of almost blind consumerism.

The lust for more of everything, but especially of wealth, is threatening the American democratic culture and immigration model as never before in history. Immigration has suddenly become all about making the most profits off the backs of the cheapest foreign labor possible, dismissing the American worker summarily (as has happened in the New Orleans reconstruction effort). Companies (from high tech to agriculture) demand that they be allowed to hire waves of the cheapest foreign labor possible (preferably on temporary work visas so that the workforce cannot set down roots), or they will take their companies offshore and hire even cheaper labor abroad. No matter which way, it's the more expensive American labor that loses out.

Being a responsible consumer not only means taking responsibility to pay a fair price for probably fewer but better-quality items produced by workers who have fair wages and working conditions. It also means that every American needs to be responsible about what labor we purchase. To maintain our American middle-class labor standards, every employer, including the home owner, must be sure that every worker they hire has the legal right to work in the country.

## Toning Down the Rhetoric

The goal of this book has been to confront the emotional hype and hysteria of the immigration debate with facts about the consequences of the life-changing decision and, it is hoped, enriching experience that is immigration. All immigrants need to be treated with the highest respect for the courage they have shown to undertake one of the most consequential acts a person can make—to leave their homeland and live and work in and commit their energies and often their offspring to another country, culture, language, and way of doing things.

It also is the goal of this book to enable all involved with immigration to understand and appreciate the tremendous responsibilities that every nation-state has in deciding who can come into their country to stay, to work, and eventually, if they choose to, to commit themselves as citizens. The nation-state has to decide how it will responsibly and fairly manage immigration and especially how it will enforce its immigration laws. These decisions are legitimate and differ from culture to culture. All immigrants know—or should know—that there are such laws in every nation-state or collection of nation-states in the world and that they need to respect and obey the laws, or they cannot stay.

The main point of this book is that to rationally discuss immigration law, numbers, qualifications, diversity, and enforcement is not being bigoted, racist, xenophobic, nativist, or against any one nationality group, and especially it is not being anti-immigrant. Such labeling of legitimate discussion only silences Americans who need to be able to participate in one of the most basic decisions of their nation. Similarly, exaggerating one side's position to extremes (i.e., evoking images of Nazi boxcars when referring to deportation) does not help answer tough questions that need to be asked (e.g., what deportation options are available, such as self- or voluntary deportation).

Deciding exactly what to do about immigration is up to every American citizen. It is up to you. What you think should be done might be different than what I think. But I hope this book has cleared up some of the confusion caused by the emotional rhetoric and strange political bedfellows that have been present in the immigration debate up to now. I hope this book will help you make your immigration decisions based on fact, not just emotion.

## The Tough Loving Parent

Political framers have suggested that using the family/parenting analogy gives everyone an image they can relate to. So perhaps it will be helpful to close this immigration debate on this thought.

For the past two decades, we Americans have acted as very permissive parents toward immigrants to our country and toward our immigration law. We all are proud to say we have immigration laws controlling temporary visas, permanent visas, work visas, and illegal entry—but we have done almost nothing (Democrats and Republicans) to enforce them. As permissive parents regarding immigration management, we have had our cake and eaten it as well.

And now we have created a monster child. Our immigration process is overwhelmed, underfunded, unsupported, and totally unfair to American workers, citizens, and immigrants—legal and illegal and especially to wannabe immigrants waiting in their homelands to follow the laws. So now our monstrous immigration mess has to be controlled.

It is probably too late to become the strict parent. Our only option now is to be the loving but tough parent. That means Americans cannot complain about cheap foreign labor "outsourced" by our major companies both inside and outside the country if we ourselves continue to hire cheap labor in our homes and gardens. Every American has to take responsibility to uphold our American standards by adhering to our immigration and labor laws (that means learning what a valid work visa looks like—you can easily look it up online—and taking the right and responsibility of an employer to ask for legal documents or to insist that your contractor hire only legal workers, or they won't be paid).

Being a citizen of our American nation of immigrants not only means being responsible to the immigrants who come to our shores, to make sure that they are treated fairly and justly. It also means that we have the responsibility to protect and maintain our American culture and democracy by adhering to the rule of law. That includes immigration laws. If we don't like the laws, then change them; but in America, we can't just ignore them and expect our society to remain a civilized one. That is the essence of the American Dream.

As one Mexican migrant farmworker told me years ago in the strawberry fields of Guadalupe, California, when I told him he would have to learn English in order to become a citizen, he nodded, smiled, and said, "*Bueno si, por supuesto. Es su país.*"—Yes, of course; it's your (or their) country.

# Notes

## CHAPTER 1

1. Rahm Emanuel and Bruce Reed, *The Plan: Big Ideas for America* (New York: PublicAffairs, 2006).

2. Thomas E. Mann and Norman J. Ornstein, *Broken Branch: How Congress Is Failing America and How to Get It Back on Track* (New York: Oxford University Press, 2006).

3. Paul Krugman, "North of the Border," *New York Times*, March 27, 2006.

4. "Is anyone for illegal immigration?" asked Arizona Governor Janet Napolitano (D) at an immigration form at the National Press Club sponsored by the Manhattan Institute on June 27, 2007.

5. Alvin Toffler, *The Third Wave* (New York: Morrow, 1980).

6. Jason DeParle, "Should We Globalize Labor Too?," *New York Times Magazine*, June 10, 2007.

7. Cullen Murphy, *Are We Rome? The Fall of an Empire and the Fate of America* (Boston: Houghton Mifflin, 2007).

## CHAPTER 2

1. There also incredibly continue to be some slave immigrants in the United States, usually women who thought they were coming in for legitimate jobs and end up being sexual and domestic servant slaves, often to their own countrymen. There is a State Department program that deals with this modern travesty

in every country in the world, according to Ambassador John Miller, ambassador-at-large on international slavery.

2. Of course "labor shortage" is a relative statement. "Throughout history, employers always say there is labor shortage," says Larry Mischel, director of the Economic Policy Institute in Washington, D.C., which focuses on living standards of working people in a prosperous, fair, and sustainable economy. "From the earliest days of our history, employers always 'needed' workers who would do the work they wanted them to do at the (usually minimal) wages they wanted to pay. And there was always a shortage and continues to be, of such workers!" said Mischel at the Women's National Democratic Club, where he was the featured speaker on March 15, 2007.

3. Congressman Luis Gutierrez (D-Ill.) said this during a talk at a press conference on immigration politics at the National Press Club on April 18, 2007, which I attended.

4. Yale University professor of history and American studies and director of the Program in Ethnicity, Race, and Migration Stephen Pitti before the House Subcommittee on Immigration, Citizenship, Refugees, Border Security, and International Law, on "Shortfalls of the 1986 Immigration Reform Legislation," April 19, 2007.

5. In fact, this is not true since any migrant—legal or illegal—who *voluntarily* exits the United States is free to apply for legal entry, whereas someone who is *forcibly* deported cannot.

6. Nathaniel Philbrick, *Mayflower: A Story of Courage, Community, and War* (New York: Viking, 2006).

7. Justia.com History of Immigration Law. See also Otis L. Graham, *Unguarded Gates: A History of America's Immigration Crisis* (Lanham, MD: Rowman & Littlefield, 2004), 9.

8. Graham, *Unguarded Gates*, 3.

9. Graham, *Unguarded Gates*, 4.

10. Graham, *Unguarded Gates*, 4.

11. Deanna Barker, Frontier Resources, "Indentured Servitude in Colonial America," online newsletter of the Cultural Interpretation and Living History Section of the National Association for Interpretation, March 10, 2004.

12. Karen Ordahl Kupperman, *The Jamestown Project* (Cambridge, MA: Belknap Press, 2007), in an interview with the author on April 28, 2007.

13. Deut. 15:12–15.

14. Barker, "Indentured Servitude in Colonial America."

15. Fredrick Kunkle, "Jamestown Fights Its Second-Rate Image," *Washington Post*, April 8, 2007.

16. Graham, *Unguarded Gates*.

17. From the first part of a four-part PBS series "Slavery and the Making of America," first shown in the nation in February 2007 and searchable at its website.

18. Graham, *Unguarded Gates*, 9.

19. William W. Freehling, *The Road to Disunion* (New York: Oxford University Press, 2007), as cited in Eric Foner, "The Three Souths," *New York Times Book Review*, April 8, 2007.

20. By 1860, 90 percent of Delaware's black population and about half of Maryland's were already free, according to Freehling.

21. Graham, *Unguarded Gates*, 6. "The Civil War and subsequent economic depression of the 1870s brought a lull."

22. Graham, *Unguarded Gates*, 9.

23. Graham, *Unguarded Gates*, 10. Here Graham quotes historian John Higham, whose *Strangers in the Land: Patterns of American Nativism 1860–1925* was published in 1954.

24. *Henderson v. the Mayor of the City of New York*, 92 U.S. 159 (1875).

25. Graham, *Unguarded Gates*, 11.

26. Graham, *Unguarded Gates*, 37.

27. Graham, *Unguarded Gates*, 38.

28. Graham, *Unguarded Gates*, 39.

29. Graham, *Unguarded Gates*, 40.

30. Graham, *Unguarded Gates*, 41.

31. Graham, *Unguarded Gates*, 67.

32. Graham, *Unguarded Gates*, 82.

33. Graham, *Unguarded Gates*, 88.

34. Graham, *Unguarded Gates*, 89.

35. Graham, *Unguarded Gates*, 90.

36. Graham, *Unguarded Gates*, 91.

37. Graham, *Unguarded Gates*, 91

38. Graham, *Unguarded Gates*, 92.

39. Graham, *Unguarded Gates*, 92.

40. Graham, *Unguarded Gates*, 95.

41. Graham, *Unguarded Gates*, 105–6.

42. *Plyer v. Doe*, 457 U.S. 202 (1982).

43. John Willshire Carrera, "Immigrant Students: Their Legal Right of Access to Public Schools. A Guide for Advocates and Educators," National Coalition of Advocates for Students, Boston.

44. Hearing before the House Subcommittee on Immigration, Citizenship, Refugees, Border Security, and International Law on "Shortfalls of the 1986 Immigration Reform Legislation," April 19, 2007.

45. From a paper by the California Coalition for Immigration Reform on the "History of Proposition 187."

46. Paul Virtue, former INS General Counsel and Executive Commissioner Partner, Hogan & Hartson, in testimony at a hearing before the House Judiciary Subcommittee on Immigration, Citizenship, Refugees, Border Security, and International Law on "Shortfalls of the 1986 Immigration Reform Legislation," April 19, 2007.

47. Krikorian, testimony before House Judiciary Subcommittee on Immigration on "Shortfalls of the 1986 Immigration Reform Legislation," on April 19, 2007.

48. Hearing before the House Subcommittee on Immigration, Citizenship, Refugees, Border Security, and International Law, February 24, 1995.

49. Hearing before the House Subcommittee on Immigration, Citizenship, Refugees, Border Security, and International Law on "Shortfalls of the 1986 Immigration Reform Legislation," April 19, 2007.

50. Steven A. Camarota, "The Open Door: How Militant Islamic Terrorists Entered and Remained in the United States, 1993–2001," report by the Center for Immigration Studies, May 2002.

51. Kupperman, *The Jamestown Project*.

52. Graham, *Unguarded Gates*, 89.

53. Joseph S. Nye, *Soft Power: The Means to Success in World Politics* (New York: PublicAffairs, 2004).

54. "Thirty-Day Truce," *Time*, April 9, 1945.

55. Philip M. Dine, *State of the Unions: How Labor Can Strengthen the Middle Class, Improve Our Economy and Regain Political Influence* (New York: McGraw-Hill, 2007), ix and x.

56. Dine, *State of the Unions*, xxvii.

57. Dine, *State of the Unions*, 258.

# CHAPTER 3

1. At a "Newsmakers" meeting "Immigration and the 2008 Elections: Are We Victims to Political Spin?" sponsored by the National Press Club and the International Center for Journalists at the National Press Club on April 18, 2007. Panelists included Congressmen Luis Guitierrez (D-Ill.) and James Sensenbrenner (R-Wis.), former INS Secretary Doris Meissner, director of the Migration Policy Institute, Pamela Constable, deputy editor, *Washington Post*, and Jose Carreno of El Universal No transcripts were made or are available at the time of printing, but the author has heard Gutierrez make the quoted statements on various occasions both in English and in Spanish. The seminar was

part of an ICJ program for 21 community journalists from Latin America to meet U.S. leaders.

2. "Immigration Facts," February 2007, No. 18; Migration Policy Institute (MPI), "Immigration Fees Increases in Context," available online at MPI website.

3. Family-sponsored preferences for green card include first tier: unmarried sons and daughters of citizens—about 23,400 visas given out annually; spouses, children, and unmarried sons and daughters of permanent immigrants—114,200; married sons and daughters of citizens—23,400; and brothers and sisters of adult citizens—65,000. A minimum of 140,000 employment-based preferences for green cards are allotted by law as follows: priority workers—28.6 percent; advanced degree holders or exceptional ability—28.6 percent; skilled worker—28.6 percent; certain special immigrants—7.1 percent; and "employment creators" such as investors in low-populated rural areas—7.1 percent.

4. Section 201-2.

5. From the testimony of Michael Hoefer, director, Office of Immigration Statistics, U.S. Department of Homeland Security, at a congressional hearing on "Government Immigration Statistics" by the House Judiciary Committee's Subcommittee on Immigration, Citizenship, Refugees, Border Security, and International Law, 110th Congress, June 6, 2007.

6. Hoefer, testimony before the House Judiciary Committee's Subcommittee on Immigration, Citizenship, Refugees, Border Security, and International Law, 110th Congress, June 6, 2007.

7. "Warehousing Refugees: A Denial of Rights, a Waste of Humanity" report by the U.S. Committee on Refugees by Merrill Smith, editor, May 2007, available on home website.

8. A statement by Kelly Ryan of the U.S. State Department's Bureau of Population, Refugees, and Migration at a conference at the American Enterprise Institute (AEI) on "Who Is Accountable for Refugee Rights?" on May 4, 2007; transcripts available at AEI website.

9. "Congress Made a Mess of Refugee Law and a Lot of Human Rights Victims Could Suffer," *Washington Post*, April 17, 2007, editorial.

10. "Iraq's Refugees," *Washington Post*, January 22, 2007, editorial.

11. The U.S. refugee program offers grantees permanent immigrant status after they have completed a successful first year in the United States. The U.S. asylum program is different in that it gives temporary residency status to qualified migrants fleeing certain recognized temporary life-threatening situations (natural disasters and local civil wars). More details are found in the section about temporary visas.

12. All temporary permits are (1) are time limited; (2) are nonimmigrant, work restricted; (3) carry the proviso that the holder has promised to leave the country once the temporary period is over; and (4) are not encouraged by the United States to be "adjusted" while in the country to another permit status such as student or scholar or permanent green card unless the holder returns home and applies from there—a proviso from which thousands of immigration lawyers throughout the country make it their often lucrative businesses to find exception to, usually at great expense to the foreign national ($1,000s) seeking adjustment without having to leave the country.

13. Here are some details about some of the most popular temporary permits. (1) tourist and visitor—unlimited in number—around 1 million issued a year; (2) H-1B high-tech workers—65,000 new ones a year—and vacation workers; (3) foreign student and scholar—600,000 a year; (4) season agricultural workers—about 300,000 are used, though more are available but farmers prefer hiring illegal workers; and (5) other interesting permits including for "fiancés," "extraordinary abilities," and "asylees of temporary national disasters."

14. Rangel is quoted in the article "Close to Slavery—Guestworker Programs in the U.S." in the *Bulletin of the NGO Committee on Migration*, June 7, 2007. Available online.

15. Here are some facts about the H-1B visa as assembled by the Center for Immigration Studies, an immigration think tank in Washington, D.C.:

- Very few H-1B workers are "highly skilled." Employers who used the Department of Labor's skill-based prevailing wage system classified most workers (56 percent) as being at the lowest skill level (Level I), as did most State Employment Security Agency wage determinations (57 percent). This suggests that most H-1B computer workers are low-skilled workers who make no special contribution to the American economy or that employers are deliberately understating workers' skills in order to justify paying them lower salaries.
- According to the applications filed in 2005, it appears that employers may be significantly understating what U.S. computer workers are earning in order to justify paying low wages to H-1B guest workers in those occupations. In fiscal year 2005, H-1B employer prevailing wage claims averaged $16,000 below the median wage for U.S. computer workers in the same location and occupation.
- Ninety percent of H-1B employer prevailing wage claims for programming occupations were below the median U.S. wage for the same occupation and location, with 62 percent of the wage claims in the bottom 25th percentile of U.S. wages.

- While higher than the prevailing wage claims, the actual wages reported for H-1B workers were significantly less than those of their American counterparts. Wages for H-1B workers averaged $12,000 below the median wage for U.S. workers in the same occupation and location.
- The reported wages for 84 percent of H-1B workers were below the median U.S. wage; 51 percent were in the bottom 25th percentile of U.S. wages.

Many employers make prevailing wage claims using wage sources that are not valid under the law. The Department of Labor routinely approves prevailing wage claims based on these invalid sources. From "The Bottom of the Pay Scale: Wages for H1B Computer Programmers" by the Center for Immigration Studies, Washington D.C., by John Milano, December 2005; available online.

16. "Their Work Ethic Is Phenomenal," *Washington Post*, July 23, 2007.

17. Here are some facts about foreign students that everyone should know:

- Foreign students are a big and lucrative business for public universities and community colleges; they are charged three to four times more tuition than U.S. students; the majority of the foreign graduate students pay for their tuition by U.S. research grants, which often cover the additional tuition.
- Foreign students earn the majority of graduate degrees in the STEM fields (science, technology, engineering, and math) and often occupy a majority if not 100 percent of all graduate STEM teaching assistantships and research assistantships.
- While many have superior secondary educations from their homelands, all of the hundreds of thousands who are accepted every year into U.S. second-tier colleges and community college programs are no brighter or better than average U.S. students.
- Many college deans say that the existence of their graduate programs depends on the body count, revenue, dedication, and single-mindedness of foreign graduate students.
- Foreign students are not allowed to work off campus during their studies but may during summers and for one year after each degree obtained.
- Many universities admit that foreign graduate students who teach American undergraduates cannot speak English well enough to be understood and are turning off U.S. majors in those fields.
- Bill Gates urged U.S. senators on March 7, 2007, in a single-witness hearing of the Senate Education Committee, to attach permanent resident green card visas to every graduate degree earned by a foreign student in STEM fields from a U.S. university.
- Some ambassadors to the United States (including from Nigeria and Switzerland) have stated on record that they are concerned that because the

United States is not enforcing the return-home requirement of the foreign student visas, their countries' young brains who were educated at their expense are being encouraged to stay in the United States against the intention of foreign exchange.

- The ambassador from India, however, said on record that his country depends on the money and the intellectual property that their scholars send back; the ambassador from Austria said she considers one Austrian genius who first studied and now is working at the Massachusetts Institute of Technology to be "Austria's gift to the world of science."

18. Permits marked with a "1" (i.e., an F1) are for the student; those marked with a "2" are normally for a dependent of the permit holder; it allows them to reside in the country but not usually to have the same study or work or other privileges.

19. The program is authorized by the Immigration and Nationality Act as amended by the Immigration Reform and Control Act of 1986.

20. From testimony by Marcos Camacho, general counsel for the United Farm Workers in Bakersfield, California, at a hearing about before the Congressional Judiciary's Subcommittee on Immigration, Citizenship, Refugees, Border Security, and International Law, 110th Congress, May 24, 2007.

21. The author attended the Senate debate and vote and noted the senator's remarks; also cited in the *Congressional Record*, June 7, 2007, CRS7318.

22. Some 40 percent of illegal aliens in the United States today have lived here less than five years. Most are single males, though increasingly they bring in families later or have relatives in the United States.

23. For instance, if an illegal alien overstays a legal visa, this is a civil offense; if he or she enters the country illegally, this is a misdemeanor; if he or she obtains false documents and uses them for any purpose such as getting a job, buying a home, getting insurance, and so on, he or she has committed a felony; if he or she purports in writing to be in the country or the state legally (such as on a voting registration form or a public college application to avoid out-of-state tuition), written statements that often are not or cannot by law be questioned at the time of signing, this is a felony; if he or she defies an order for deportation, then his or her residency becomes a felony; if he or she reenters after deportation, this is a felony; if he or she fails to depart, this is a civil offense penalized with a formal order of removal and 10-year bar.

24. There are two kinds of deportation: *voluntary* and *forced*. First, an illegal alien who voluntary deports (even after a deportation hearing if he or she is not a criminal felon) will have a clean record and will be eligible to apply for a legal visa and permit into the Untied States once he or she has returned to one's homeland. Second, any alien who is deported involuntarily, however, is not allowed to return legally to the United States.

25. Examples include Anchorage; Los Angeles; Chicago; Cambridge, Massachusetts; Portland, Maine; Tacoma Park, Maryland; Detroit; Minneapolis; New York; Houston; Seattle; Madison, Wisconsin; and New Haven, Connecticut.

26. Statistics from U.S. Census Bureau and Department of Homeland Security as reported by the Migration Policy Institute (available on the MPI website) and other U.S. immigration data.

27. Richard Kluger, *Seizing Destiny: How America Grew from Sea to Shining Sea* (New York: Alfred A. Knopf, 2007).

28. "Economic Anxiety and the American Dream: Is the Dream at Risk in the 21st Century?," report by Change to Win and Lake Research Partners presented at the Brookings Institute on July 13, 2007, transcript online at Brookings Institute archives and at Change to Win.

29. John Tirman, *The 100 Ways Americans Are Screwing Up the World* (New York: HarperPerennial, 2006).

30. Anne-Marie Slaughter, *The Idea That Is America: Keeping Faith with Our Values in a Dangerous World* (New York: Basic Books, 2007).

31. Celinda Lake at the presentation of her Lake Research Partners report on "Economic Anxiety and the American Dream: Is the Dream at Risk in the 21st Century?," Brookings Institute, July 13, 2007.

32. Lake, "Economic Anxiety and the American Dream."

33. Lake, "Economic Anxiety and the American Dream."

34. EPI President Lawrence Mischel, "What's Wrong with the Economy?," Economic Policy Institute report, June 12, 2006. Also in 2005, the unemployment rate by racial and ethnic groups was whites, 4.3 percent; Latinos, 6.8 percent; and non-Hispanic blacks, 10.9 percent, according to the Pew Research Center's Rakesh Kochbar, "Latino Labor Report 2006: Strong Gains in Employment," September 27, 2006. By the second quarter of 2006, the unemployment rate of whites steadied around 4.6 percent, Latinos hit historic low level of 5.2 percent, and blacks hit 8.6 percent in 2006, according to Kochbar. By July 2007, the unemployment rates for whites was 4.2 percent, blacks 8.0 percent, Hispanics 5.9 percent, and Asians 3.0 percent, according to the U.S. Census Bureau database for 2007.

35. Mischel, "What's Wrong with the Economy?"

36. Center for Labor Market Studies, Northeastern University in Boston.

37. The U.S. economy in the first half of 2007 experienced modest job growth but by July 2007 began to slow and "appeared likely to continue slowing the rest of the year," according to economists quoted in Abby Goodnough, "Census Shows a Modest Gain in U.S. Income," *New York Times*, August 29, 2007. The U.S. Labor Department reported that businesses and governments added 92,000 jobs in July, down from 126,000 in June—the slowest pace of job creation since February when employers hired 90,000. While some of the downturn was due to normal seasonal government jobs—such as teachers—still

most of the jobs lost were in construction (both residential and commercial) and in retail. The job market's strength was in financial and business services, hospitality, and health care. "[While] the labor market as of now is OK, the issue is will the current rate of job growth sustain income at a fast enough rate to offset the other factors in the economy that don't look so good?" said Joseph LaVorgna, chief U.S. economist with DeutscheBank. Jeremy W. Peters, "Jobs Growth Slid in July, Echoing Drift," *New York Times*, August 4, 2007.

38. Bob Herbert, "Who's Getting the New Jobs," *New York Times*, July 23, 2004.

39. Gary Rivlin, "In Silicon Valley, the Crash Seems Just Like Yesterday," *New York Times*, Sunday Week in Review, June 3, 2007.

40. In August 2007 it was reported that wages were still up over the past year. Workers in nonmanagement jobs (about 80 percent of the American workforce) earned an average of $17.45, according to U.S. Labor Department. But that wage had peaked at $17.52 in February and had since fallen. In recent months the growth in nominal wages (the actual amount people see in their pay check) had slowed somewhat while inflation had jumped. Strong continued consumer spending provided a buffer against a recession (but the report did not mention at what rate consumer credit card debt rose in that period as a result). Productivity also slowed in 2006, which some economists attributed as the reason that employment rates did not slow down at the same time the growth slowdown did. This and the latest statistics are available at the Bureau of Labor Statistics website at http://www.bis.gov.

41. Cornell University economist Frank H. Rich's book *Falling Behind: How Rising Inequality Harms the Middle Class*, July 9, 2007 (Aaron Wildavsky Forum for Public Policy) review of the thesis in August 4, 2007, "Concurring Opinions," "What Lies Beneath: The Inequality-Commodification Nexus" by Frank Pasquale.

42. "The Land of Opportunity?," *New York Times*, July 13, 2007.

43. "The Misery Strategy," *New York Times*, August 9, 2007.

# CHAPTER 4

1. Frank I. Luntz, *Words That Work: It's Not What You Say It's What People Hear* (New York: Hyperion, 2006).

2. George Lakoff, *Don't Think of an Elephant! Know Your Values and Frame Your Debate: The Essential Guide for Progressives* (White River Junction, VT: Chelsea Green, 2004); George Lakoff, *Whose Freedom? The Battle over America's Most Important Idea* (New York: Farrar, Straus & Giroux, 2006).

3. Brooks Jackson and Kathleen Hall Jamieson, *Un-spun: Finding Facts in a World of Disinformation* (New York: Random House Trade Paperbacks, 2007).

4. Lakoff *Don't Think of an Elephant!*, from chaps. 1 and 2, esp. 11, 13, 25–27.

5. Congressman Dana Rohrabacher (R-Calif.) before (an almost empty) House on May 1, 2007, just before it adjourned at 10:30 P.M.

6. Under the definition of *amnesty*, in *West Encyclopedia of American Law*, vol. 1,186–87.

7. 100 Stat. 3359, 8 U.S.C.A.§1101.

8. Often cited by Mark Krikorian, director Center for Immigration Studies in Washington, D.C., at conferences and in writings such as "Harvesting Illegal," FrontPageMagaxzine.com, April 8, 2005. On April 9, 2007, the AIC (Americans for Immigration Control) Weekly News and Commentary, "Kennedy's Broken Promise," reports, "In 1982, in a letter to his colleagues on the Senate Judiciary Committee, Sen. Edward Kennedy addressed the issue of legal status for illegal aliens in a pending bill. That measure foreshadowed the 1986 immigration bill that granted amnesty, for the first time, to illegals. Said Kennedy, 'A critical feature of [the bill] is the proposed legalization program. . . . It is both humane and sensible to undertake a one-time legalization program, as was unanimously recommended by the Select Commission.'"

9. Thomas Sowell, "More Amnesty Fraud," July 27, 2006, posted on his website.

10. "Debate Could Turn on a 7-Letter Word," *Washington Post*, May 30, 2007; "Amnesty Becomes Archilles Heel," *Washington Post*, June 8, 2007.

11. Janet Napolitano, "The Myth of Amnesty," *Washington Post*, June 10, 2007.

12. At one point in 2006, even the *Washington Post* started to change its anti-immigrant label to "anti illegal immigrant legislation supporters." For example, in an article by Dan Balz, *Washington Post* political staff writer, on May 6, 2006, headed "In Speech: A Balancing Act of Policy and Politics," he writes in the lead paragraph, "The immigration debate that reopened in the Senate yesterday offers Republicans an unpalatable political trade-off. Disappointing conservative, anti-illegal-immigration forces could demoralize a crucial constituency and depress turnout in the November elections at a time when every vote appears important to the GOP."

13. Almost every night for the past four years, Lou Dobbs on his nightly CNN show talks about legislators and lobbyists who advocate for illegal aliens. He labels them variously "The pro-illegal alien lobby" (May 1, 2007), "Pro-amnesty Senators" (June 26, 2007, et al.), "Illegal alien supporters," and "Pro-amnesty open-border Senators" (June 27, 2007).

14. Jackson and Jamison, *Un-spun*, 1.

15. This is not a bigoted subject. It is a serious matter when public issues such as universal health care are debated. In California, the giving of publicly paid doctor visits to illegal immigrants became a huge issue in the new universal

health plan proposed by Governor Arnold Schwarzenegger. A question about whether illegal immigrants would receive universal health care benefits under Democratic presidential candidates' health plans was the only question about immigration that made it onto the CNN-selected YouTube debate in July 2007. For the record, an "American" in this book refers to a U.S. citizen.

16. Carrie Budoff, "Tough, Fair and Practical: Magic Words," Politico.com, June 27, 2007.

# CHAPTER 5

1. Elizabeth Dickson, immigration services manager, Global Mobility Services Team, Ingersoll Rand Company, on behalf of the U.S. Chamber of Commerce, was a witness at a congressional hearing at the House Education and the Work Force Committee on "Guest Worker Programs: Impact on the American Workforce and U.S. Immigration Policy," July 19, 2006.

2. Luawanna Hallstrom, vice president of Harry Singh and Sons, a family-owned farming operation in Oceanside, California, at a congressional hearing at the House Education and the Work Force Committee on "Guest Worker Programs: Impact on the American Workforce and U.S. Immigration Policy," September 19, 2006.

3. *The Crisis*, monthly publication of the NAACP, cover story of July/August 2006, The Crisis Interviews: Immigration. Five Black leaders respond to the furor over immigration, commenting on its economic and political relevance to African Americans. Interviews by David C. Ruffin.

4. As quoted in Karin Brulliard, "AFL-CIO Aligns with Day-Laborer Advocates," *Washington Post*, August 10, 2006.

5. Pew Hispanic Center, "Unauthorized Migrants: Numbers and Characteristics: A Background Briefing Prepared for the Task Force on Immigration and America's Future" by Jeffrey S. Passel, June 13, 2005, charts on 26 and 27; note that the report explains their use of the term "unauthorized migrant" instead of illegal immigrant in a footnote on page 2: "This report uses the term 'unauthorized migrant' to mean a person who resides in the United States but who is not a U.S. citizen, has not been admitted for permanent residence, and is not in a set of specific authorized temporary statuses permitting longer-term residence and work (see Passel, Van Hook, and Bean 2004 for further discussion). Various labels have been applied to this group of unauthorized migrants, including 'undocumented immigrants,' 'illegals,' and 'illegal aliens.' Many migrants now enter the country or work using counterfeit documents and thus are not really 'undocumented' in the sense that they have documents but not completely legal documents. While many will stay permanently in the United States, un-

authorized migrants are more likely to leave the country than other groups (Van Hook, Passel, Zhang, and Bean 2004). Thus, we use 'migrant' rather than 'immigrant' to highlight this distinction."

6. The source is a journalist colleague who told the author this off the record at a private social gathering.

7. At the founding presentation of the Choose Black America organization at the National Press Club, May 23, 2006, Chooseblackamerica.com.

8. Nenaji Jackson, former commissioner on the City of Los Angeles Human Relations Commission and assistant professor of political science at Howard University, on a C-SPAN Washington Journal interview focusing on African Americans and immigration, April 15, 2006.

9. A quote of Tommy Pines, a young Washington, D.C., carpenter who asked the author for work in Washington in the fall of 2005; the author does not know anything more about him.

10. Quote by the mayor in Leslie Eaton, "Study Sees Increase in Illegal Hispanic Workers in New Orleans," *New York Times*, June 8, 2006; story of laid-off worker was told in Eaton, "In Louisiana, Worker Influx Causes Ill Will," *New York Times*, November 4, 2005.

11. U.S. Department of Labor, Bureau of Labor Statistics, "Charting the U.S. Labor Market in 2005," June 2006, 48, from chart 4-5, "Unemployment Rates for Blacks, Hispanics and Whites," and information from Kochbar, "Latino Labor Report 2006." Note that by late 2007, the strong gains of Hispanics in construction work were beginning to decline because of the subprime mortgage crisis and consequent credit crunch. Bob Herbert cited the statistics for black males in his column "The Danger Zone," *New York Times*, March 15, 2007.

12. Rachel L. Swarns, "A Racial Rift That Isn't Black and White," *New York Times*, October 3, 2006, the second article in the series, "The Latino South: A New Rivalry."

13. Actually many NPR shows besides the cited show on September 7, 2006, have dealt with immigration issues and civil rights; for instance, it was the focus of an hourlong discussion on *Talk of the Nation* on November 1, 2006, "Towns Get Tough on Immigration" and on a *Talk of the Nation* show on September 26, 2006, "Should a Voter ID Be Required at the Polls?"

14. Phil Martin, professor of agricultural economics, University of California, Davis, witness at a congressional hearing at the House Education and the Work Force Committee on "Guest Worker Programs: Impact on the American Workforce and U.S. Immigration Policy," July 19, 2006.

15. Mark Krikorian, director of the Center for Immigration Studies, speaks often about how the reliance of American employers on cheap unskilled foreign labor inhibits the development of mechanization and genetic engineering

that would make their products less reliant on human labor, as in most of Europe. He says this often in interviews and panel discussions.

16. Rebecca Smith, coordinator, Immigrant Worker Project, National Employment Law Project, witness at a congressional hearing at the House Education and the Work Force Committee on "Guest Worker Programs: Impact on the American Workforce and U.S. Immigration Policy," July 19, 2006.

17. Michael Chertoff, secretary, Department of Homeland Security, at the American Enterprise Institute, June 29, 2006.

18. A comprehensive cover article in the *New York Times Sunday Magazine* on July 9, 2006, "The Immigration Equation" by Roger Lowenstein, lays out the arguments on both sides in a fairly unbiased manner.

19. Klaus F. Zimmerman, director, IZA (a labor study institute in Germany), in conversation with the author at the Migration Policy Institute on March 8, 2007, after the presentation of his institute's new book *Immigration Policy and the Labor Market* at the conference "Lessons from Europe? Immigration Policy and the Labor Market."

20. The Statue of Liberty has become a symbol of the mantra, with much regard for the romantic idealism of the mantra and with little if any question of the historical intentions and consequences. Historical details of the creation of the statue and its fund-raising, construction, mounting, and public responses all are found easily online. In regard to the immigration mantra, however, some relevant points from "Liberty's" official history are as follows:

1871. The idea for the Statue of Liberty first took hold in the mind of French sculptor Monsieur Frederic Auguste Bartholdi during a dinner party at the home of Eduoard-Rene Lefebvre de Laboulaye, a French intellectual and activist. Lefebvre wanted to sponsor an enormous monument, a new Colossus such as the one that stood in the harbor of Rhodes during ancient classical history. The statue would serve as propaganda against the conservative leaders of the then shaky French government. Bartholdi, an admirer of America's freedoms, had always wanted "to create a large structure in honor of U.S. principles; so Laboulaye named him to create what he envisioned as a powerful political lever for shaping French government and society—a statue representing liberty," to be displayed ideally in New York City.

1875. The Franco-American Union was formed in Paris to make plans, secure funds, and implement the project. Laboulaye was named president of the Union. French representatives responded positively to the idea that the project would be jointly funded by the two nations (the statue and its transportation by France, the base and mounting by the United States). Work began immediately to raise funds and to construct the statue (wonderful photos exist and can easily be found online showing the monument's construction).

1876. A model of the completed statue was displayed at the Centennial Exhibitions in Philadelphia and New York City.

1877. In January 1877, the American committee for the construction of the pedestal was formed, made up of 400 prominent American men. The majority of the national press was hostile toward the project, however, and most Americans did not think they should be asked to finance "New York's Lighthouse."

1884. Joseph Pulitzer, who became owner and editor of the *New York World* in 1883, undertook the flailing campaign to fund the Statue of Liberty pedestal. He tried to "nationalize" the project, pointing out that the statue was a gift to the whole American people from France. The result was that other port cities such as Philadelphia, Boston, Cleveland, Boston, and even San Francisco offered to entirely fund the construction of the statue's pedestal if it was located in their port entrances.

By the summer of 1884, the American Committee had collected $125,000—but it also was broke since prior contracts had consumed all the money. This was awkward because by 1884, France had raised enough money to put all the pieces of the statue together. "It stood a veritable colossus overlooking all the roof tops of Paris," according to official brochures.

On June 11, 1884, Levi P. Morton, the minister of the United States to France, gave a banquet in honor of the Franco-American Union to celebrate the completion of the statue. Bertholdi said he was honored to have given "ten years of his life to the great work, putting into it both his ability as a sculptor and his LOVE OF LIBERTY." In his acceptance speech, Levi Morton said in part, "God grant that it [the statue] may stand until the end of time AS AN EMBLEM OF IMPERISHABLE SYMPATHY AND AFFECTION BETWEEN THE REPUBLICS OF FRANCE AND THE UNITED STATES."

1885. Back in New York, the statue completion ceremony of 1884 in France posed a problem. In March 1885, it had been announced that unless $100,000 could be raised for the pedestal, the "generous gift of the people of France would have to be abandoned." Mr. Pulitzer stormed at everyone from men of wealth to America's working people "who failed to support the gift from France—the most generous gesture one nation had ever offered to another." In April, word was received that the statue had been reduced to 350 individual pieces and packed into 214 crates, ready for its transatlantic voyage aboard the French frigate *Isere* to Bedloe Island, the selected site in New York Harbor. Finally the national press rallied to the cause with a national campaign (stirred on undoubtedly by growing media mogul Mr. Pulitzer). Money poured in—some in pennies—from throughout the country. The statue arrived on June 19. By August 11, the needed funds to construct the pedestal had been raised.

1886. "LIBERTY," as the Statue of Liberty was called, arrived in the United States and was efficiently mounted on her pedestal. President Grover Cleveland unveiled the statue to an audience of thousands on October 28, 1886. He said in part, "We will not forget that LIBERTY here made her home; nor shall her chosen altar be neglected."

So how did the statue become a symbol of immigration? Because of a poem. In brief, the poem was written in 1883 by a New York poet as a fund-raising piece for the statue's base, forgotten, then found in 1903 by a patron of the New York arts who had five lines of the poem mounted on the statue on a plaque. In 1945, the entire poem was placed over the statue's entrance portal, and after the war, the statue became a symbol of immigration to the United States by the world's poor.

In 1883, the poem *The New Colossus* was written by Emma Lazarus, a moderately popular, very wealthy, self-identified Communist Party member (according to a piece done on Lazarus the poet on NPR in 2006) and socialite and female poet in New York. She composed it to help raise funds for the construction of the statue's pedestal. It consisted of 14 lines:

### The New Colossus

Not like the brazen giant of Greek fame,
With conquering limbs astride from land to land;
Here at our sea-washed, sunset gates shall stand
A mighty woman with a torch, whose flame
Is the imprisoned lightning, and her name
Mother of Exiles. From her beacon-hand
Glows world-wide welcome;
Her mild eyes common
The air-bridged harbor that twin cities frame.
"Keep ancient lands, your storied pomp!" cries she
With silent lips. "Give me your tired, your poor,
Your huddled masses yearning to breathe free
The wretched refuse of your teeming shore.
Send these, the homeless, tempest-tost to me,
I lift my lamp beside the golden door!"

Lazarus's sonnet to the Statue of Liberty was hardly noticed. In 1903, after Lazarus's death, a patroness of the New York arts, Georgina Schuyler, found it tucked into a small portfolio of poems. She was struck by the poem and arranged to have its last five lines become a permanent part of the statue itself.

The lines were placed on a plaque directly on the statue. Children's textbooks began to include the sonnet, and Irving Berlin wrote it into a Broadway musical. By 1945, the 14 lines of the poem were engraved over the Statue of Liberty's main entrance. Today many people think of the Statue of Liberty and the ninth and tenth lines of the poem as inseparable: "Give me your tired, your poor, Your huddled masses yearning to breathe free." "It may now be indelibly engraved into the collective American memory," states the official Statue of Liberty pamphlet.

21. "Latinos" is a term that grew out of so-called ethnic studies departments in universities. According to academics, Latinos are really only those people who grew up in Spanish-speaking Latin America of all racial, socioeconomic, and ethnic backgrounds. People from Brazil, Spain, and the Caribbean islands usually are not considered to be (nor do they consider themselves to be) "Latino." But spokespeople from Latino political groups such as the National Council of La Raza (National Council of the Race—an astoundingly politically incorrect name one might say if it were in English) have said that "anyone who is sympathetic to Latinos *is* a Latino."

22. "Hispanic" is a term coined by the U.S. Census Bureau to distinguish people with a Spanish surname. There is no particular geographic origin connected to the term, but some Latin Americans don't like the term because it refers to Spain's colonial dominance over the continent.

23. "Chicano" was a pejorative term referring to Mexican immigrants (Mejicanos) in the Southwest until the 1970s, when it was recreated to be a symbol of ethnic pride by student activists of Mexican indigenous blood. The student movement MECHA (Movimiento Estudiantil Chicano de Aztlan) that pushed the term distinguished Chicanos as being neither of Spanish nor of Mexican heritage but stemming from the "Land of Aztlan"—geographically large parts of southern California, Arizona, and New Mexico as well as northern and central Mexico. The term was rejected by the older generation in the 1970s, but now the young Chicanos have become that older generation, and academic departments and many schools in the area teach Chicano history. The University of California at Santa Barbara in 2005 established the first Ph.D. program in Chicano studies. Many Californians use the term "Chicano" instead of "Latino" or "Hispanic."

24. "Espanoles" is an old term in Texas and California that refers to original settlers in those states who were from Spain—soldiers, ranchers, and missionaries—and who created the rich Spanish culture in those states.

25. 42,687,224 out of 296,410,404.

26. Figure 4, "Annual Immigration to the United States from Selected Countries or Regions of Birth Based on Census 2000, ACS and CPS Data: 1991–2004," report by the Pew Hispanic Center's Jeffrey S. Passel and Roberto

Suro, "Rise, Peak and Decline: Trends in U.S. Immigration 1992–2004," September 27, 2005.

27. U.S. Census Bureau report on 2004 election patterns released on May 26, 2005, quoted in various publications, including in Brian Faler, "Census Details Voter Turnout for 2004," *Washington Post*, May 26, 2005.

28. The foreign student visa was developed after World War II to enable bright young potential leaders to be able to pursue higher education at America's best universities. The foreign student permit is temporary, time limited, and nonimmigrant. The visa requires every student to return home after their studies, and it contains strict work restrictions—foreign students can work on campus only during the academic year, their spouses are not allowed to work at all, and after graduation they are allowed up to one year of "practical training" in their field of study before returning home.

There are three kinds of foreign student visa permits that vetted educational institutions are allowed to issue to foreign nationals whose applications they have accepted: J permits for foreign scholars, researchers, professors, and post-graduates (issued by research universities and institutions, such as the National Institutes of Health, that have been vetted by the U.S. State Department); F permits for associate, bachelor's, master's, and doctoral students (issued by accredited degree-issuing institutions vetted by the U.S. State Department); and M permits for specialized training in trade schools giving certificates in everything from cosmetology, bartending, graphic design, and flight training (vetted by the Immigration Enforcement Bureau).

Hosting foreign students has become a lucrative business in the U.S. world of postsecondary education. Most public colleges charge foreign student three to four times more annual tuition than they do Americans and legal residents and have become dependent on that revenue. Many C-grade private colleges aim their expensive programs exclusively to foreign students. In fact, American colleges have become the most expensive in the world for foreign students. There is no limit to how many foreign student visas can be issued in the United States by any or all educational institutions. Today some 600,000 foreign nationals are registered as students in the United States at every kind of postsecondary educational institution, from elite university to beauty school.

29. Robert Samuelson, *New York Times*, September 6, 2006, calls it our unique "system of learning."

30. One might assume that most foreign students are usually elite at least in that they come from wealthy families in their countries and/or their education is sponsored by their governments. The International Institute of Education reports that most foreign undergraduates finance their studies with "personal" funds. What they don't say is that those personal funds come mainly from two sources: work and/or credit cards. In truth, foreign student advisers report that

many foreign students have a lot of financial problems and financial stress once they are in the United States. While their visas specifically do not allow foreign students to work off campus, the fact is that many must and do—often illegally (it doesn't take much asking around in off-campus retail stores and restaurants in any college community to meet foreign students working in these "shadow" jobs). Many foreign students are disappointed and even upset that they are forced to work illegally in jobs that do not pertain to their studies as they had expected to have and that their off-campus, in-the-shadows, low-paying jobs are often approved by a wink and a nod by sympathetic foreign student counselors. Many foreign students also soon learn "the favorite American solution of paying for their college expenses—credit cards," according to Robert D. Manning, author of *Credit Card Nation: The Consequences of America's Addiction to Credit* (New York: Basic Books, 2000). These cards are often urged on them by credit card companies on campus using university-affiliated cards that also are fund-raising devices for campus fund-raisers.

31. According to a November 2003 study prepared for the Division of Science Resources Studies for the National Science Foundation by Michael G. Finn of the Oak Ridge Institute for Science and Education titled "Stay Rates of Foreign Doctorate Recipients from U.S. Universities, 2001." Some specifics reported include that more than two-thirds (71 percent) of foreign citizens who received science/engineering doctorates from U.S. universities in 1999 were in the United States in 2001. Among discipline groups, the highest stay rates were recorded for computer/electrical and electronic engineering, computer science, and physical sciences. The stay rates in economics and the other social sciences were lowest. Ninety-eight percent of doctorate recipients from China and 86 percent from India stayed on in the United States after their studies in 2001.

32. From the "Open Doors" report by the International Institute of Education (IIE), which every November issues a report on foreign students. In academic years (AY) 2000 and 2001, the number of foreign students increased to record highs in total numbers and in percentage of growth—a 6.8 percent increase in both years. In those years, the IIE reported a record number 585,000 registered foreign students at U.S. accredited universities and colleges on F and J visas. (The IIE does not count the number of foreign students who enter the country on M visas and actually attend trade schools in the United States.) In AY 2002–2003, the percentage of increase of foreign students dropped for the first time in decades. Foreign student numbers increased "only" by 2 percent in those years. Nevertheless, this was greeted by headlines even in major newspapers referring to the "foreign student crisis." In AY 2003–2004, the total number of foreign students dropped for the first time—by 2.4 percent. The drop occurred only among undergraduates, however, which dropped by 5 percent; the number of foreign graduate students increased by about 2.5 percent. In AY

2004–2005, the total number of foreign students remained about the same as the previous year. In AY 2005–2006, the number of foreign students at accredited universities and colleges rose by 3.2 percent to 582,984 (the all-time record in 2002–2003 was 586,323). New international student enrollment increased by 10 percent, with again more graduates than undergraduates, according to the IIE's "Open Doors 2007" report released on November 13, 2007.

# CHAPTER 6

1. Joseph E. Stiglitz, *Making Globalization Work* (New York: Norton, 2006).
2. Stiglitz, *Making Globalization Work*, 4.
3. Ralph E. Gomory and William J. Baumol, "Globalization: Prospects, Promise and Problems," *Journal of Policy Modeling* 26, no. 4 (June 2004): 425–38.
4. Stiglitz, *Making Globalization Work*, xii and xv.
5. Stiglitz, *Making Globalization Work*, 89.
6. According to the World Commission on the Social Dimensions of Globalization, which was established in 2001 by the United Nations' International Labour Organisation that sponsored the study. The report, "A fair globalization: Creating opportunities for all," can be accessed at http://www.ilo.org/public/english/fairglobalization/report/index.htm.
7. Warren Hoge, "Nations Benefit from Migration, U.N. Study Says," *New York Times*, June 7, 2006, A8.
8. John J. Sweeney, president, AFL-CIO, quoted in John Zarocostas, "Job Outsourcing 'Serious Problem,'" *Washington Times*, June 12, 2006, A15.
9. Michael Kinsley, "Free Trade but . . .," *Washington Post*, January 9, 2004.
10. "Remarks at a White House Meeting with Business and Trade Leaders" (September 23, 1985). The full text of President Reagan's remarks can be found at http://www.reagan.utexas.edu/archives/speeches/1985/92385a.htm.
11. Ron Hira and Anil Hira, *Outsourcing America: What's Behind Our National Crisis and How We Can Reclaim American Jobs* (New York: American Management Association, 2005), 16.
12. Senators Byron Dorgan and Sherrod Brown, "How Free Trade Hurts," *Washington Post*, December 23, 2006, A21. The wonky term for all this is "comparative advantage." Trade agreements used to be built on a few products that one nation could produce better than another because of demography or climate or some natural reason. Comparative advantage is gained by the country that can produce and sell what everyone else makes (from agricultural to computer software to service products) cheaper than anyone else (or "more efficiently" or with "higher productivity" in economically politically correct speech).

13. Steven R. Weisman, "After Six Years, the Global Trade Talks Are Just That: Talk," *New York Times*, July 21, 2007.

14. Stiglitz, *Making Globalization Work*, 271.

15. Lori Wallach on PBS's *NewsHour*, July 27, 2005, "Free Trade Fight" with commentator Ray Suarez.

16. Byron L. Dorgan, *Take This Job and Ship It: How Corporate Greed and Brain-Dead Politics Are Selling Out America* (New York: Thomas Dunne Books/St. Martin's Griffin, 2006), 30.

17. Louis Uchitelle, "NAFTA Should Have Stopped Illegal Immigration, Right?" *New York Times* (February 18, 2007). The article can be accessed at http://www.nytimes.com/2007/02/18/weekinreview/18uchitelle.html ?partner=rssnyt&emc=rss.

18. Uchitelle, "NAFTA Should Have Stopped Illegal Immigration, Right?"

19. Wallach, *NewsHour*, "Free Trade Fight: Discussion," with Ray Suarez, correspondent, and John Murphy, vice president, U.S. Chamber of Commerce.

20. "Is CAFTA Good for Costa Rica? Two Views on the CAFTA Referendum," conference at the Economic Policy Institute in Washington, D.C., cosponsored by the Carnegie Endowment for Peace, the Global Policy Network, and Oxfam America, July 25, 2007. Otton Solis was introduced as the former presidential candidate, head of the Costa Rican Citizen's Action Party, and leader of the CAFTA opposition in Costa Rica. The quote cited was also quoted in the blog of Jim Wallis on August 10, 2007, "God's Politics," in an article, "Pro-Prosperity, Anti-CAFTA."

21. Council on Foreign Relations, "Task Force Urges Measures to Strengthen North American Competitiveness, Expand Trade, Ensure Border Security," news release, May 17, 2005, also released in Spanish.

22. "USA Population Hits Milestone Number," *USA Today*, October 17, 2006.

23. Haya El Nassar, "A Nation of 300 Million," *USA Today*, July 28, 2006.

24. Pew Hispanic Center, "From 200 Million to 300 Million: The Numbers behind Population Growth," *Fact Sheet*, October 10, 2006.

25. See "Interview with Linda Jacobsen on the U.S. at 300 Million: Challenges and Prospects" (October 11, 2006), available at http://discuss.prb.org/content/interview/detail/673.

26. Steve Camarota, "100 Million More: Projecting the Impact of Immigration on the U.S. Population, 2007–2060," *August 2007 Backgrounder* (Center for Immigration Studies, Washington, D.C.), available at http://www.cis.org/articles/2007/back707.html.

27. "Social Security: Gambling with Your Future," a Social Security debate essay by the Stanford University Department of Biological Sciences Tuljapulkar Lab, found at http://popstudies.stanford.edu/socsecurity.html.

28. Camarota, "100 Million More."

29. Steve Camarota projects the positive impact if that age increase to 66. See table 7 of his report available at http://www.cis.org/articles/2007/back707.html.

30. John Fonte, "It Is Time for Americanization," testimony before the House Judiciary Committee, Immigration Subcommittee (May 16, 2007), available at http://www.hudson.org/files/publications/Fonte_Congressional-TestimonyMay_07.pdf.

31. Gary Gerstle, "Becoming Americans—U.S. Immigrant Integration," testimony before the House Judiciary Committee, Immigration Subcommittee (May 16, 2007), available at http://judiciary.house.gov/media/pdfs/Gerstle070516.pdf.

32. The transcript of this event is available at http://www.webprodserv.brookings.edu/~/media/Files/events/2007/0713u%20s%20economics/20070713.pdf. The quote is in the author's notes of the event and was discussed with Ms. Lake during the question-and-answer period and afterward person to person.

33. Victor Davis Hanson, *Mexifornia: A State of Becoming* (San Francisco: Encounter Books, 2003), 46.

34. Pamela Constable, "For Many Immigrants, No Answers," *Washington Post* (March 20, 2007). Available at http://www.washingtonpost.com/wp-dyn/content/article/2007/03/19/AR2007031901906_pf.html.

35. Analysis by the author after synthesizing the many sympathetic and poignant descriptions by Dr. Victor Hanson in his book *Mexifornia* of the "strange newshizophrenia" (51), especially illegal immigrants from Central America; read especially chaps. 2 and 3.

36. Z.-C. Qian and D. T. Lichter, "Social Boundary and Marital Assimilation: Evaluating Trends in Racial and Ethnic Intermarriage," *American Sociological Review* 72 (2007): 68–94.

37. Jeffrey S. Passel, "Growing Share of Immigrants Choosing Naturalization," Pew Hispanic Center, March 28, 2007, available at http://pewresearch.org/pubs/439/growing-share-of-immigrants-choosing-naturalization.

38. Passel, "Growing Share of Immigrants Choosing Naturalization." "An increased acceptance of dual nationality in Mexico and other countries" is also mentioned as a reason for increased naturalization, according to the study. The study also states that eligible immigrants from Latin America and Mexico naturalize at lower rates than those of other nationalities: "Among immigrants eligible to become citizens 77% of those from the Middle East had done so by 2005, compared with 71% from Asia, 69% from Europe and Canada, and 46% from Latin America. The high citizenship rates of immigrants from some Latin American countries are offset by Mexico's comparatively lower rate of 35%" (v).

39. Quoted in an Associated Press story in Juliana Barbassa, "U.S. Naturalization Rate Hits 25-Year High," *San Mateo County (Calif.) Times*, March 29,

2007, which was covering the Pew Hispanic Center's report on naturalization trends by Jeffrey Passel based on federal census and immigration data.

40. Barbassa, "U.S. Naturalization Rate Hits 25-Year High."

41. Pamela Constable, "Sometimes, a Labor Day: A Trailer in Gaithersburg Is a Haven for Immigrants Hoping for a Better Life," *Washington Post*, August 30, 2007, B01.

42. Testimony by Gary Gerstle, Ph.D., professor of history at Vanderbilt University, at the May 16, 2007, hearing of the Subcommittee on Immigration, Citizenship, Refugees, Border Security, and International Law. Hearing on Comprehensive Immigration Reform: "Becoming Americans—U.S. Immigrant Integration."

# CHAPTER 7

1. Google these two phrases, and you get 185,000 sites for "immigrants do jobs Americans won't do," including President Bush as reported by the Associated Press on his visit to a Texas border station on November 29, 2005, and 326,000 sites for "immigrants will help with Social Security problem," such as an article in the *American Chronicle* by Donna Poisi, president of Live and Thrive Press, on September 26, 2007, who wrote typically, "Fifty years ago, it took 20 workers to keep enough tax money flowing in to keep a retiree on Social Security. By 2030 there will only be two workers to cover each retiree. All the baby boomers will be in that group of retirees and more will be getting ready to retire. Add the fact that people are living much longer and it's easy to see why we need more young workers now. We also need a steady supply of young workers coming into the system. The young immigrant workers who are already here may be the answer to the Social Security funding problems of the future" (she means illegal workers).

2. Roger Lowenstein, "The Immigration Equation," *New York Times Magazine*, July 9, 2006. It particularly highlights two leading economists whose studies differ on the impact of illegal immigrants on the U.S. economy—George Borjas of the Kennedy School of Government at Harvard University and David Card of the University of California at Berkeley. The article can be accessed at http://www.nytimes.com/2006/07/09/magazine/09IMM.html?_r=1&oref=slogin.

3. Lou Dobbs, *Exporting America: Why Corporate Greed Is Shipping American Jobs Overseas* (New York: Warner Business Books, 2004).

4. For example, see Paul Streitz, *Outsourcing America: How Outsourcing, Free Trade, and Open Borders Are Destroying the American Middle Class and What Can Be Done about It* (self-published, 2005); Ron and Anil Hira, *Outsourcing America: What's behind Our National Crisis and How We Can Reclaim American Jobs* (New

York: American Management Association, 2005); Stiglitz, *Making Globalization Work*; and Dorgan, *Take This Job and Ship It*.

5. In 2006, the median annual income of middle-class American males was $48,201. Households in the top quintile had incomes exceeding $91,705, 77 percent of which had two income earners. Households in the middle quintile had a mean of one income earner per household and an income between $36,000 and $57,657. This is a slight increase over 2005.

6. Steven A. Camarota, "Immigration's Impact on American Workers," testimony prepared for the House Judiciary Committee, May 9, 2007. Available at http://www.cis.org/articles/2007/sactestimony050907.pdf.

7. Press release, January 23, 2007, Committee on the Judiciary, Ranking Member Lamar Smith.

8. Evan Perez and Corey Dade, "An Immigration Raid Aids Blacks for a Time," *Wall Street Journal*, January 17, 2007.

9. Robert J. Samuelson, "We Don't Need Guest Workers," *Washington Post*, March 22, 2007, A21.

10. The quote is from U.S. Senate, Subcommittee on Immigration and Naturalization of the Committee on the Judiciary, Washington, D.C., February 10, 1965, 1–3. Available at http://www.cis.org/articles/1995/back395.html. The original record is in the National Archives at http://www.archives.gov/research/guide-fed-records/groups/046.html#46.15.

11. T. Willard Fair, "Mass Immigration vs. Black America," Statement before the Subcommittee on Immigration, Committee on the Judiciary, U.S. House of Representatives (May 9, 2007). Available at http://judiciary.house.gov/media/pdfs/Fair070509.pdf.

12. Carmen DeNavas-Walt, Bernadette D. Proctor, and Jessica Smith, "Income, Poverty, and Health Insurance Coverage in the United States: 2006," U.S. Census Bureau, August 2007. Available at http://www.census.gov/prod/2007pubs/p60-233.pdf.

13. Robert J. Samuelson, "Importing Poverty," *Washington Post*, September 5, 2007. Available at http://www.washingtonpost.com/wp-dyn/content/article/2007/09/04/AR2007090401623.html.

14. His prepared testimony is available at http://judiciary.house.gov/media/pdfs/Feinstein070524.pdf.

15. Michael J. Wilson, "Labor Movement Perspectives on Comprehensive Immigration Reform," Testimony before the Subcommittee on Immigration, U.S. House of Representatives (May 24, 2007). Available at http://judiciary.house.gov/media/pdfs/Wilson070524.pdf.

16. Vernon M. Briggs Jr., "Immigration Policy and Organized Labor: A Never-Ceasing Issue," Testimony before the Subcommittee on Immigration,

U.S. House of Representatives (May 24, 2007). Available at http://judiciary. house.gov/media/pdfs/Briggs070524.pdf.

17. See http://judiciary.house.gov/oversight.aspx?ID=333.

18. William R. Hawkins, "Comprehensive Immigration Reform: Business Community Perspectives," Testimony before the Subcommittee on Immigration, U.S. House of Representatives (June 6, 2007). Available at http://judiciary. house.gov/media/pdfs/Hawkins070606.pdf.

19. Congressman Howard Berman (D-Calif,) in Hawkins, "Comprehensive Immigration Reform: Business Community Perspectives."

20. Congresswoman Maxine Waters (D-Calif.) in Hawkins, "Comprehensive Immigration Reform: Business Community Perspectives," questioning Laslo Bock, People Operations, Google Inc. She also asked Mr. Bock, "What are you doing—these jobs include management and otherwise as well—to ensure that Americans who need the work are getting the work?" And "Do you have a history—and I would like you to give it to me in writing—of recruiting at African-American—historically Black colleges?"

21. Byron Dorgan and Sherrod Brown, "How Free Trade Hurts," *Washington Post*, December 23, 2006. Available at http://www.washingtonpost.com/wp-dyn/ content/article/2006/12/22/AR2006122201020.html.

22. Michael Kinsley, "Free Trade Butters," *Slate*, January 8, 2004. Available at http://www.slate.com/id/2093649/.

23. Harold Meyerson, "Can Free Trade Be a Fair Deal?" *Washington Post* (February 22, 2007). Available at http://www.washingtonpost.com/wp-dyn/content/ article/2007/02/21/AR2007022101587.html.

24. From a news release from Congressman Walter B. Jones, August 20, 2007, available at http://www.house.gov/jones.

25. This is a common point of disagreement between Bill O'Reilly and Geraldo Rivera.

26. There are some 11,000 border agents patrolling the 327 ports of entry into the United States.

27. Presidential candidate Rudolph Giuliani (R) discussed the noncriminality of illegal immigrants at length with Glenn Beck on CNN Headline News on September 7, 2007. Transcript available at http://www.glennbeck.com/news/ 09072007.shtml.

28. For example, the DDI, CIA, and other intelligence agencies, including Interpol, deal with international terrorists in the United States and the development of terrorist cells, plots, and plans carried out in conjunction with foreign terrorist organizations; foreign consulate officers and diplomats issue consulate registration cards for their citizens in the United States illegally and increasingly represent their citizens regarding their illegal status; federal, state, and local

public housing authorities, social welfare personnel, division of motor vehicle officers, and university and college registrars are all charged by law to deny services to illegal aliens; FBI, Internal Revenue Service, Social Security Administration, and consumer protection organizations deal with identity theft, low-quality or dangerous products, and fraudulent document use by illegal aliens; sheriffs, marshals, and state, county, and local police investigate, detain, and identify illegal aliens involved with criminal activities, especially drug-related violent gang activities; and state, county, and local legislative bodies shape and vote on legislation that deals with local and state business licensing and housing rental regulations; public nuisance issues such as loitering, drinking, noise, and aggressive unwanted soliciting; housing density and the use of some specific public services by illegal aliens; and increasingly the use of English for official businesses. Many new regulations will undoubtedly be challenged in the courts, some successfully, some not. The U.S. Border Patrol at times, especially in border cities, will be called to help ICE with large raid operations, as will the Bureau of Alcohol, Tobacco, and Firearms and the Food and Drug Administration, to help identify illegal substances and tainted food products. ICE is also the agency charged with training local law enforcement officers to help with immigration enforcement if the local jurisdiction requests such training under Section 837b of the national immigration code. Some Catholic and evangelical churches, nonprofit ethnic immigrant advocacy groups, private-sector nonprofit organizations, and a few self-declared sanctuary cities give out food, clothing, temporary housing, job search and interpreter services, English and computer classes, and free legal and immigration advice to illegal aliens. Some also offer those facing deportation sanctuary and protection from law enforcement actions as long as they stay within a certain geographic area (a building or even a city limits).

29. Samuel P. Huntington, *Who Are We? The Challenges to America's National Identity* (New York: Simon & Schuster, 2004), 185.

30. Huntington, *Who Are We?* (see chap. 4).

31. Peggy Levitt, *God Needs No Passport: Immigrants and the Changing American Religious Landscape* (New York: New Press, 2007).

32. From question and answer period of the May 15, 2007, hearing of the House Judiciary Subcommittee on Immigration about "Becoming American— U.S. Immigrant Integration." Page 86 of the transcript is available on the committee's website.

33. Huntington, *Who Are We?*, 214.

34. Catholic Legal Immigration Network, Inc. "A More Perfect Union: A National Citizenship Plan," available at http://www.cliniclegal.org/DNP/citzplan.html.

35. Georgie Ann Geyer, *Americans No More* (New York: Atlantic Monthly Press, 1996).

36. Huntington, *Who Are We?*, 204.

## CHAPTER 8

1. Borosage is the codirector of the new Campaign for America's Future (a liberal Democratic, neo-Progressive organization). His assessment is in the July/August 2007 issue of *The American Progress*.

2. They include the U.S. Chamber of Commerce, the U.S. Hispanic Chamber of Commerce, and the American Manufacturing Association. Smaller business lobbyists and associations represent agricultural and construction contracting groups, such as the National Roofers Contracting Association, the National Restaurant Association, and the Plumbing, Heating and Cooling Contractors National Association. Sympathetic organizations include think tanks like the CATO Institute in Washington and the Manhattan Institute in New York City and respected media like the *Wall Street Journal*, *Reason* magazine, and *The American Spectator*.

3. Margaret Orchowski, "The Student Visa Loophole," *The Weekly Standard*, January 27, 2003, 31 (and mentioned on the cover under a small banner "Homeland Security").

4. Ramensh Ponnuru, "Getting Immigration Right—A Headache and a Half for the GOP," *National Review*, October 8, 2007. Traditional conservatives generally believe the following:

- All foreign-born visitors and non–green-card holders in the country who want to get a job in the United States should have identity cards that plainly show their work permit (or not).
- Those with work permits should be readily verified on a national database.
- All employers who hire a foreign-born visitor without a work permit should be punished.
- All foreign nationals who are in the country must choose which deportation they will take—voluntary or involuntary.
- Local police must be trained to help with the detention of illegal immigrants who are committing offenses against communities' laws and regulations governing standards of neighborhood cleanliness, noise abatement, loitering, solicitation, overcrowding of housing, and the use of public services limited to legal residents, such as low-income housing and the like.

- Publicly subsidized education for children of illegal aliens must end at the end of secondary school; no adult who is illegally in the country, no matter what age they came in, should get a publicly subsidized college education.
- Social Security payments should never be paid to illegal immigrants or to relatives of legal immigrants who have never lived or worked in the United States.
- Birthright citizenship—granting citizenship to the children of illegal aliens—should end; we are the only country in the world that still grants it foolishly.
- All the borders should be secured from illegal entry in the best way possible with a variety of options, including a wall in certain strategic places (few people support the walling off of the entire U.S. border) and manned and unmanned procedures.
- Those who are arrested for crossing over illegally should be deported immediately.
- No trucks from Mexico should be allowed more than 25 miles into the country until safety standards are assured to be the same as in the United States.
- American safety and worker hygiene standards must be assured for all products sold in the United States, especially including those produced by foreign workers in U.S. fields and construction sites and restaurants where English is not spoken and a dominant nationality is hired and managed only by bosses of that nationality.
- American businesses must prove at a much higher standard that they cannot find an American worker to take the job—this especially includes office jobs at American universities.
- American universities must take responsibility that the foreign students from whom they derive so much revenue comply completely with U.S. immigration laws, including their return after their studies; if the universities won't take that responsibility, then they should to be allowed to "host" foreign students.

5. For example, starting in about 2004, CNN economist Lou Dobbs suddenly took up the cause of illegal immigration limitation in his daily primetime show. He claims that he has become a "advocacy journalist," as he focuses on illegal immigration outrages in segments with titles such as "Outsourcing American Jobs," "Broken Borders," and "Assault on the Middle Class."

6. Rahm Emanuel and Bruce Reed, *The Plan: Big Ideas for America* (New York: PublicAffairs, 2006). Talked to author in a one-on-one interview.

7. Sam Youngman, "'08 Dems Push Immigration," *The Hill*, September 20, 2007, and Gabe Martinez, "Local Votes Could Be Immigration Kingpin," *The Politico*, October 30, 2007.

8. Matt Bai, *The Argument: Billionaires, Boggers and the Battle to Remake Democratic Politics* (New York: Penguin, 2007), 138.

9. Brink Lindsey, *The Age of Abundance: How Prosperity Transformed America's Politics and Culture, Why the Culture Wars Made Us More Libertarian* (New York: HarperCollins, 2007).

10. John B. Judis and Ruy Teixeira, authors of *The Emerging Democratic Majority* (New York: Scribner, 2002), in "Back to the Future: the Re-Emergence of the Emerging Democratic Majority," *The American Prospect* (July/August 2007).

11. For a comprehensive look at the history of liberalism, see Paul Starr, *Freedom's Power: The True Force of Liberalism* (New York: Basic Books, 2007).

12. Charles E. Schumer with Daniel Squadron, *Positively American: Winning Back the Middle-Class Majority One Family at a Time* (Emmaus, Penn.: Rodale Books, 2007).

13. The name "Blue Dog" came about partly to reflect their difference from the southern Democrat "Yellow Dog" loyalists (they, who it was said, would vote for a "yeller dog" if it was listed as a Democrat on the ballot). Blue Dogs are the opposite—the stubborn Democrat donkeys who had been chocked blue by their party's liberal knee-jerk positions leading up to the 1994 elections. They are Democratic elected representatives who would not and will not toe the party line if it doesn't suit their constituencies.

14. From Angela Kelley, director, Immigration Policy Center of the American Immigration Law Foundation, at the telephone press conference "Immigration in an Election Year" for members of the ethnic press on December 5, 2007, moderated by the New America Media.

15. Thomas L. Friedman, "High Fence and Big Gate," *New York Times*, April 5, 2006. The first line is often quoted: "America today is struggling to find the right balance of policies on immigration. Personally, I favor a very high fence, with a very big gate."

# CHAPTER 9

1. Ted Hayes, homeless activist, speaking at the Choose Black America joint press conference with the American-Latino group You Don't Speak For Me at the National Press Club, June 19, 2007.

2. Fishman spoke at a September 11, 2007, meeting of the American National Council on Immigration Reform, a grassroots organization based in Washington, D.C., organized by Republican Party activists from California, Virginia, and the District of Columbia.

3. Anita Kumar, "Va. GOP Seizes on 'Red-Hot' Concern: Illegal Immigration Fuels Campaigns across the State," *Washington Post*, September 24, 2007, B01.

4. Kumar, "Va. GOP Seizes on 'Red-Hot' Concern."

5. The quotes are from Frank Sharry, executive director, National Immigration Forum, and Angela Kelley, director, Immigration Policy Center of the American Immigration Law Foundation, at the telephone press conference "Immigration in an Election Year" for members of the ethnic press on December 5, 2007, moderated by the New America Media.

6. Robert D. Novak, "McConnell's Immigration Failure," *Washington Post*, July 2, 2007.

7. Jill Zuckman, "GOP in an Uphill Fight on Capitol Hill," *Chicago Tribune*, December 2, 2007.

8. Quotes are from a December 14, 2007, immigration panel discussion at the National Press Club in Washington, D.C.

9. December 14, 2007, immigration panel discussion at the National Press Club, from the author's notes.

# Acknowledgments

This book is the result of years of personal interactions I have had with hundreds if not thousands of immigrants and those concerned with their welfare. It also comes from my personal experience with the impact of immigration law on my family in the United States and abroad and its impact on the quality of life in the various communities and countries where I have lived and worked. It also is the product of the many knowledgeable people who have shared their expertise on immigration with me in private and in public forums.

While it is impossible to list all those who helped me indirectly with this book, I would like to acknowledge in print some of those who helped me directly to formulate and clarify the concepts in this book and to check the facts. They include especially Bill Buchannon of ANSIR (American Council on Immigration Reform), a Washington, D.C.-based immigration fact-finding organization formed by Joan Heuter of California and headed by Bob Shoemaker of Virginia. Jessica Vaughan of Boston, Massachusetts, helped me with fact checking; she is an associate of the Center for Immigration Studies (CIS) in Washington, D.C., which was founded by former University of California, Santa Barbara, professor and longtime friend Otis Graham. CIS director Mark Krikorian and research director Steven Camarata were constant helpful sources of sensible and factual information on immigration whom I often cite and want to thank for their constant accessibility.

I must also thank with profound gratitude the librarians of the National Press Club, especially Beth Shankle, who helped me check and validate many of the press references in the book. The library and the club is a treasure for me and any working journalist in Washington, D.C., with its professional, personal, and fully equipped press library; its constant press conferences of newsmakers, many of whom spoke on immigration; and its efficient and friendly staff that provided me with constant support, a place to meet and eat with news sources, a readily accessible high-speed computer network, and a chance to meet journalist colleagues from around the world. The Press Club helped me immeasurably to physically produce this book.

I also want to acknowledge with admiration what I came to realize is an institution that is almost as maligned as it is venerated: the U.S. Congress. I strongly disagree that Congress "does nothing" and "is broken." I found that the democratic legislative process is alive and well particularly in the committee hearing rooms of the House and the Senate. In 2007 alone, Zoe Lofgren (D-Calif.), chair of the House Subcommittee on Immigration, held some 20 hearings on the impact of immigration on almost every segment of American society, bringing in over 100 international, national, state, and local experts to present often comprehensive and even cutting-edge testimonies followed by hours of intense questions, answers, debate, and follow-up in the committee rooms and halls by members. As a reporter, I benefited greatly from attending these congressional "seminars," the opportunity to interview the witnesses, and the frequent chance to engage in discussion afterward with the participating representatives, particularly Steve King (R-Iowa). The committee staffs of the Judiciary Committee and of the Education, Foreign Affairs, and Labor committees and their subcommittees, were always helpful with transcripts, background information, and follow-ups. Similarly, the facilities of the press gallery and the helpful services of their staffs of both chambers were invaluable to me as a credentialed member of the press, as were the services of the Senate Law Library and the Library of Congress. I am grateful to all.

Finally, I want to acknowledge my close friends such as Robin Homet and Priscilla Friedersdorfer and especially my twin sister and her husband Anna and Ron Lafferty, all of whom listened attentively—and most of the time patiently—to what must have seemed at times my endless permutations of immigration issues. They constantly shared their knowledge, critiqued me gently, and constantly encouraged me to write this book. Anna, who is also my identical opposite as a graphic designer, helped me immeasurably to visualize the concepts I was conceiving.

Lastly, I need to assure all that while I did my best to validate all citations, facts, and statements in this book, I of course take full responsibility for any errors that are included. None are intentional. I welcome any corrections and comments, provided that they are made civilly.

My intention in writing this book is to provoke knowledge-based discussion about immigration management. Who can come in, stay, work in, and even have the eventual privilege of becoming a citizen of one's country is a vital and legitimate decision that citizens of any nation-state are obliged to make for the sake of the quality of life and prosperity of their family, friends and countrymen. To immigrate is one of the most life-changing choices any human can make. Both immigrants and citizens of the host country must be respected in the debate about immigration control. In encouraging this discussion, I in no way mean to insult or harm anyone.

# Index

(John F.) on, 35; progressives on, 174; relatives eligible for, 57–58, 207n3
Union Pacific Railroad, 29
United Automobile Workers (UAW), 47
United Farm Workers, 37, 65–66
United Food and Commercial Workers International Union, 153
United Mine Workers of America (UMW), 46–47
United Nations High Commission on Refugees, 60
United States: as job magnet, 113–17; as nation of immigrants, 17, 99–101
U.S. Citizenship and Immigration Services (USCIS), 39, 43, 56
U.S. Committee for Refugees and Immigration, 60
U.S. Customs and Border Protection Agency (CBP), 55–56
U.S. Supreme Court: on education for minor illegal aliens, 37; on federal jurisdiction over immigration, 22, 29–30, 41
universal health care, 188–89
University of California at Berkley, 72
University of California at Davis, 109–10
*Un-spun* (Jackson and Jamieson), 84, 89
"unstoppable" illegal immigration, 113–17
*USA Today*, 139

vacation employees, 63–64, 208n13
Valentine, Victoria, 104
vertical issues, 15, 176, *176*, 176–77
Virginia: colonial immigration to, 41; immigration politics in, 185–86;

indentured servants in, 25; Jamestown experience in, 25, 26
Virtue, Paul, 39
visa(s), 53–56: categories of, 52; consular interviews for, 40, 42, 43–44, 54–55, 127; countries oversubscribed for, 58–59; definition of, 53; fast-track, 54, 125–26, 127; flexibility in, 196; multiple-entry, 55; overstaying, 69–70, 106, 111–12, 128, 145, 210n23; "soft power" of, 43–44, 127; verification and checking of, 115–16, 125–26, 127–28. *See also specific laws*
visa-waiver countries, 53–54, 55, 56, 62
visitor visa, 52, 61, 62, 208n13
visualizing message, 85
vocabulary of immigration, 83–98, *86*
vocational certificate programs, 64
voluntary deportation, 210n24
volunteerism, 6
voter fraud, 98
voting: dual-citizen, 165; by Latinos, 120–23
voting blocs, 120–23, 175
voting rights, 56, 121

wages: growing gap between, 79–80, 226n5; growth in, 78, 212n40; illegal workers' impact on, 111–12, 148
Wagner Act, 46
waiting list, for green cards, 58–59
Wallach, Lori, 135
wall along border, 158–59, 195
*Wall Street Journal*, 36, 150, 229n2
Walters, Ronald, 105
"War on Poverty," 151

# About the Author

Margaret "Peggy" Sands Orchowski, Ph.D., is the vice president of programs of the National Democratic Woman's Club and the Washington correspondent and columnist for the *Hispanic Outlook on Higher Education*. She is a former international journalist with the Associated Press and was with the United Nations press corps in Geneva, Switzerland. She is an active member of the National Press Club, the American Newswomen's Club, and JAWS—Journalism and Women's Seminar.